PIETY AND DISSENT

✢

✝

PIETY AND DISSENT

RACE, GENDER, AND BIBLICAL RHETORIC IN EARLY AMERICAN AUTOBIOGRAPHY

Eileen Razzari Elrod

University of Massachusetts Press

AMHERST

Copyright © 2008 by University of Massachusetts Press
All rights reserved
Printed in the United States of America

LC 2007022044
ISBN 978-1-55849-629-3 (paper); 628-6 (library cloth)

Designed by Dennis Anderson
Set in New Baskerville by BookComp, Inc.
Printed and bound by The Maple-Vail
Book Manufacturing Group

Library of Congress Cataloging-in-Publication Data

Elrod, Eileen Razzari.
Piety and dissent : race, gender, and biblical rhetoric in early American autobiography / Eileen Razzari Elrod.
p. cm.
Includes bibliographical references and index.
ISBN 978-1-55849-628-6 (library cloth : alk. paper) — ISBN 978-1-55849-629-3 (pbk. : alk. paper)
1. United States—Church history. 2. Christian biography. 3. Church and minorities. 4. Social integration—Religious aspects—Christianity. 5. Race relations—Religious aspects—Christianity. 6. Sex role—Religious aspects—Christianity. I. Title.
BR515.E47 2008
277.3092'2—dc22
2007022044

British Library Cataloguing in Publication data are available.

To Mary Heywood Razzari

In Memory of John Serafino Razzari

CONTENTS

    List of Illustrations   ix

    Acknowledgments   xi

1 Margins and Centers, New and Old Narrations: Biblical Voices, Great Awakening Christianity, and American Autobiographical Traditions   1

2 "I Did Not Make Myself So . . ." : Samson Occom and American Religious Autobiography   21

3 John Marrant, John Smith, Jesus: Borders, Tangles, and Knots in Marrant's 1785 *Narrative*   38

4 Moses and the Egyptian: Religious Authority in Olaudah Equiano's *Interesting Narrative*   62

5 Gender, Christian Suffering, and the Minister's Voice: Submission and Agency in Abigail Abbot Bailey's *Memoirs*   85

6 Devotion and Dissent: Jarena Lee's Rhetoric of Conversion and Call   117

7 Finding a Way in the Forest: The Religious Discourse of Race and Justice in the Autobiographies of William Apess   146

8 Religious Imperatives, Democratic Voices, and Autobiographical Preoccupations   171

    Notes   187

    Works Cited   201

    Index   217

ILLUSTRATIONS

Samson Occom	26
Olaudah Equiano	69
Jarena Lee	121
William Apess	153
Phillis Wheatley	173

ACKNOWLEDGMENTS

WARM THANKS to colleagues and friends who have helped me do the work I love to do and complete this project. The questions that energized this study began during a National Endowment for the Humanities seminar on Religion and Diversity in American Society at Haverford College, and then took shape during a sabbatical year funded by Santa Clara University and a Pew Grant. I am indebted to colleagues in the fields of American literature, American studies, autobiography, religious studies, and cultural history; their legacy is evident. More particularly and personally, I thank Emory Elliott, whose generous, thoughtful reading of the manuscript at a critical moment was enormously helpful; and William L. Andrews, whose interest in the project in its earliest stages was a great encouragement. The sound advice of the anonymous readers for the University of Massachusetts Press helped me clarify and conclude the book. Clark Dougan and Carol Betsch at University of Massachusetts Press shepherded the manuscript through final revision and publication, and Patricia Sterling copyedited with precision and care. I am grateful to Don Dodson and the Provost's Office of Santa Clara University for funding support, and to many other truly excellent colleagues: my friends in the Ignatian Faculty Forum, the Women Faculty Group, the American Studies Group, and the Program for the Study of Women and Gender. English Department colleagues Ann Brady (now at Michigan Technological University), Phyllis Brown, Michelle Burnham, Julie Chang, Marilyn Edelstein, Linda Garber, and John Hawley offered critical readings of chapters, consultation, thoughtful questions, and kindness along the way. The interest and insights of Judy Dunbar and Juan Velasco helped me to be mindful not only of this project but also of how it is situated within larger endeavors. Laurie Robbins and Ed Schaefer are the best lunch companions anyone could ask for.

I note my debt of gratitude to other sorts of colleagues as well: my undergraduate students at Santa Clara University, who have on occasion shared my interest in American religious autobiography and pursued their own commitments to justice and faith in ways that have inspired and sustained me. These students, who have worked with me in many courses and asked about the work I was doing when I wasn't teaching, include in particular Andrea Friaz-Gallardo, Trevor Gibson, Mary Lee, Christine Lupo, Ashante Martin, Elizabeth Ojeda, Jen Re, Emily Ryan, Virginia Suarez, Elissa Stebbins, Nate Swinton, and Jill Yamasawa, plus a host of resourceful research assistants: Julie Jigour, Michael Moul, Kathryn Ortiz, Rebecca Rissman, Ava Schlossmacher, Stefanie Silva, David Van Etten, Melissa Whippo, and especially Melissa Franklin and Shiaw-Ling Lai.

Most important, I acknowledge my nearest neighbors. Marta Gardner, Doug Gardner, and Bridget Levich remained interested and concerned well past all reasonable obligations of love, family, and friendship. Stephen Elrod, Adriana Elrod, and Maria Elrod persistently reminded me of what matters and who counts, compelling me to take far more time with the manuscript than I might have. Perhaps the book is better for that; certainly I am better for that. Finally, Roger Razzari Elrod always appreciates my questions; his partnership, love, generosity of spirit, intellect, faith, and unfailing good humor have been a sustaining presence for so many years that I have started to lose count. I am more grateful than I can say that my scholarly work takes place within the loving chaos of this particular family, these particular people.

EARLIER VERSIONS of chapters 2 and 4 appeared in previous publications: "I Did Not Make Myself So . . .": Samson Occom and American Religious Autobiography," in *Historicizing Christian Encounters with the Other*, ed. John C. Hawley (New York: Macmillan, 1998), reproduced with permission of Palgrave Macmillan; and "Moses and the Egyptian: Religious Authority in Olaudah Equiano's *Interesting Narrative*," *African American Review* 35.2 (2001): 409–25.

PIETY AND DISSENT

1

MARGINS AND CENTERS, NEW AND OLD NARRATIONS

Biblical Voices, Great Awakening Christianity, and American Autobiographical Traditions

☦

> The great subject of thought was, of course, theology; and woman's nature had never been consulted in theology.
> Harriet Beecher Stowe, *Oldtown Folks*

> Where theorists and philosophers tread with sublime assurance, women often follow with bleeding footsteps.
> Harriet Beecher, Stowe, *The Minister's Wooing*

IN THE MIDDLE of the nineteenth century, Harriet Beecher Stowe, the most popular writer in America, described how women—disenfranchised by traditional Protestant theological systems—contended with grave discrepancies between what male theologians and religious philosophers argued and what they themselves lived. Specifically, Stowe's narrators suggested that patriarchal Christianity refused and resisted women's experience and, at the same time, entrapped and injured them as they complied with a system they did not author. Stowe's incisive insider critiques of mid-nineteenth-century New England religion regularly featured an opposition between firsthand experience (and stories told about that experience) and abstract theological argument, with narrative always coming out ahead, revealing the deficiencies and even viciousness of theology and, by extension, traditional Protestantism (in which Stowe was a sincere, if not always orthodox, believer). Despite Stowe's family credentials as an American evangelical insider (she was, after all, the daughter of one famous preacher, the sister of another, and wife of a theology professor), her narrators frequently imagine themselves as outsiders—female interlopers in a male tradition that they didn't design, a tradition, ironically, from which they derive profound meaning and from which they express profound dissent. But Stowe, arguably the most famous American Christian of the nineteenth century, was simply articulating what earlier writers—earnest Christians marginalized from mainstream American Protestantism by gender and race—had long known and compellingly described, not through fictional narrators such as Stowe's but in their own voices in life narratives, complex texts that frequently alternate between earnest religious piety and enraged religious dissent.

This book examines six autobiographies published in the United States between 1765 and about 1830, specifically, narratives by Samson Occom, Olaudah Equiano, John Marrant, Abigail Abbott Bailey, Jarena Lee, and William Apess. Each writer was an eager convert to Christianity; each one (though to varying degrees) experienced Christianity as an outsider because of race or gender. That is, they were excluded from the authority of their traditions and articulated their outsider status with different levels of awareness and degrees of dissent. Whereas, for example, William Apess and Jarena Lee spoke from positions of Christian social conscience that anticipate in some ways the biblical oratory of Martin Luther King, Jr., Abigail Bailey resisted seeing her own suffering (a lifetime of domestic violence) in any but deeply personal and entirely spiritualized terms. The diverse and complex conceptions of self and Protestant Christianity presented in these narratives enrich existing characterizations of both American religious rhetoric (and, in particular, early American life-writing) in eighteenth- and early nineteenth-century America and, indeed, the legacy of American Protestantism.

The presence of religious traditions other than Protestant Christianity in early America has become an important piece of the rethinking of facile narratives about American religious (and literary) identity, which have typically featured American Puritanism, New England, and English settlers at the center. Such groundbreaking, decentering work leads to a complex presentation of religious experience and cultural production in the early period in North America and quite specifically informs this work. My focus remains on Protestantism, but I am interested here in examining the power relations in texts by individuals from nondominant groups who self-consciously entered the dominant

Anglo-American, even primarily northern New England, Christianity of the period. That Protestant Christianity (and specifically New England Puritanism and its legacies) dominated the national narrative about early America for several generations reinforces the need for a study of how non-English, non-European, and even white female writers (recalling Stowe's narrative critiques, for example) made sense of that tradition in their own life narratives from within its marginal spaces.[1]

These writers confronted experiences of racialized and gendered violence, prohibitions, and silencing in the context of religious ideals they earnestly embraced, ideals that they believed condemned such experiences. At the same time, they reflected on the way their religious traditions actively endorsed, tolerated, or helped design the suffering they endured. They made use of biblical texts, biblical rhetoric, and, quite specifically, biblical voices to understand, explain, or oppose violence, suffering, and injustice, but they came to different and, sometimes even within the same autobiographical text, shifting conclusions. The complex ironies and careful rhetorical presentations of their experiences provide a kind of map of some of the muddy cultural conflicts that mark American Protestantism's social and religious history. In particular, these texts presage the conflicted experiences of later Americans of color and white women who adopt the dominant U.S. religion of Protestant Christianity but find themselves excluded from exercising personal authority or even agency, subordinated to an official authority that they represent as living out a less authentic vision of the faith described in the approved religious rhetoric of the tradition, indeed, colonized by the very system of meaning that they embraced as liberatory, redemptive.

The writers discussed here ground their life-writing in Christian rhetoric, theology, and piety, and each may be understood in the legacy of the U.S. eighteenth-century revivalism and religious fervor identified with what historians have called the "Great Awakening." Although in the last two decades scholars have argued about the set of events and corollary effects in the religious and popular culture of the period, they seem to agree, for the most part, in identifying a significant shift in the terrain of religious practice and popular belief among American Protestants in the period before and after the English evangelist George Whitefield's popular U.S. tour in 1739. As Susan Juster explains, the "mass revivalism [of the 1730s and '40s] . . . has occasioned as much controversy now as it did then" (*Disorderly* 17).

Although one historian, Jon Butler, has dismissed the Awakening as "interpretive fiction," scores of others have argued about its particulars.[2] In general the period has been understood as a time of revived religion and renewed spiritual fervor, emphatically displayed in a more expressive religion, a religion of experience or (in the pained rhetoric of Jonathan Edwards's early circumspect defense of the shift) of "affections." Great Awakening analyses have frequently typified the effects of revivalism as not only including but depending upon a radical shift in notions of authority. As revivalism asserted the primacy of experiential religion, competing hierarchies of authority were displaced or challenged. As the actual physical space of religious encounter moved out of the church and into barns, fields, and tents, the symbolic and social spaces—including well-practiced exclusions and hierarchies associated with the structure of the meetinghouse and the institutional authority it represented—were challenged as well. Revivalist Christians in many communities worshiped together across the lines of race, class, and gender, emphasizing the immediate (and experientially understood) spirit of God as the only pertinent reality.

This relative, temporary fluidity of social roles, grounded in theological assertions about the universal availability and the mysterious, surprising locations of divine grace and its effects, are hallmarks of early American evangelical religion for both its original participants and historians of religion. Juster (discussing Rhys Isaac's important study of religion in mid-eighteenth-century Virginia) relates that "rich and poor, men and women, black and white all communed together in the presence of the Lord, often without a minister" (*Disorderly* 19). And, for his part, Jonathan Edwards, describing the Northampton revival, calls it "extraordinary on account of the universality of it, affecting all sorts, sober and vicious, high and low, rich and poor, wise and unwise" (*Faithful Narrative* 64). The disorderliness and multiple dislocations of Great Awakening religion and its legacies—the move from church to field, the loosening of bonds between minister and parish which was due to widespread itinerancy, the accompanying weakening of official ministerial authority, the upsetting of accepted hierarchies of gender, class, and race—threatened the social order in profound ways, to the extent that they were directly addressed by contemporary ministers who grasped the potentially radical social consequences. Anglicans and "Old Light" Protestants (see chapter 5) warned against both the social disorder (especially the empowerment of women via expanded ecclesiastical roles and public discourse) and the theological messiness of Awakening religion. Revivalists were characterized as theologically unsophisticated, personally vulgar, and sexually promiscuous.[3] Ultimately, revival religion and all its messy, embarrassing features were placed on the margins of the social and cultural history of early America. And the temporarily loosened social roles were thoroughly reinscribed in nearly all the religious communities born from Great Awakening revivalism, even as their theological rhetoric continued to espouse a New Testament egalitarianism that they imagined characterized an authentic Christianity such as Paul spoke of in Galatians (3.28) where "there is neither bond nor free, there is neither male nor female: for ye are all one."

This is to say not that the religious revivalism associated with eighteenth-century awakenings resulted in an egalitarian social order but rather that the rhetoric and theology—particularly the emphasis on experience and on the immediacy and universal availability of divine grace—invited less hierarchical ways of thinking, which occasioned some loosening of roles. George Whitefield preached that God was no respecter of color, urging African Americans to take part in the work of the church even as he simultaneously defended slavery (Lovejoy 199). Profoundly limited as it was, the spirit of egalitarianism in religious matters played a part in the controversies and texts that ensued from the Great Awakening.

The legacy of the popular evangelicalism of mid-eighteenth-century America, understood in social practices and theological assumptions, leads—perhaps quite directly—to the voices examined here, to the particular rhetoric of these writers, their complex presentations of self and their assumptions about their relationships with readers. They all addressed white readers; some addressed communities of color as well.[4] I am particularly interested in the rhetorical relationship between the writers of color (that is, all but Abigail Bailey) and their white readers, the way they constructed authority, the way they positioned themselves within the traditions and communities emerging from revival religion, the way they challenged readers' presumptions and autobiographical conventions.

The historical particulars of just what constituted the Great Awakening, and how accurately one may generalize local effects to a wide movement concerning all the colonies, may continue to be a point of argument.[5] But this set of texts, spanning a considerable period of years that encompass enormous political and social changes, reflects a shared language and theology of religious revival. Despite significant differences of circumstances, historical contexts, and local communities, the texts mention consistent concerns, creating an intriguing narrowing of scope despite the broad span of years. This book observes this recurring significance of experiential religion in the rhetoric, motifs, and allusion of autobiographical texts by women, Native Americans, and African Americans, noting the repeated, conflicted function of religion for these writers. The discussion begins with Samson Occom, whose writing occurred in the late 1760s just after the French and Indian Wars concluded, and moves on to John Marrant and Olaudah Equiano, whose 1785 and 1789 autobiographies were published just after the American War for Independence ended and as the abolition movement became an organized force in Britain and America. During this same decade, Abigail Abbot Bailey was writing a prayer diary that would become the sourcebook for her 1815 *Memoirs*. The last two writers, Jarena Lee and William Apess, published their autobiographies in the 1830s as abolition, Indian removal, and woman suffrage developed into significant and often overlapping social, political, and religious debates in the United States. Both the span of years and the crucial differences in political, philosophical, and social contexts get compressed in this sample of texts, where external, material, and political realities are always informed and understood (and on occasion ignored entirely) via a Protestant pietism that is highly personal, importantly social, and absolutely dependent upon the outsider sensibility of the writers. Even some of their more educated and privileged contemporaries, such as Thomas Jefferson and Mary Wollstonecraft, found the piety in evidence in these autobiographies both embarrassing and emphatically over—historically and philosophically. Such dismissals are cut from the same cloth as the neglect of writers outside the mainstream, which has been rethought and redressed in recent decades.

Important points of convergence and conflict occur particularly around the twin effects of a pietistic sensibility that both empowers and silences. The language about and experience of religion seems, to an extent, shared here. For example, even the personal presence of George Whitefield (and his friend and patron Selina Hastings), frequently represented as a pivotal public figure in eighteenth-century Awakening religion in both England and America, is well represented in the pages of two of these autobiographies. (He also figures prominently in the work of and reception to Phillis Wheatley, the subject of the concluding chapter.) The significance of Whitefield's influence and theology for eighteenth-century black Atlantic writers is addressed fully in two recent anthologies of African American writing from the period, by Adam Potkay and Sandra Burr and by Vincent Carretta (*Unchained*). Whitefield himself, along with his particular brand of evangelical Christianity, which emphasized predestination (rather than Wesleyan free will), is a frequent, nearly ubiquitous presence in early black spiritual autobiography. And so, more important, is the theological assumption that spirit and experience trump all else—including, some of these writers insist, hierarchies and prohibitions that threaten to silence the voice of that spirit in the testimony of the individual. The language of the spirit would be heard through the ordinary individuals in the pew in these communities that were "wedded to the transforming power of the word, spoken, written, and sung . . . supremely confident that the vernacular and the colloquial were the most fitting channels for religious expression" (Hatch 127).

Contradictory strains of liberation and oppression were manifest long before eighteenth-century revivalism in Anglo-American Christianity. Even a cursory glance at early American Protestantism reveals a host of individuals armed with biblical texts and similar theology who nevertheless reached very different conclusions about particular issues of social justice. In 1700 John Saffin and Samuel Sewall—both New England Puritans—argued vigorously with each other about slavery and race, for instance. Sewall (who opposed slavery on biblical grounds) went on to call for the humane treatment of Indians, though he stopped far short of articulating a vision of racial equality. Meanwhile, Cotton Mather, in a position that Phillis Wheatley seems at times to echo, envisioned the enslavement of Africans as a positive force for Christian conversion. Others argued that it was theologically contradictory for any baptized person—black or white—to be enslaved, a contention leading to an increasingly tangled set of positions on conversion, baptism, and slavery. On more theoretical questions of freedom of expression and religious dissent, Roger Williams and Anne Hutchinson fought with colonial leaders of Massachusetts about the role of the authority of the individual conscience and religious freedom.

Arguably, the core assertions of Protestantism, and more specifically of American Protestantism, not only allow for but encourage acts of dissent on the part of the faithful. Because Protestantism emerged on a foundation—a doctrine, even—of resistance to established tradition, it has frequently, despite near constant and aggressive strains of racism, sexism, and violence, acknowledged, at least (and sometimes only) on a theoretical or theological level, individual acts of conscience and the right to voice dissent as a result of the same. Dissent—political, ideological, ecclesiastical—as an act of faith in response to God and in defiance of human authority is a tradition established and contradicted vigorously in New England (and elsewhere as well). Puritan Protestants were notoriously intolerant of dissent, whether it occurred inside or outside their own religious community. But the presence of dissenters—voices such as those of Samuel Sewall, Roger Williams, and Anne Hutchinson—who unsuccessfully pressed the tradition in a direction it might (but emphatically did not) take, demonstrates that traditions that silence can also empower. Contemporary readers may be less familiar with evangelical Christianity as a site for individual acts of conscience in the name of a commitment to social justice, and much more familiar with the strains of American Christianity that helped shape the aggressive and systematic racism and sexism of America's history—strains that still influence the experience of nation and religion for many individual Americans—but such contradictions are ever present. The contradictions of near contemporary expressions of earnest evangelical Christianity—the simultaneous existence, for instance, of the still vigorous Christian white supremacy movement and the Southern Christian Leadership Conference—are part of an old, conflicted conversation among American Protestant writers about what it means to be a person of faith in a biblical tradition. Many early writers, including white women and persons of color within Protestantism such as those discussed here, took part in this dialogue in a much more forceful way than is usually represented.

The writers this book is concerned with encountered the religion of English America somewhat as outsiders but ultimately had earnest conversion experiences; then, despite what seem to be a set of profoundly contradictory experiences with and in Christianity, they all became proselytizers themselves, often taking a specific interest in other outsiders, typically members of their original communities whose experiences with white Christianity paralleled theirs. A number of early American writers fall into this category, many of whom have been historically neglected by literary scholars—perhaps specifically because of the overt piety and religious zeal of their texts—and who are now being recovered by literary historians and critics interested in presenting a fuller and more diverse picture of early American letters.

Reading these autobiographies through feminist and postcolonial literary critical lenses affords insight into the riches of text and context that constituted early American Protestantism for these writers. All the subjects here write in the space suggestively identified by Mary Louise Pratt as "the contact zone," that complex space of interaction between empire and colony—material, political, and psychological—visible in the histories of nations and cultures and in individual narratives (in Pratt's study, those of travelers). In Pratt's terms these writers produced what might be described as autoethnographic texts, describing themselves in part by engaging precisely the representations that they know others have made of them. Further, they both collaborate with and appropriate the idioms of the conqueror, a relationship most accurately understood not in a straightforward "dynamics of possession and innocence" but in the untidy dialectic of the contact zone.[6] And although I am neither able to identify nor interested in doing so with precision which argumentative strain or rhetorical practice within these texts belongs to which community or tradition, I am concerned with analyzing the complex textual dynamic that results. The corollary psychological dynamic described by Frantz Fanon in his early groundbreaking studies *Black Skin White Mask* and *Wretched of the Earth* comes into play in the complex selves presented by these life writers. Fanon's articulation of a progression from assimilation to the colonizer's cultural model, to an internal self-questioning, to a commitment to liberatory struggle on behalf of the colonized provides a descriptive paradigm for many of the individual writers of these texts.

Further, Abdul JanMohamed's discussion of the commonalities of voice and stance among diverse minority perspectives informs the readings of texts drawn from disparate traditions and communities. These writers share common strategies, particularly as they appropriate religious authority and theorize about racial and cultural difference in the context of their own religious conversions to Anglo-American Christianity. In examining the consequence of domination in contemporary minority discourse, JanMohamed argues that oppressed persons indeed appropriate the oppressors' views of them: "Coerced into a negative, generic subject position, the oppressed individual responds by transforming that position into a positive, collective one. Therein lies the basis of a broad minority coalition: in spite of the enormous differences among various minority cultures, which must be preserved, all of them occupy the same oppressed and 'inferior' cultural, political, economic, and material subject-position in relation to the Western hegemony" (JanMohamed and Lloyd 10). In situating minority discourse within poststructuralism and postmodernism, JanMohamed argues that rather than deconstructing its identity formations from within the Western tradition, as some poststructuralisms do, minority discourse "must begin from a position of objective nonidentity that is rooted in their economic and cultural marginalization vis-à-vis the 'West'" (15). These autobiographers begin, indeed, with two somewhat paradoxical foundations: one, an experience of marginalization; two, identification of the injustice of that marginalization, which, to varying degrees, they critique in light of Western tradition, specifically Christianity and, even more specifically, the biblical text. Positing an alternative identity vis-à-vis the sacred text of the colonizer places them in a dual position: outsiders by virtue of race, culture, gender, and class; insiders by virtue of the central authority of the tradition and their personal experience of sacred text.

Sharon Harris's work with nontraditional autobiographical writing of early American women (specifically her notion of *discours décousu*), as well as Françoise Lionnet's work with autobiography (specifically her notion of *metissage*), provides helpful lenses for these nontraditional texts. A reader may approach these narratives—some of which (in Harris's terms) do not satisfy a traditional set of expectations for conventional published autobiography (although all except Occom's were published texts and all have now been reissued)—by way of Lionnet's notion of a boundary space, a complex space that encompasses the writers' multiple and multiply conflicted racial, gendered, and (in these cases, as I argue) religious selves. Like the subjects of Lionnet's study of autobiography, these "divergent" individuals exist in boundary spaces that empower them to speak in, of, and to the social locations of their multiple identities. They speak, in Lionnet's terms, from "within the straightjackets of borrowed discourses," and yet they endorse religious/theological discourse even as they uncover its severe constraints. The ambivalence of their texts—what Lionnet would call their "braided" voices—in fact becomes a source of their power for readers, enriching the sense of early American spiritual autobiographical practice.

We gain insight into the ambivalence, even the contradictoriness, of these narratives by way of Harris's articulation of *discours décousu*, an important paradigm for perhaps the most troubling one for contemporary readers, that of Abigail Bailey. Like many of the early American diarists that Harris discusses, Bailey (and to a certain extent the other writers discussed here) may be described as having a discontinuous voice; her text is associative, interruptible, characterized by "intellectual looping" and resistance to closure rather than a more traditional kind of continuity that readers might prefer to privilege, and which we are more likely accustomed to reading in the context of traditional (European, masculine) autobiographical texts. Harris describes her appreciation of this discursive form of writing by way of now traditional feminist metaphors of quilting (used by Hedges, Showalter, even Alice Walker), Bhaktinian theory of patchwork, and Luce Irigaray's concern with the facets of subjectivity and language. As Harris describes the diary genre, "Its restrictive nature (its insistence upon privacy) undermines the overt control of authority figures other than the author herself. Patriarchal systems and ideologies may be *momentarily* abandoned, challenged or supplanted. Thus while the diarist explores multiple facets of subjectivity, she can simultaneously engage in acts of creating meaning for herself" (29). The writers discussed here are not precisely diarists, but such a description works nevertheless toward an understanding of the simultaneous private and public task which engaged them in these religious texts that seem to move both toward a private meaning that will nurture and sustain the writer in the midst of oppression and even abuse, and a public meaning that both asserts the credentials and authenticity of the writer and questions the validity of the community's religious values. Like Harris's use of *discours décousu*, my strategy is to "tease out the threads of discursive patterns" in these separate texts (29).

This book depends upon previous discussions of early American religious life-writing, including Daniel B. Shea's 1968 study of early American spiritual autobiography, which helped establish a sense of what might be called the dominant modes of religious life-writing found within Puritan and Quaker traditions.[7] Shea's study provides a preliminary sense of context for the traditions of American Protestant religious life writing. Notably, in his 1988 update, Shea addressed some of the changes in American literary studies by recontextualizing his work in light of literary theory and the boom in autobiography studies. He did not, however, address the central concern here: that is, how rediscovered works by writers of color and women shift the ground of religious autobiography in the early period. Other writers have examined Protestant religious life-writing in early America. Patricia Caldwell describes the evolution of the American Puritan conversion narrative, which in some ways is a precursor genre to the spiritual autobiography taken up by later Puritan and Quaker writers and by the writers examined here. Of particular importance to my discussion is Caldwell's recognition of the ways the first generation of writers of American conversion narratives used biblical voices and texts, the ways they constructed a sense of authority, and the ways they articulated a sense of perplexity. Rodger Payne's study of later (1740–1850) life-writings of early American Protestants examines an element of the paradox important to the writers here—the apparent contradiction between a speaker's commitment to Christian self-effacement and, at the same time, to exercising his or her own sense of personal authority by way of textual construction. But these examinations of spiritual autobiography have not taken into consideration the significance of life-writing by people of color in the early period, nor have they investigated the dynamics of personal authority and nascent political protest or religious dissent. Indeed, in talking about the authority and the psychological function of these narratives for their writers, I want to suggest the broader relevance of Rodger Payne's specific argument. He looks at conversion as a type of discourse that allowed late eighteenth- and early nineteenth-century evangelicals to "speak purposefully of themselves," suggesting that the text itself (in his discussion, conversion narrative) constitutes experience: "By speaking (or writing) the language of conversion, evangelical autobiographers were called to 'baptize' the modern concept of the independent and autonomous self into the larger discourse of Christian orthodoxy." Further, "texts *of* conversion (as opposed to texts *about* conversion) served to constitute self, experience, and community for early American evangelicals" (2).

Other writers have examined religious and other forms of autobiography by writers we might regard as outsiders to the Anglo-American tradition. In his now classic *To Tell a Free Story*, William L. Andrews examined the shared features, circumstances, and significance of early African American life-writing. Andrews's work, in particular, informs much of the discussion that follows. His individual readings of key texts, his analysis of the sticky issues of editors and amanuenses, of the authority and use of metaphor, and of the problematics of discussing the authorship of these early texts is essential to discussions particularly of Jarena

Lee, Olaudah Equiano, and John Marrant. Further, it is important to recognize the issue of authorial control for the writers in this study. Occom's was not a published text; the others were, and to a great extent they were under the control of their authors. Marrant's apparent control of the edition I have selected for discussion, evident not only in the bibliographic history of the text, but in dramatic textual differences as well, is crucial. Both Jarena Lee and William Apess struggled against particular religious authorities to ensure that their life stories were published the way they wanted them to be. And Equiano's authorial control is fully documented in carefully examined bibliographic records of his text. Only Bailey's, in many ways the most difficult text in this discussion, less clearly evidences its author's control. In her case (and her editor's), the difference or development between text proper and appended letter becomes an important part of my discussion of agency in that work.

The dynamics of authority, authorship, and social critique come into play in other ways as well. To a certain extent I am examining the dynamic that Andrews identified in 1986 when he argued that although "early black autobiographers usually celebrate the acculturation process, the process itself does not go uncritically examined. Some white-controlled narratives imply that acculturation changed black outsiders into insiders, but a few early black autobiographies resist this easy conclusion. In these latter works the acculturation process leaves the narrator with a dual perspective, that of the insider who remains outside in some crucial sense," a dynamic that, as Andrews notes, parallels W. E. B. Du Bois's "unreconciled strivings," his now classic articulation of the "double-consciousness" of race for African Americans (39).

The dynamic identified in Du Bois's classic analysis of U.S. race consciousness parallels that explored by feminist scholars interested in autobiography studies. Sidonie Smith, for example, examines women autobiographers' use of a double-voiced structure to reveal their simultaneous desire for narrative authority and fear of self-exposure; Leigh Gilmore identifies a wide range of women's life-writing in a strategy she names "autobiographics," a construction of experimental, conflicting, multiple identities that allow the autobiography itself to become an act of resistance. Whereas most Protestants in this period saw themselves as inheritors of a biblical tradition and as deriving their religious authority from their experiences with God and the Bible, and whereas most of them gained a sense of identity by imagining themselves typologically—reenacting the experiences of biblical narrators—white women and non-European writers emphasized different sets of texts that spoke to and about the oppression and silencing they experienced inside and outside of traditional Christianity. Like Leigh Gilmore's women autobiographers and Rodger Payne's white evangelical Christians, the writers here assert their life narratives as enactments of resistance and self-definition. Discourse itself becomes agency.

I look at this literature from a perspective informed by postcolonialism, feminism, border theory, and Critical Race Theory—approaches that all share a concern with interrogating systems of power and issues of justice for the disenfranchised; I depend, as well, upon historically contextualized close readings of the individual texts. In each case a close reading of the text or a portion of the text allows readers to appreciate these writers' use of biblical voices, narratives, tropes, and hymn language to express their piety along with their perplexity, rage, and dissent. The literature—that is, the autobiographies themselves—is central here, as is an attempt to understand and appreciate the diverse religious and personal experiences and perspectives (the voices) of these writers. I began the project with a strong sense of their complex rhetorical situations, of the way they negotiated a sense of self both spiritual and political in what appeared to be profoundly unaccommodating terrain. That sense of appreciation for their fraught rhetorical circumstances, informed sense of audience, strategic textual work, and complex commitment to faith continues to inform my discussion.

I am especially interested in attending to the faith perspectives of these writers, aware that this element of early texts has not been examined as carefully as it might have been. Some years ago, at the beginning of a senior seminar in early American literature, I asked a group of undergraduate English majors to write a preliminary response to the *Journal* of John Woolman, which they had just finished reading. What stood out to them in Woolman's work, what features of his style had they noted? What were the pivotal structural moments in the *Journal?* I had in mind, for the most part, simply jump-starting our first day of discussion in a course on autobiography. What I got, instead, was a demonstration of undergraduate resistance to religious texts and religious rhetoric. Student after student expressed in vigorous prose that they found Woolman's relentlessly religious sensibility annoying, distracting. Many wished they could have read about what he did but not *why* he did it; they found his resistance to slavery compelling, and his insistent commitment to living peaceably and working toward justice remarkable, but his discussions of his motives were "unnecessary," they thought. His "overly religious" rhetoric was "hard to get past," they said, as if that was what any sensible reader would do when encountering descriptions of a writer's religiosity. We had, to be sure, a lively discussion as I asked them to interpret *their* texts, to examine their assumptions about literature, about religion, and about interpretation. Would one try to "get past" other sorts of language in an assigned reading, for instance? And how, exactly, had they come to believe that although representations of other experiences and sensibilities were legitimate, authentic stuff and worth their attention as students, representations of religion needed, apparently quite obviously, to be discarded as one made one's way to something more—what? Interesting? Complicated? Literary? In fact, until quite recently, I found my students' perspectives on this matter remarkably similar to that of more sophisticated readers, despite their shared sense of the way these qualifying terms have been problematized by several decades of conversation about aesthetics, canon, literary theory, and autobiography studies.

Occasionally, and especially in texts by writers of color and women, earnest (if conventional) religiosity gets characterized by contemporary critics as the writer's regrettable or simple (and entirely uncritical) acquiescence to the dominant culture; readerly response to religiosity then seems reminiscent of a now thoroughly problematized dismissal of racial or cultural inauthenticity. As I was finishing this project, for instance, I heard a speaker at an academic conference, assert that the "only" way to teach or, indeed, read Frances Ellen Watkins Harper's extraordinary attack on American racism in her 1890s novel *Iola Leroy* was to dismiss altogether the main character, because of her "ridiculous" piety, and to focus instead on "less annoying" peripheral characters.

Scholarly examinations have often failed to appreciate the appeal of traditional and creative employment of Protestant Christianity— its ideals, rhetoric, traditions—for early women and writers of color, sometimes assuming that the Christian piety self-consciously reflected upon in a personal narrative, for instance, is really nothing more than a narrative pose, designed to appeal to and perhaps deceive the original audience. Historically contextualized close readings reveal instead, however, that ideas and ideals at the heart of some writers' experience of Christianity—and, perhaps even more specifically, biblical narratives that contain enactments of those ideals—allowed certain writers a tradition in which to articulate their own pain and rage, a hermeneutical lens for violence, a voice with which to express their experience, and a theoretical justification for resistance. The strategies of appeal to biblical figures of dissent, in many cases, provided legitimation for resistance to traditional discourse and beliefs that threatened to silence those writers. In Joanna Brooks's words, this work is both crucial and challenging: "Early African-American and Native American literatures demand that we grapple not only with race but also with the value of religion to early communities of color. Engaging the vital religious aspects of these writings is an enterprise fraught with its own complications" (17). Traditional and emerging revisionist Christianity often becomes a site of both contest and liberation in these texts, especially in the writers' interpretive work with violence and in their uses of biblical voices and imagery. The complexity of religious life-writing in this period consists not only of diverse and divergent views within the broad traditions of evangelical Christianity, for example, but within individual religious persons themselves, who interpret their own experiences and their contemporary religious cultures in the context of opposing strains of thought within historical Christianity.

In contrast to arguments that present religion as a mask for a critique that is antireligious, thus subordinating religion to other issues in the narrative, these texts suggest that to a certain extent, religion and religious discourse must be understood as being among the primary sources of identity here, that the biblical voices these writers appropriated allowed them a powerful framework within which to understand and articulate their own conflicted identities and their difficult relationships to the forces that shaped their experiences. I am not suggesting that religion be understood as distinct from other forces, or, to be sure, from crucial material circumstances, but rather that religion must be understood as a significant part of the personal and cultural dynamic that their texts reveal.

Occasionally, contemporary literary critics have attempted to ignore religion in or to excise it out of American texts, with the unspoken assumption that somehow one could thereby discover another text unsullied by what might seem at first a quaint but finally embarrassing religiosity. There is much evidence of literary critics' postmodern discomfort with earnest religious expression, a discomfort that is not as apparent in other disciplines, for example, cultural history, art history, sociology, and anthropology. There is a particular need for a deeper understanding of religion in American literary studies. In a 1995 issue of *American Literature* focused on "The Next Century," Jenny Franchot persuasively argued, for example, that scholars of American literature have effectively avoided religion as a location for serious inquiry and interpretation. Until recently, this avoidance was especially true regarding texts produced by women and writers of color in the early period of American literature.

Criticism that produced insightful and contextualized readings of difference frequently attended to issues of religious identity and meaning with somewhat less sensitivity and insight. Franchot's 1995 article identifies a significant gap, which, as she explains, "produced a singularly biased scholarship" marked by a refusal to "engage intensively with the religious questions of the topic at hand *as religious questions.*" In the discipline of literary studies, she explains, "religious questions . . . are peculiarly subject to silencing." Recently, scholars such as Katherine Clay Bassard, Joanna Brooks, Helen Thomas, Hilary Wyss, and Gauri Viswanathan have moved into that gap to consider issues of religious meaning and writers' experiences of difference.[8] My discussion attempts to take seriously both the religious rhetoric and the religious questions of these writers—questions of salvation and sanctification, divine sovereignty, personal agency, religiously inflected hierarchies of race and gender, suffering and violence, and justice—and to contextualize these questions in their historical and literary moments.

The common strategies and strikingly similar theological concerns of these religious life writers resembles the theorizing at the core of some contemporary theological critiques of traditional Christianity from communities of men and women of color. Womanist and *mujerista* theologians within African American and Latina communities, respectively, rely, for instance, on a theoretical foundation that not only includes but often foregrounds the life experience of the writer and the concrete experience of the historical community from which the writer draws her sense of identity and theological location. Ada María Isasi-Díaz and María Pilar Aquino, for example, both begin their discussions of *mujerista* theology from the vantage of their own autobiographies. Similarly, Delores Williams and Katie Cannon initiate their discussions of womanist theology by discussing the historical exclusion of women of color from traditional theology, and by insisting upon contemporary women's concrete experiences of oppression and silencing as an authoritative starting point for theology. Such a starting point leads them, further, to reject religious justification of symbolic or actual violence as for example, they reinvision a theology of sacrificial atonement. In all this work the narrative of personal experience provides a location from which to voice opposition to theological systems that have failed to account for the actual historical and personal experiences of people who suffer. Cannon goes on to use African American writers, notably Zora Neale Hurston, as sources for religious reflection and argument. The biblical hermeneutics at work here and the sense of authority by which the writer articulates theological arguments concerning traditional Christianity rest in large part on an insistence (and this is always posed as a corrective) on justice for marginalized people whose experiences of exploitation and abuse have been either justified or ignored by Christianity. Indeed, this shared approach to religion looks remarkably like the strategies Mary Bednarowski uncovers in her study of contemporary American women's religious thought and practices, particularly in her emphasis on the significance and even power of ambivalence for women who write and speak publicly about conventional religion, specifically U.S. Christianity.

This kind of reliance on the life experience of the writer and the historical community with which he or she identifies is a feature of disparate theological arguments from diverse religious communities that share a sense of earnest assent and, equally, a sense of profound disenfranchisement. The liberation theologies that emerged in the Latin American Roman Catholic Church with Gustavo Gutiérrez, Juan Luis Segundo, José Míguez Bonino, and José Porfirio Miranda, for example, began with a fundamental concern for justice and a profound identification with the poor, as well as a depiction of God (primarily through the use of Old Testament prophetic text and imagery) as unwaveringly on the side of the marginalized and oppressed. These activist-writers insisted that theology must begin not with abstract arguments about authority or with tradition but with a clear sense of one's specific historical location in an unjust world, and with questions shaped by one's experience in and with the world. Spiritual liberation here becomes of a piece with political liberation. Without conflating the significant distinctions among these movements, I want to point out the relevant shared elements within this group of writers and texts. All these theological perspectives share a commitment to methodologies and conclusions resting on the actual experience of particular individuals and groups outside the dominant Western Christian tradition of European America, a commitment shared by the writers I discuss.

Although I examine shared contexts—historical, theological, experiential, psychic—I do not suggest that these writers constitute either a group or a movement in a historical sense. A number of these writers knew, or knew of, one another, or read each other's autobiographies. Apess had likely read Equiano; Phillis Wheatley knew and corresponded with Samson Occom. Occom and Marrant experience conversion in historically and culturally proximate circumstances. Some of these writers did, to a certain extent, share a network of ideas and affiliations associated with revivalist Christianity, but that connection did not extend to all of them. (Bailey—despite her evangelical piety and revivalist experience—vigorously separated herself from the embarrassing excesses of the Methodists.) And the writers' relationships to that legacy vary in important ways that would be elided by such a generalization. Nor is there, necessarily, a progression or development. Important specific differences within this group have to do, certainly, with the passage of time, with political and theological change, but also with the degree to which the writer gained a level of economic freedom, a public and specifically political persona, and, perhaps most important, what Abigail Bailey was denied: a sense of collectivity—affiliation with a community of others who shared their experiences of prohibitions, exclusions, and violence.

In the end, Stowe's critique of traditional male Christianity, quoted at the outset of this chapter, seems to resonate with the nonfictional presentations of the writers in this discussion and with contemporary voices as well. Like Stowe, the earlier writers insist on expanding and reshaping traditional Christianity by way of personal stories that seem to suggest alternative, sometimes roomier, sometimes subversive versions of the master narrative of patriarchal Christianity. Surfacing in their texts is a range of issues relevant to religious life-writing—recurring, overlapping issues of authority, including the authority of the church pulpit, biblical identity, dissent, social justice, psychological trauma and denial, religious ecstasy, violence, narrative tensions between internal and external worlds, and experiential versus theoretical theology.

Their dissenting yet still insistently participatory voices suggest many of the postmodern concerns of contemporary religious writers: they frequently value ambivalence over orthodoxy, and they locate the source of authority for meaning as centrally in the individual's experience and conscience as in text or traditions.

2

"I DID NOT MAKE MYSELF SO..."

Samson Occom and American Religious Autobiography

✠

> Christians are some times worse than the Savage Indians.
> Samson Occom

IN 1772, SAMSON OCCOM composed what LaVonne Ruoff calls the "first Indian best-seller": an execution sermon before the hanging of his fellow Christian Mohegan, Moses Paul (62).[1] The most famous student of Eleazar Wheelock—a New England preacher turned Indian educator—Occom himself had become a missionary, teaching and preaching to Native Americans, and raising significant sums of money on a British tour on behalf of missionary efforts among Native Americans.[2] An articulate and persuasive speaker, Occom was successful in ministry and marketing, inspiring jealousy in white colleagues (who worried that his popularity undermined theirs) and generosity for "Wheelock's Indians" in British audiences (who marveled at the civilized Christian savage). Occom preached over three hundred sermons in England between 1765 and 1768, and raised more than 12,000 pounds. Funded significantly by that revenue, Wheelock's educational venture in New Hampshire was subsequently transformed into Dartmouth College and its mission of Indian education dissolved. Occom vigorously, angrily, opposed Wheelock in this venture, which he viewed as a violation of the trust of the donors to whom he had successfully appealed.[3]

Occom's inadvertent role in the founding of Dartmouth and his sermon vilifying his fellow Indian both for the crime of murder and for drunkenness—a vice he himself had been accused of—are merely the beginnings of the perplexing story of Samson Occom and the New England missionaries.[4] In order to begin to appreciate the complexity of Occom's situation and, by extension, the stories of thousands of other non-European Christian converts in early America, one needs to examine his fascinating autobiographical piece, "A Short Narrative of My Life."[5] Occom's brief account (which he began to compose years before his final break with Wheelock over Dartmouth) provides a kind of rhetorical map of the difficult notion of self wrought by his conversion, and of the complexities and contradictions of, for example, values of justice and compassion—crucial to Christianity—and the practice of racism as it was entrenched in the Christian tradition. The intricacies of this particular autobiographical narrative, which remained unpublished long after Occom's lifetime, forecast the issues that recur and resonate in life-writing by women and writers of color in the Christian tradition in North America.

Occom's story challenges the assumptions underlying much of the religious life-writing in the early period of American literary history; his story, and in particular his interesting and unfinished rendition of that story in "A Short Narrative," interrogates a traditional Protestant set of answers about how and why one composed a life story. The differences in tone, style, and structure between Occom's narrative and those of his contemporaries with whom he shared a great deal, most notably a bedrock of pious Calvinism, reveal what is unspoken and unquestioned in some of the texts more familiar to readers of early American religious autobiography. Occom's alternative narrative undercuts what became the dominant mode of discourse in early American religious life-writing: the story of the interior self in its spiritual progression toward rebirth and sanctification, the approved Puritan narrative, which continued to evolve through the revivalism of the Great Awakenings and which informed both religious and secular autobiography long into the nineteenth century. If, in the late twentieth and early twenty-first centuries, some readers of Jonathan Edwards's *Personal Narrative*, for instance, wonder (as my students always do) what actually "happened" in the Puritan writer's life—that is, what were the actual life circumstances that accompanied, even caused, the interior narrative—then Occom's narrative provides them with a telling counterpoint in its focus on the material circumstances resulting from the racist treatment he experienced at the hands of his fellow Christians. Occom's "Short Narrative," along with published, autobiographical texts by women, African American, and Native American writers, interrogates the autobiographical mode of writing, requiring readers to enlarge the frame around early American autobiography as a genre and to reconsider religious autobiography, including the conversion narrative, the form that has been viewed as the "center" of religious autobiography in the early period (Shea, "Prehistory" 31, 42).

A discussion of Samson Occom must begin with the circumstances that shaped his story.[6] Occom remained within the tradition whose vicious practices he experienced firsthand. In his own words, though he was "Born a Heathen and Brought up In Heathenism," he was a faithful Christian for the rest of his life after his conversion, eager to introduce Western civilization, literacy, and Christ to his fellow Indians.[7] Despite his split with Wheelock over the founding of Dartmouth, and his anger at his mistreatment by white missionaries (expressed both in the "Short Narrative" and in many personal letters), Occom remained a loyal Christian, completing his missionary effort by establishing the Brothertown community of Christian Indians in New York near the end of his life. His adherence to traditional Protestantism notwithstanding, Occom was held suspect throughout his career by white missionaries and ministers who accused him both of having too strong an allegiance to his kinsmen and of arrogance.

Samson Occom's preliminary move toward an autobiographical account seems to have been provoked by specific accusations in his string of ongoing troubles with church and mission authorities concerning his identity and character. For instance, he was a participant in a long-running land dispute (the Mason Controversy) between Native Americans and colonists. A group of Mohegans, sponsored by the Mason family, lobbied for compensation for or the return of stolen Mohegan lands. In 1765, after charges from (among others) a schoolmaster, Robert Clelland, and his patron, Rev. David Jewett, pastor of the North Church of New London, Connecticut, that he was inappropriately involved, Occom withdrew from the dispute with an apology for misconduct.[8] His quarrels with Jewett and Clelland lasted many years, however. Before their complaints about his involvement in the Mason affair, Occom had accused Clelland of favoring the English over the Indians in his school (Blodgett 78–80). A year earlier, Jewett had lodged complaints, first, that Occom did not attend his sermons and, second, that he held his own Sunday meetings in his schoolhouse, which Jewett felt had the immediate effect of depleting the attendance at his (Jewett's) sermons. And even after Occom's return from England, not only Jewett and Clelland but Wheelock and others repeatedly complained that he had become arrogant and independent; his troubles in getting along with his Christian brethren worsened dramatically.

As he prepared to leave on his fund-raising tour of England in 1765, Occom was attacked by the Boston commissioners of the London missionary society sponsoring the tour. There were rumors that he was Mohawk rather than Mohegan, that he had been converted immediately before (and purposely *for*) the British tour, and that he drank. Discouraged by accusations that he was not who he seemed to be, Occom wrote to Wheelock in 1765:

> They think it is nothing but a Shame to Send me over the great Water, they Say it is to Impose upon the good People. . . . Some say I can't Talk Indian, orthers say I can't read. . . . O that God wou'd give us grace and Wisdom to conduct aright before him and before all men,—I have a Struggle in my Mind At times, knowing not where I am going, I dont know but I am Looking for a Spot of ground where my Bones must be Buried, and never to see my Poor Family again. (Richardson 75)

Occom roused himself to respond to the attacks; he had to defend himself for the good of his cause—education of his fellow Indians—and for the sake of his reputation. And so he wrote his personal story, drafting a preliminary narrative prior to the English tour in 1765, then expanding and completing it after his return, in 1768, in a climate of even greater controversy and accusation. Occom's English and American friends were wary of his confidence and self-direction—more pronounced than they had been before his great success in England. According to Harold Blodgett's 1935 account of Occom's life, he was carefully watched, and Wheelock and others reminded him of his humble origins and proper place under their authority. In spite of their corrections, Occom took the part of his fellow Mohegans in yet more disputes, clashing with Wheelock and others in increasingly vigorous disagreements that resulted, finally, in Occom's losing his only source of steady income: Wheelock wanted Occom to settle in the wilderness with the Iroquois; Occom refused. And this is the point at which Occom and Wheelock clashed over the founding of Dartmouth (Blodgett 105–9). There were personal troubles, as well: in addition to his being accused of public drunkenness, one of his many children was rebellious; his wife, Mary, became seriously ill; and he himself suffered a shoulder injury that prevented him from riding a horse. Compounding all these real troubles, rumors about Occom spread throughout the community so that, increasingly, he lost credibility with other missionaries and ministers, especially Wheelock (Blodgett 109–11). It was in this context—of accusation, suspicion, and terrible discouragement—that Occom returned to the task of setting down the circumstances of his life experience. He must have felt pressure to defend himself and to correct the misconceptions fostered by years of both direct accusation and rumor.

In contrast to the more extensive, formal, and internally focused personal narratives of other early American Puritan writers, Occom's is shaped by these constraints of experience and, indeed, by the larger cultural and religious constraints that he specifically addressed in his narrative. In defending himself, Occom might have been expected to defend the New England missionary enterprise with Native Americans, with which he had had so much to do. But he did not. Instead, he wrote a scathing indictment of his white missionary colleagues. In the process, he called into question his own sense of identity—as it was inextricably linked to New England Christianity—just as he meant to assert his own version of an authentic self in the face of multiple accusations of inauthenticity (that he was neither a proper Mohegan, nor a proper Christian). The emphasis of the narrative thus seems to shift over the course of the text: rather than insisting on its author's own actual identity in the face of the lies being told about him, it progressively focuses on exposing the lies around him, on the hypocrisy of his missionary colleagues. In the end the work not only presents his own understandably decentered self, but decenters the model religious self of many of his contemporary religious writers and readers.

I want to situate Occom's account historically by acknowledging the personal narrative of one of his near contemporaries, Jonathan Edwards.[9] Both men were important participants in the Great Awakening of the 1740s: Edwards as both preacher and interpreter of the "Surprising Work of God" he witnessed; Occom as one of the model converts during what he describes in his narrative as the time of "Strange Concern among the White People."[10] The two men knew many of the same people and shared many beliefs. But by comparing them, I do not mean to ignore the significant differences between their texts or to suggest that there is a sameness of purpose, tone, or circumstance. Indeed, it is the important differences between the two that interests

Samson Occom. Courtesy Boston Public Library.

me. Occom had neither the spiritual leisure nor the relative security of circumstance of Edwards, and the differences in level of introspection and in tone between these two works result, in large part, from the differences in situation and, just as important, purpose of their writers. Edwards's narrative reflects its pensive, earnest author, who endeavors to get closer and closer to the ultimate meaning of his own spiritual journey, and to represent that journey in a way that will bring glory to God. Occom, in contrast, sees his own troubles and their cause most clearly, despite the set of beliefs and spiritual concerns he shares with Edwards.

Edwards's "Personal Narrative" recounts his progression from an unenlightened spiritual condition to a state of increasing spiritual confidence. At every turn and every reversal (and there are many in this brief narrative), Edwards reevaluates the spiritual state that he had, only sentences before, found, if not satisfactory, at least a marked improvement over his former state. Each reevaluation brings new insight into his own sinfulness and a deeper sense of joy in a central theological concern: the sovereignty of God. And Edwards's narrative (like many seventeenth- and eighteenth-century American religious autobiographical texts) is almost entirely focused on his internal condition, with very few references to his life circumstances. This is not to say, however, that the external world is not present. In fact, Edwards comes to depend upon the spiritual meaning inherent in the natural world, a dependence, as so many readers have noticed, that anticipates the transcendentalism of Emerson. Edwards looks at the sky from his father's pasture, and the meaning of the sovereignty of God becomes clear to him; Emerson crosses a bare common at twilight and is transformed into a "part or particle of God," one who sees all clearly without the distractions of egotism (*Nature* 10). Still, the beauty and spirituality of the natural world notwithstanding, ultimate meaning for Edwards depends upon a mode of progressive internal revelation which is characteristic of other early American religious autobiographical writing. Edwards weights the end of the account with interpretive authority. The reader, who has all along been asked to reevaluate each of the author's "former" states, must depend upon the end of the narrative for the most authoritative vision of Edwards's self and God.[11] Edwards presents his religious self in a recursive way, circling back into the narrative with a deepening, increasingly certain sense of spiritual development.

In Occom's text, too, the reader can observe a progressive revelation, with the authoritative interpretation occurring in the final paragraphs. But there the comparison with Edwards and with most other white, New England Christian autobiographical writers must end. Edwards's narrative depends upon internal revelation and upon a natural world imbued with spiritual meaning; Occom's spiritual revelations, although earnest, seem prefatory—almost parenthetical—and the rest of the meaning of the text is inextricably bound to and by the very specific, discrete difficulties of his everyday life. Whereas Edwards resides in a natural world that catapults him into a spiritual reality of abstract doctrines, Occom lives in a relentlessly material world of circumstance shaped by his racist brethren, a world of circumstance that distracts him from the spiritual transformation he seeks. This shift or relocation of tension, where the autobiographer's difficulties—a source of rich meaning in this genre—are located in the material, rather than exclusively in the spiritual world, characterizes the writing discussed in the rest of this study, accounting for a crucial difference at the foundation of style and purpose.

Occom's introductory paragraph consists of a very brief account of his "Heathenish Ways" when he could neither read nor write and was "unacquainted with the English tongue." From the beginning, then, Occom clearly and emphatically speaks from the perspective of the colonized native. This makes sense in light of his purpose: in order to justify himself to his audience, he needs to identify himself as one of them. But in order to underscore that affiliation, Occom seems, throughout the account, to present other Indians as "other," using the third person, referring repeatedly to "these Indians" and to "them"—language consistently suggestive of a profound separation between his current and original selves, between his religious and racial identity. Indeed, despite the increasing anger toward white Christians that his letters take on in this same time period, the sense of identification with white Christianity remains consistent. In fact, Leon Richardson in his 1933 account describes Occom as the only one of Wheelock's Indian charges who seemed to bear out his theories that a properly Christianized Indian would be distinguishable only by color from white New England Puritans: "In attire, in mannerisms, in language, in habits, even in mental attitude, Occom, upon superficial observation, was hardly distinguishable from the traditional New England divine" (12–13). Wheelock, who at one point baldly described his attempts to "purge all the Indian out" of another student, seems to have lamented that he was unable to produce a greater number of properly Christianized Indians such as Occom (qtd. in Axtell 98; M. Elliott 241). Occom seems, at times, to be the quintessence of cultural betrayal, a case study of the effects of conquest and colonization. But to dismiss him as failing an authenticity standard is to miss both the circumstances and achievement of this text and of Occom's legacy at Brotherton.

What is most surprising here is that Occom's conversion to Christianity—the main stuff of so many contemporary religious figures' autobiographical accounts—is referred to only briefly in the second paragraph of the narrative. After providing some necessary details concerning the religious climate of the Great Awakening—"there were Extraordinary Ministers Preaching from Place to Place and a Strange Concern among the White People"—Occom mentions his conversion only briefly and in a subordinate clause: "These Preachers did not only come to us, but we frequently went to their meetings and Churches. After I was awakened & converted, I went to all the meetings, I could come at; & Continued under Trouble of Mind about 6 months; at which time I began to Learn the English Letters; got me a Primer, and used to go to my English Neighbours frequently for Assistance in Reading." This initial account of his conversion to Christianity consists of a preliminary mention, a quick fact embedded in his acquisition of habits of churchgoing and literacy. Occom does go on to say briefly that he had a "discovery of the way of Salvation" and to describe a deepening of his spiritual state whereby he "found Serenity and Pleasure of Soul, in Serving God" ("Short" 13). But again, the focus is only very briefly on his spiritual awakening, and these comments seem buried in descriptions of his continued educational progress and earnest declarations of concern for his "Poor Brethren." Much of the subsequent narrative consists of a recounting of the details of Occom's life and ministry: how he kept school, how he held religious meetings, how he served as an arbiter in disputes.

Even though in the introductory paragraphs Occom clearly aligns himself with English Christians—as eager as they are to christianize the Native Americans—he also consistently presents himself, in subsequent paragraphs, as one under the unfortunate and unjust control of white church leaders and missionaries. He emphasizes that he has no control over his circumstances, and that decisions are made for him, by using passive constructions repeatedly, saying "I have been obliged" or "I was obliged" and explaining how he "was allowed" to supplement his inadequate income. The emphasis throughout the piece is on his lack of control and his dependence on authorities who mistreat him and then fail to exercise compassion concerning his circumstances. He is not an agent of action here; rather, he is consistently acted upon.

Interestingly, this same stylistic feature, frequent use of passive voice, occurs in a number of other early American religious autobiographies (particularly among those by Puritan and Quaker writers), including Edwards's "Personal Narrative." But most often in those other texts, the agent is God, the narrator being acted upon by the divine. In contrast, Occom is acted upon by other missionaries, the result being hardship and discomfort for himself and his family. He does not name those who do the obliging and allowing, however, nor does he directly accuse his colleagues of mistreatment. Instead he catalogues his own extraordinary need, along with his faithful service, in increasing detail. It is not until the very end of this catalogue, near the conclusion of the narrative, that he begins to present his interpretive conclusions regarding the meaning of his misfortunes.

Occom describes his hardships and the ways he has been mistreated by quoting the Apostle Paul in the second letter to the Corinthians. (Corinthians, and the Apostle Paul's anger, may have had a particular appeal for Occom: Michael Elliott notes his use of another section of the same epistle in a confrontational letter to Wheelock concerning the founding of Dartmouth [245–46].) In the biblical text, Paul himself speaks as an angry missionary, confronting his Corinthian readers with claims that they have mistreated him. He places himself and his faithful service in the context of those he calls "false apostles" and "deceitful workers," arguing further, in words that Occom literally repeats, that he speaks "as a fool" (2 Cor. 11).[12] Because Occom actually quotes Paul here, it is difficult to imagine that he would *not* have been identifying with the angry, accusatory tone of this section of the biblical epistle. And as he catalogued the particulars of his hardship, he must have recalled Paul's litany of peril from the same passage, in which he recounts beatings, imprisonment, stonings, and shipwrecks. Occom, for his part, recalls in parallel fashion how he has lived in a wigwam, traveled two miles for wood and eighteen miles for meal, has had to "contrive every way" to feed his family as a result of his meager pay: fishing, keeping pigs, raising corn and potatoes and beans, binding books, selling feathers, and making pails and spoons. Like Paul, Occom establishes his authority by listing his hardships and establishes his virtue by describing the vicious behavior of others. Occom confronts the missionaries with rhetoric from their own authoritative text, using the language and circumstances of the apostle to draw a parallel to his own. And in his reconfiguration of things here, the missionaries are the ungrateful and recalcitrant Corinthians, while he is the faithful and long-suffering apostle, the "true" missionary. Occom's audience would have heard the language of the biblical text, particularly in the Pauline description of the angry, ranting fool, constrained to name the vile behavior of brethren who have, for the moment, become adversaries.

Just as many early American writers of spiritual autobiography present themselves as travelers who arrive, by reflective turns, at an increasing sense of revelation in their narratives, so Samson Occom, after reflecting on his own experience of financial need and oppression, moves toward an ultimate revelation at the end of his narrative. He begins to accuse his audience of intentional racist abuse: "I Can't Conceive how these gentlemen would have me Live. I am ready to impute it to their Ignorance, and I would wish they had changed circumstances with me but one month, that they may know, by experience, what my Case really was; but I am now fully convinced, that it was not Ignorance" ("Short" 17). Though he asserts that it was *not* ignorance that led to his mistreatment, Occom stops short of naming the cause in precise terms: he does not explicitly identify issues of race until the final paragraph of the narrative. Here, instead, he goes on to contrast the vast difference between his pay and that of white missionaries who have fewer qualifications. Wheelock had, in fact, called for the training of Indian missionaries, in part, precisely because he saw them as needing only half the pay of English missionaries (M. Elliott 241). But "what can be the Reason that they used me after this manner?" Occom rhetorically asks. And then, in an intriguing response to his own previously repeated assertions concerning his relationships with and position in regard to the white missionaries, he asserts that "I am not under obligations to them" ("Short" 18). Of course Occom means financial obligation here, but his word choice, echoing their experiences of the earlier "obliged," which he had used to describe the extraordinary constraints of circumstance caused by the "gentlemen" to whom he now says he is not obliged, is notable. He reveals a distinct sense of self here, one that must be separated from his audience, from those who have mistreated him so severely.

The final revelation that Occom presents in his "Short Narrative" is one that would have had a profoundly discomfiting effect on his audience. In an attempt to answer his own questions (concerning why those with whom he has faithfully worked for years have abused and exploited him), he recalls a story told by a "Poor Indian Boy," whose white master regularly beats him. When asked to explain the violence of his master, the boy says that his master might beat him because of his poor performance, or he might beat him because he is inclined to do so, but finally, that he "Beats me for the most of the Time 'because I am an Indian.'" Occom follows his fable of abuse with his own reflection, explaining, finally, the meaning of his own experiences, which parallel the boy's beatings: "So I am *ready* to Say, they have used me thus, because I Can't Influence the Indians so well as other missionaries; but I can assure them I have endeavoured to teach them as well as I know how;—but I *must Say*, "I believe it is because I am a poor Indian." I Can't help that God has made me so; I did not make my self so" ("Short" 18). In this remarkable conclusion, Occom defends himself by leveling his aim directly at his accusers, attributing years of abuse and exploitation to the overt racism of his Christian colleagues, a racism which, in the context of a racist culture, spawns the story of the Indian boy and fuels the repeated accusations against Occom.

Occom's life narrative becomes a list of grievances. And it is as if over the course of the text he comes to the conclusion, the final insight or truth, which he presents to readers. Occom's truth, however, in contrast to that of Edwards' and others, is not a revelation about the state of his soul but rather an insight concerning others and the meaning of his own circumstances. His defense of himself, finally, rests not on his authentic identity but on the authentic identity of his audience, which has fostered ongoing abuse of Occom in particular and of other "poor Indians" in general. Whereas normative English Christian narratives progress toward an accumulation of spiritual insight, with the end result of self-revelation designed to encourage and challenge the larger religious community, Occom's narrative ends with a revelation about the community, an unmasking of the community ethos that has legitimated the calculated cruelty and false accusations to which the wrier has been subject throughout his career.

In the end, Occom's account of his life effectively undercuts the expected form of religious autobiographical narratives from the early period of American literary history and forecasts the dynamics that occur in texts by many writers, including those in this discussion, who embrace but are simultaneously "othered" by Christian traditions. The truth that Occom presents here opposes the assumption at the foundation of much traditional Western Christian autobiography: that one can tell the truth of one's spiritual life without recourse to the larger social and political realities that shape one's notions of spiritual truth. Whereas many of Occom's contemporaries and seventeenth-century predecessors in their life-writing present hardship as God's chastening hand, sanctifying them and deepening their faith, Occom's halting narrative insists on the truth of his daily experience, reminding readers that the conventional approach of other Christian autobiographers depends upon the identities of tellers who are not in the margin but in the mainstream of the Anglo-Christian community.

There are, of course, crucial exceptions, early American religious autobiographical writers who set their self-knowledge in the context of a larger, not exclusively internal and spiritual, reality. John Woolman, for instance, the remarkable eighteenth-century American Quaker journal writer, relates how he came to realize the injustice of slavery and then lived a life of such alarming integrity as to make those around him (who cooperated, even unwittingly, with an unjust society) profoundly uncomfortable. But Woolman's Quaker social and political awareness concerning the rights of African American slaves, displaced Indians, and poor workers, which he sees as part of his spiritual development and which dominates his text, stands in contrast to Puritan autobiography—the tradition that Occom, as a Great Awakening convert, participates in—in which notions of conscience, for the most part, are limited to purely personal moral and ethical concerns.

In articulating his final angry complaint against the missionaries, Occom severely qualifies the certain definition of himself presented at the beginning of the narrative, where he took pains to distinguish himself from his Indian origins. Exposing race as the grounds for the inequity he has endured, he realigns himself with the Mohegan community, implicitly arguing that despite the missionaries' rhetorical claim of fluidity of identity by means of "conversion," they continue to see all Indians not only as Indians but as other, and subordinate. Moreover, Occom's use of the story of the Indian boy as a template for his own experience effectively dismantles not only his earlier assertions of identity but also the tidy dualism of "heathen" and "Christian," the terms that have given meaning to his life as an Indian missionary to the Indians and Indian spokesman to the Christians. By describing the racism he has experienced, Occom challenges the assumptions of the superiority of the Christian culture, assumptions that he seems, at other times, to share with his audience.[13]

Occom's complex and not fully articulated representation of self and experience here can be appropriately understood not only in the historical contexts of the specific cultural encounter that produced it—featuring Wheelock's and his fellows' uncomplicated attempts to erase the cultures and languages of Native converts, to supplant them with English Christianity—but also in the contexts of the ongoing account of contact and conflict between European and Native Americans. The concept of Native American intellectual sovereignty articulated by Robert Allen Warrior is particularly pertinent here. A recognition of intellectual sovereignty would require us, rather than seeing Native American converts to Christianity as simply hybrid individuals refusing to compromise or even clearly define multiple identities, to read accounts of Christian conversion as a part of the work of Native American self-determination. Hence, even (or perhaps especially) conversion narratives ought to be read as expressions of Native Americans acting within and on behalf of their own cultures. Indeed, Warrior has noted that Native writers "going back at least as far as Samson Occom have grappled with many of the same issues that remain with us today. Finding in their work not only resources for self-determined Native engagement but also political commitments and intellectual praxes that are at times troubling is a double-edged sword that reminds us constantly of our own challenges and fallibilities" (*Tribal Secrets* 44). Jace Weaver examines sovereignty in the specific contexts of Christian conversion as he argues not only for intellectual sovereignty but hermeneutical sovereignty as well, calling for further reflection on the interpretive system and commitment to community employed by Native American writers.

Such work by today's Native American scholars and activists elucidates the contrary pulls in Occom's narrative (and it speaks to the much more fully developed tension in the writing of William Apess, discussed below). As Hilary Wyss argues, both Occom and Apess envision Christianity not as a European religion but as a basis of their ethnicity as Native Americans (161). Joanna Brooks examines Occom in precisely this context—"Even English language literate Christian converts like Occom should be viewed primarily not as intercessors with the white world but as proponents of new and powerful definitions of Indianness"—and goes on to stress that his later experience underscores a new self-definition (55), which I argue he began to articulate in in the personal narrative. Occom became a leader in the Brotherton movement, a pantribal Christian separatist movement that established its own settlement in upstate New York and drew upon the theology and practices of white Christian revivalism, even as it established its own unique religious forms.[14] In this context we might see Occom, in the personal text, as imagining the sense of sovereignty that he would go on to realize more fully at Brotherton.

Finally, then, what should contemporary readers make of Occom's seeming self-hatred in the last two sentences of his narrative, when he cites the reason for his own mistreatment by quoting the words of the Indian boy: "'I believe it is because I am a poor Indian.' I Can't help that God has made me So; I did not make my self so." The tone of this last bit of Occom's text seems pathetic to some readers; Occom's self-figuring as "poor"—a modifier not present in the boy's original self-description at the end of the story—and helpless (in the face of God's choice of his racial identity) seems apologetic, perhaps even pitiful. It may be. But there are other, more likely, nuances to Occom's concluding sentences as well. First, it is worth noting that the phrase "poor Indian/s" is a favorite of Occom's. He uses it repeatedly in his letters to refer to himself, his family, and his own and other Native communities. His tone seems somewhat inconsistent across these instances, but he frequently uses "poor" quite literally to mean impoverished circumstances. And that seems surely to be the case here.

Further, by insisting that he is not who he is by his own making, he confronts his contemporaries with their own self-making: in Occom's and his audience's view of things, race may be God-ordained, but human behavior, or what Occom calls "use" in this passage, is emphatically not. By describing himself as "poor," he reminds readers of the rest of his narrative, of the poverty imposed upon him by mission authorities: God may have ordained his racial identity, but the missionaries have ordained his poverty. And both circumstances occur—equally, it seems—outside of Occom's power. In this reading, then, he reveals not self-hatred but instead a chafing against his powerlessness and against the religious sensibility that continues to ensure his powerlessness. His "I did not make myself so" is as much an indictment of the missionaries who have shaped his experience as it is an appeal to the sovereign God who ordained his race. Indeed, the Calvinist preoccupation with sovereignty, an important theological context for this and all Great Awakening texts, suggests a particular self-consciousness concerning control and responsibility or culpability. Occom's detailed account of his troubles and their cause leaves no room for speculation concerning the unambiguously human origin of this decidedly unspiritualized set of trials.

Occom describes himself as a man who has been thoroughly changed by cross-cultural contact, but he presents himself, consistently and unmistakably, as a Native American. And his insistence on this provides a corollary to his colleagues' insistence on the distinction of race, even in the midst of educational ventures that they envisioned as designed to eradicate such a distinction. In the end, Occom's presentation of himself, rather than the synecdochic self that Arnold Krupat posits as a model for Native American autobiography ("Synecdochic" 176), is closer in tone and apparent purpose to a modernist, ironic presentation of self. This is in part because of Occom's ideological and cultural distance from non-Christianized Indians, and in part because he can not derive from his Christianity the same meaning that whites would have: the "sweetness of the Sovereignty of God" that overcomes Jonathan Edwards, for instance, cannot impress Occom. Instead, he experiences the harsh sovereignty of his white missionary coworkers, who prevent him from experiencing what has been by his own reports one of the primary appeals of Christianity: material gain and financial security. He has learned the truth bluntly articulated by Jace Weaver 250 years later in his account of Christian and Native American contact: "The attempts at acculturation did not matter. The profession of Christianity did not matter. In the end, it only mattered that they were Indian" (3).

In discussing early American autobiographical texts by Samuel Sewall, William Byrd, and Landon Carter, Shea says that the "'I' in their writing is confident that it speaks from the center of the real world, whereas, in contrast, in the autobiographical succession from Anne Hutchinson, the 'I' finding itself set out at an apparent margin, disputes the given real and invents a text that acknowledges a journeying rather than a fixed center" ("Prehistory" 37). Occom participates in this latter tradition; his "Short Narrative" reads as a preliminary description of the discovery that shaped his life: not the discovery of Christ but the discovery of the vicious racism of Christians.

Samson Occom's narrative, and the circumstances that shaped it, form part of a rich tradition in American autobiographical writing, and of course it is part of a larger tradition of multicultural contact and conflict characterized by irony and contradiction at the outset. The Puritans, for instance, religious dissenters themselves, arrived in America and immediately established a zero-tolerance policy on dissent and a violent response to most forms of difference: Quakers were executed; slavery was viewed as a Christianizing force for heathen Africans; and Native Americans were seen, by turns, as devils, as latter-day Canaanites to be driven out of the promised land (with violence justified by the Old Testament), and as missionary projects. Occom's life-writing does not fit the paradigm set up by those whose religious views he came to share. Their interior journeys, their notions of a spiritual self—defined and determined by supernatural action, personalized for their sanctification by a sovereign God who ordained suffering as well as success—were built on the presumptions of privilege, on the facts and circumstances of their Anglo-American experience, which, even when characterized by hardship or oppression, were founded upon an assumption of religious, intellectual, and cultural superiority to those around them. Occom's narrative insists on the circumstances of his life and on the human meaning, the human causes, of those circumstances. Ultimately, Samson Occom's narrative, and the larger story of his experience of Christianity present the story of a religious self decentered through cultural contact, a cultural self who refused the subordinating effects of that contact, and a community whose identity is contradicted by that story.

3

JOHN MARRANT, JOHN SMITH, JESUS
Borders, Tangles, and Knots in Marrant's 1785 *Narrative*

✇

> He crosses the fence, which marked the boundary between the wilderness and the cultivated country.
>
> William Aldridge, on John Marrant

JOHN MARRANT'S 1785 autobiographical *Narrative* was one of the most popular eighteenth-century Indian captivity narratives—the best-selling early American genre that held readers captive for over a century, serving up an irresistible blend of adventure, religious instruction, autobiography, ethnography, and horror. Frequently categorized as a captivity narrative, Marrant's autobiography fits into other genre classifications as well. The captivity narrative as a genre that overlaps or coincides with the authorial concerns and readerly appeal of the spiritual autobiography is particularly important not only to this discussion of Marrant but also to the subject matter of this book as a whole. Captivity narratives provided Anglo-American readers with an interpretive paradigm for making sense of the harrowing experiences of life in settlement culture, specifically modeling straightforward and surely comforting ways of understanding complex, distressing experiences: hardship and suffering, including actual and threatened violence, and contact with racial and cultural others. The captivity narrative form was especially important for early American readers, and recent studies of the genre have expanded critical understanding of the writers, their audiences, and the era that shaped their work. Adam Potkay and Sandra Burr, along with Richard VanDerBeets, document the popularity of Marrant's text in particular, classifying it as one of the three most widely read captivity narratives in early America; Rafia Zafar discusses the work in this context as well.[1]

Popular in its own moment for historically meaningful reasons, *A Narrative of the Lord's Wonderful Dealings with John Marrant, a Black* is equally compelling in the early twenty-first century because of its persistent connections to contemporary concerns of both popular and more scholarly readers. Central to Marrant's story are the multiple selves and subjectivities he experienced as he lived the metaphor of crossing and recrossing boundaries, defining and redefining himself in religious, cultural, linguistic, and racial terms. Forging his multiple identities as an outsider in a biblically inscribed world allowed him to construct a theory or, in his own contextual terms, a theology informed by his experience of the biblical texts he found meaningful; furthermore, Marrant's theology both reinforced and interrogated the traditional Christianity to which he and his readers gave assent. The experiential theology that his *Narrative* argues addresses the larger forces that shaped his life, including both his isolation from and his identification with the Anglo-American culture of his religion. Ultimately, Marrant presents a surprising theological vision which may seem paradoxical at best to contemporary readers but which was unusually expansive in the context of his immediate tradition of eighteenth-century Methodism. His *Narrative* implicitly argues that true religious conversion cannot occur in the context of violent cultural eradication, which he identifies as the context for much of the missionary activity of his religious peers.

The complex dynamic of Marrant's autobiography anticipates an argumentative stance and rhetorical authority similar to those of writers identified with border theory, who insist on the multiplicities of voice and experience shaped by the literal and figurative boundaries they live in and on, who appropriate the border metaphor to express their own cultural circumstances and identity. Marrant's identity emerges in his *Narrative* as a puzzle for those he encounters in the text, and perhaps for readers as well. His refusal to resolve or simplify the self he presents anticipates the voice, for instance, of Gloria Anzaldúa in *Borderlands/La Frontera*, insisting that "[she] will have [her own] voice: Indian, Spanish, white . . . [whose] serpent's tongue . . . will overcome the tradition of silence." Anzaldúa and other border writers such as Cherrie Moraga and Richard Saénz engage in autobiographical, reflective writing that explores complex ethnic and cultural selfhood. In the context of a boom in life-writing and, as a corollary, increased awareness concerning the complexity of ethnic and racial identities in the United States, these writers insist on retaining what appear to be conflicting identities in the face of cultural and linguistic erasure. Emerging in Chicano literature and from the geography shared by the United States and Mexico, the "borderland" constitutes both physical and psychic realities. According to Anzaldúa's preface:

> The psychological borderlands, the sexual borderlands and the spiritual borderlands are not particular to the Southwest. In fact, the Borderlands are physically present wherever two or more cultures edge each other, where people of different races occupy the same territory, where under, lower, middle and upper classes touch, where the space between two individuals shrinks with intimacy.

Moreover, although the "dominant features of this metaphoric and actual border are "hatred, anger and exploitation," there are corollary "joys" and "compensations," what Anzaldúa has called an "exhilaration in . . . the sense that certain 'faculties'—not just in me but in every border resident, colored or noncolored—and dormant areas of consciousness are being activated, awakened . . . [T]he 'alien' element has become familiar—never comfortable, not with society's clamor to uphold the old, to rejoin the flock, to go with the herd. No, not comfortable but home." The resulting stance speaks to and of writers of color who articulate their identities in the context of the threat of cultural and linguistic erasure, including the racial obliviousness of whites eager to look beyond race who naively insist upon a colorblind society in which the historically powerful structuring categories of race and ethnicity have simply (and happily, for the white readers who find them discomfiting and obviously unnecessary) disappeared.

In contrast, of course, John Marrant's white contemporaries were more interested in reifying boundaries of identity than arguing that one could overlook or simply move past them. But the messiness of identifications in Marrant's narrative and the anxious responses to his identifications by those he encounters in his text who attempt to reestablish the borders he both violates and embodies call to mind the very strategies of twenty-first-century contemporary border writers who insist that there is no keeping identities distinct in the midst of cultural encounter, who insist on seeing, among other metaphors posited as examples, "cultural knots," rather than fixed borders that remain intact as they are crossed and recrossed (Johnson and Michaelsen 9).

In this, Marrant's imagination is decidedly complex; his renderings forecast today's assumptions about the autobiographical task, about the complexities of identity, and about the racial anxieties of readers then and now.

A freeborn African American originally from New York, John Marrant moved as a young boy with his family to the area of Charleston, South Carolina. He converted to evangelical Christianity in response to the preaching of George Whitefield in 1769 or '70, when he was fourteen years old. Nearly immediately thereafter he exiled himself from his family in response to their disapproval of his evangelical religious zeal. He fled the community he knew and endured a harrowing experience in the wilderness (which in his newly converted state he regarded as a literal manifestation of a biblical metaphor, even as the material reality of it threatened to kill him). After meeting up with a hunter who helped him survive and taught him some rudimentary Cherokee language, he encountered a band of Cherokees, was taken captive, and nearly executed. He relates that his preaching, however, resulted first in a dramatic stay of execution, then in the Christian conversion of the Cherokee chief and his daughter, and, finally, in Marrant's adoption of Cherokee dress and manner of living. With the approval of the now friendly Cherokee leaders, and as a kind of Christian-Cherokee ambassador, he next evangelized neighboring Creek, Choctaw, and Chickasaw tribes.

In 1772, again in consultation with Cherokee authorities, he returned to his family in slaveholding settlement culture, where he resumed his trade as a carpenter and established a church school for slave children on a nearby plantation. When the violence of the plantation owners drove him away, he was impressed on a British war sloop during the Revolutionary War. After being discharged in 1782, he lived in London for three years and in 1785 was ordained a minister in one of the Countess of Huntingdon's chapels. Initially, he told his life story to William Aldridge as a part of that ordination process, and Aldridge then published (in fact, in many editions) the text that is the subject of this chapter, the *Narrative*, focusing on the events of his life up to this point. After its very successful publication, Marrant became a missionary to black Loyalists living in Nova Scotia, where he endured violence and sectarian opposition for two years, and then moved on to Boston, where he preached regularly to whites and blacks. In Boston he met up with influential African Americans such as Prince Hall, the community organizer and activist who founded the first black Masonic lodge. Marrant returned to England in 1790, and died in 1791.[2]

The rhetorical situation in the *Narrative* is decidedly complex. The author had an undeniably sensational story to tell. His audience consisted of, first of all, religious authorities on the occasion of his ordination. These authorities would have included Selina Hastings, the Countess of Huntingdon herself, the powerful and wealthy Methodist patron who at her own expense established Trevecca House, a theological college in South Wales, in 1768. An earnest Methodist eager to see the Church of England more robustly under Methodist influence, Hastings provided positions in her own chapels for evangelical preachers who had been banned from other pulpits. In 1779 she was required to register her chapels as "nonconformist meeting houses," after which they became known as "the Countess of Huntingdon's Connexion."[3] Horace Walpole nicknamed her "St. Theresa of the Methodists."

Hastings's piety proved no more progressive on race and slavery, however, than that of most of her white English peers. She owned black slaves, and although she had approved the ordination of another black preacher a decade earlier than John Marrant, doing so had not worked out according to her plans. In 1774 after David Margate had been ordained as a minister in Huntingdon's connection, she sent him to her Bethesda orphanage in America (bequeathed to her by George Whitefield) to preach Christianity to the slaves. He had done so, but his message, far from the one his patroness authorized, also urged aggressive rebellion against the slave system, and after narrowly escaping pursuit by a white lynch mob, he returned to England. Marrant would have needed to distinguish himself from Margate and thereby keep the favor of the countess, establish his spiritual authority, secure his ordination, and appeal to subscribers interested in purchasing his extraordinary tale of adventure and survival. Aldridge, fellow minister, editor, and amanuensis, who shared not only Marrant's spiritual concerns but his commercial interests as well, would have been sensitive to the complex circumstances.

The *Narrative* expresses Marrant's concern with racial injustice in the context of his relationship to a primarily white European religious tradition and culture, embedding his concerns in his earnest Christian zeal to convert, convince, and uplift his readers by means of his text. Furthermore, Marrant's thoroughgoing use of biblical overlays would surely have shaped white readers' dispositions toward his racial identity and corollary issues of power and authority. A close reading reveals Marrant's attention to matters of justice and race in the context of his theology; his use of biblical texts constructs an image of a God intensely concerned not only with spiritual redemption but with the material realities of human suffering and justice as well. His presentation of his religious beliefs and experiences—which he straightforwardly ascribes to his conversion experience via Whitefield, followed by his direct and ongoing experience of the scriptures as a lens through which he interprets all other experiences—speaks to the characteristics of African American Christianity as described, for example, by the historian Charles Joyner. Joyner argues that from the inception of the tradition in the United States, black Christians invoked ethical beliefs as an inextricable part of the Christianity they endorsed, even though this particular ethical strain had not been presented by white preachers. Marrant's autobiography constitutes an example of this dynamic; he makes Whitefield's revivalist Christianity new by way of his complex identity and experience as a freeborn black in a slaveholding society and then as an African American missionary to Native Americans.[4]

Three pivotal dramatic scenes in Marrant's *Narrative* allow readers to appreciate the popular appeal of this eighteenth-century text: first, the miraculous stay of execution effected by the young Indian girl and then the subsequent conversion of the Cherokee band who held the narrator captive; second, the riveting reunion of the narrator with his own family, who fail at first to recognize him because of his cultural markings as a Cherokee; and third, the violent encounter at the plantation between slaveholder and Christian slaves. All three scenes assert, to some extent, the fluidity of Marrant's and his audience's identities. The *Narrative* interrogates polarized binaries, along with inflections of power and status that likely were presumed by his contemporaries; both civilized and savage, Christian and heathen, family and stranger, even child and adult. Indeed, it is not only our postmodern preoccupations that dispose us to attend to such fluidity. As William Aldridge noted in his preface to Marrant's original readers: "He crosses the fence, which marked the boundary between the wilderness and the cultivated country; and prefers the habitations of brutal residence, to the less hospitable dwellings of enmity to God and Godliness. He wanders, but Christ is his guide and protector.—Who can view him among the Indian tribes without wonder?" (75). Marrant's fence-crossing in race, culture, and religion, and his doing so not only as a captive but willfully, unsettles easy identifications—of himself, of his family, perhaps of readers as well. And, given Aldrige's observations in his preface, designed to sell the book, after all, such boundary-crossing must have had a particular appeal for eighteenth-century readers whose tastes were reflected in the robust market for novels of sensation as well as captivity tales.

When, for instance, Marrant describes in the *Narrative* his reunion with his original family (while he himself was still dressing, as he says, "purely in the Indian Stile"), he explains that his own family members could not recognize him, even his brother, who asked, as Marrant recalls, "who I was and what I was?" His brother's pointed query (which goes unanswered for nearly a page in the brief, dramatic account of this reunion) speaks to the multiple and finally indeterminate identities that Marrant gains through his multicultural sojourn. His contemporary readers may well have shared his brother's question, for to an audience accustomed to clearly delineated racial and cultural boundaries, Marrant seems to present a bewildering puzzle of identities and allegiances. His own self-presentation, however, suggests his sense of a fairly coherent identity, despite his multiple subjectivities. In constructing the self of the autobiography, he confidently relies on biblical interpretive paradigms, readily figuring himself as various scriptural characters. His identification with these biblical figures affords him an interpretive frame that speaks to but does not define, explain, or settle his multiple selves, though it dismantles the hierarchies of race and culture assumed by his readers. Furthermore, Marrant's Christianity and his use of the Bible allow him paradoxical moves of simultaneous self-assertion and abject humility, the latter likely appealing to white readers unaccustomed to the authoritative narrative voice of an articulate, adult African speaker.

Some readers have assumed that Marrant presented his culture-crossing without much straightforward engagement of larger issues of justice and race, particularly when examining his text in the context of other eighteenth-century black Atlantic autobiographers (including his near contemporary Olaudah Equiano, who argued explicitly that the violent brutality of slavery was unjust on religious grounds). This mistaken impression occurs in part because versions of Marrant's *Narrative* published before Potkay's and Burr's 1995 reissue present a text not obviously concerned with issues of race and justice. In those earlier, less complete editions, Marrant's racial identity and the racially inflected circumstances he describes often go without comment in the text. As Rafia Zafar comments on the 1995 edition, "For many years readers had to look to a different text [the 1789 sermon] to confirm Marrant's pride in his African origins and his hatred for white hypocrisy," adding that readers of the "earlier versions of the book have pointed to the lack of references to chattel slavery in Marrant's narrative" (62). In earlier editions Marrant's race was revealed in the title (hence requiring readers to acknowledge the identity of the author) but not specifically spoken of elsewhere, leading some to assume that race was something of a peripheral concern, subordinated to and perhaps distinct from the more obvious religious aims of the autobiographical speaker.

Race is at the heart of Marrant's unspoken and spoken narrative concerns in this text, however, and the fuller edition reveals the extent of those concerns. Because of its popularity and sales, Marrant's *Narrative* was frequently republished and amended. Consequently, the editors Potkay and Burr note, its publication history is "tangled." The "undated fourth" edition, the one they reprint and on which my discussion depends, is "unique."[5] As they explain, this edition is not only the most complete—including material that did not appear earlier—but also characterized by a higher degree of direct authorial control than both previous and subsequent editions:

> The title pages of the first six "editions" [all from 1785, some of which may have been multiple copies or conflations of other texts] . . . indicate that William Aldridge, Marrant's amanuensis/editor, had direct control over Marrant's story because he "ARRANGED, CORRECTED AND PUBLISHED" it to be sold to his parishioners at the Jewry street Chapel where he was pastor. He did not, however, sell the undated "fourth edition"—a clear indication that he did not take responsibility for its contents. (72–73)

The speculation (based on textual evidence in the features of this edition) is that Marrant may have asked Aldridge for permission to have a personal edition (also from 1785) printed before he left London for Nova Scotia; in it he describes feelings and experiences that may not have been approved by his editor, feelings and experiences that were not, at any rate, included in any other edition (as far as is now known), providing a voice "apparently untouched by Aldridge's editing" (73). The singular material includes descriptions of domestic violence in his family of origin, Native American antipathy concerning white settlement, and a graphic description of plantation violence: a vicious beating inflicted on slaves who were part of Marrant's church school. The fuller text of this fourth edition presents a life narrative deeply concerned with issues of race and experiences of violence, and my assumption is that the material exclusive to the fourth edition was not a part of the life story that constituted the original ordination sermon, directed, at least in part, to Selina Hastings.

Scenes of violence shape the text and imply an argument in this fuller edition. Marrant endures and then witnesses violence in his own family at the outset of the *Narrative*, and scenes of violence repeat and intensify with meaningful distinctions in his own experiences, first as a captive himself with the Cherokee and then as he witnesses the captivity of plantation slaves. In fact, Marrant's religious concerns are portrayed in the context of violence, initially within the hierarchy of a family and then in imperial encounter—European settlers' aggression against Native Americans, and plantation violence used to control and exploit African slaves. In the telling of each incident, Marrant condemns the actual violence while making meaning by way of biblical accounts of violence, particularly the violent sacrifice of Jesus at the heart of the Christian story.

Marrant relates that soon after his Christian conversion he faced familial persecution, which the text suggests included violence. He refers specifically to his brother and sisters calling him names, to his mother and neighbors joining his siblings in tormenting him, and to his profound sense of isolation among his own kin: "There was not a friend to assist me, or that I could speak to." Subsequently, his difficulties intensify, leading up to his flight from home. His family and neighbors think he has lost his mind, and his youngest sister weeps as she watches her family mistreat him. Readerly assumptions concerning the oblique "persecutions" his sister witnesses must shift after the family reunion scene following his sojourn with the Cherokee, which is dramatically marked not only by this same sister's isolated recognition of her brother but by the accompanying domestic violence against the girl. The violent reaction of Marrant's family to what they at first insist is his sister's mistake or deception (actually her recognition of her brother) sheds further light on Marrant's earlier decision to flee his home after his conversion in order to "avoid the persecutors" (80). The account of family violence in the recognition scene, where one sister threatens to and then does beat the other sister, and the unremarkable way that violence is framed in the *Narrative*, suggest that those "persecutions" which made his younger sister weep (earlier in the text) were physical. This possibility helps contextualize Marrant's flight from his family and, more important, undercuts any notion that his story concerns exclusively religious realities, isolated from larger questions of identity, compassion, and social justice. The threatened and actual violence of these familial encounters and of the subsequent encounters with the Cherokee and the plantation slaves structures Marrant's story, implying a nascent argument concerning cultural identity, Christianity, and violence. Each encounter features unjust, unnecessary physical brutality enacted on the basis of the victim's inherent or claimed identity, an empathetic witness who attempts to disrupt or intervene in the scene of violence, and then the subsequent correction/redemption of that violence.

Marrant's analysis is shaped by his religious concerns, by his own experiences as an outsider, and by the larger context of contact between white English settlers and people of color in North America: Native Americans in the early part of the *Narrative*, African slaves in the latter part. When, for example, he leaves the Cherokee for his missionary sojourn with other Indian nations—Creek, Catawar, Housaw—he comments on their receptivity to Christianity in this way:

> These nations were then at peace with each other and I passed among them without danger, being recommended from one to the other. When they recollect, that the white people drove them from the American shores, they are full of resentment. These nations have often united, and murdered all the white people in the back settlements which they could lay hold of, men, women, and children. I had not much reason to believe any of these three nations were savingly wrought upon, and therefore I returned to the Cherokee nation, which took me up eight weeks. I continued with my old friends seven weeks and two days. (88)

Marrant provides a rich, conflicted set of comments here as he asserts that, first, the Indian nations he visits are at peace with each other and that, second, they behaved peaceably toward him. The Indian violence he recounts here has occurred specifically in retaliation, provoked by the land theft of white settlement and in a context of unity among different Indian nations, requiring readers to acknowledge white aggression as the cause of Indian hostility and countering eighteenth-century English American notions of Indian aggression; those notions were frequently supported by captivity narratives, which typically (though not always) included anti-Indian propagandistic elements that portrayed whites as innocent victims and Indians as brutal aggressors.

Furthermore, Marrant emphasizes his own ambiguous cultural identity as he passes among different Indian nations on their recommendations to each other (founded on his relationship with the Cherokee) and without threat of violence. Juxtaposing his safety with the violence he notes, he distinguishes the race of both the aggressors who initiated the violence and the victims slain in retaliation: these are "white people" who have driven Indians from "American shores" and been "murdered" as a result. Furthermore, the consequence that most obviously concerns Marrant is that these nations are not interested in Christianity: they are not, in his words, "savingly wrought upon." He begins to argue here for a cause-and-effect relationship: the hostility of whites, specifically their violent displacement of Indians, has caused Indian resistance to Marrant's (and presumably his readers') Christianity.

Although he stops short of developing this argument (which anticipates rhetorical moves by Jarena Lee and William Apess concerning the social and spiritual effects of Christian aggression toward women and Native Americans), Marrant's comments nonetheless distinguish him and his relationship with Indians from the whites who stole Indian land. Moreover, his comments suggest that he imagines a gospel quite distinct from, perhaps even in opposition to, the one represented by the white settlers who initiated acts of aggression against Native Americans. In contrast, Marrant models an entirely different sort of cross-cultural relationship in his traveling peacefully from nation to nation, depending on the goodwill of his hosts. The argument here, identifying the injustice of white racial violence against Native Americans and the way such violence has hindered Christianity, is fundamentally linked to an overall argument presented in the *Narrative*: that in Marrant's presentation, justice must be inextricably linked to Christianity; conversion cannot be equated with violent eradication of culture.

Marrant makes clear, though he does not fully articulate, connections between himself and the Native Americans whose experience he describes. This perspective, the fact that the narrator recounting Indian-white conflicts is himself a man of color who is at one point culturally identified as Cherokee, is crucial. Marrant's religious argument, the point he wants to make about Indian receptivity to Christianity and about white accountability for violence, is also an argument about his own racial identity, tied to questions of his position and power as the author of a didactic religious text. The ideological dynamic of an implicit connection between marginalized individuals and communities is present in varying degrees in the other writers discussed here. Marrant features himself enacting such an alliance, which is then woven into the fabric of the religious testimony he provides.

Like the other autobiographers I examine, Marrant's narrative strategies are multiple and complex; he earnestly describes Christian conversion at the same time as he indicts the practices of the white Christians by whose invitation he was converted. His story suggests that he easily separates violent cultural practices and, perhaps even more broadly, culture from the spiritual narrative he unfolds, and in fact the separation is self-consciously acknowledged in ways that invite readers to make the same, to Marrant, crucial distinctions. The biblical text then becomes a means of gaining a voice, a sense of reality, and a place from which to speak critically of the traditions inspired by the Bible. For his readers it becomes a lens through which to see the distinctions Marrant's text insists upon.

In his 1785 editor's preface to the *Narrative*, William Aldridge anticipated the biblical typology that characterizes the text by presenting Marrant as an intensified David slaying the giant: "Here the child just turned fourteen, without sling or stone, engages, and with the arrow of prayer pointed with faith, wound[s] Goliah and conquers the King" (76). In the biblical narrative that he references (1 Sam. 17), David is a young boy and a shepherd, not a soldier, the least likely person to confront a powerful warrior, such an absurd match for Goliath that he is scolded by his brothers and laughed at by his opponent. David's famous victory is remarkable, even miraculous, because of its implausibility. The near mythic story of the boy who defeats the terrible giant challenges readers to trust the strength of faith rather than physical power. By establishing Marrant as a parallel for David, Aldridge heightens readers' interest in the autobiography, but he also suggests a particular sort of nonthreatening narrative authority for its author. He encourages readers to view Marrant as a boy, at first glance an even less powerful boy than young David, since he faces his own Goliath lacking even the shepherd's weapons ("without sling or stone"). The David figure intensifies Marrant's outsider identity at the same time as it makes it more inviting to readers; they are asked to envision him in this narrative not as a mature, well-traveled African American preacher and writer but as a child, analogous to a biblical child whose faith despite overwhelmingly negative odds has inspired readers for centuries. Such figuring fits into a set of biblical motifs that would have been familiar to readers of the book, motifs in which the expected hierarchies of power and prestige are inverted, where the last become first, where the great—even, specifically, God—is identified with the "least" of all, where the weak become strong to the point of vanquishing the powerful, as in David's action.

Aldridge's figuring of Marrant as the boy David is complex, however. Even as the parallel emphasizes his lack of power, his unlikely status as a hero, it places Marrant in a powerful though paradoxical role. He is both child and conqueror; the conversion of the tribal leader is a vanquishment, a death, even; the converted Cherokee is consequently imagined as the slain giant. Marrant's acts—his prayer and his preaching as well as his faith—are envisioned as potent weapons, parallel to the sling and stone of the biblical narrative, and Marrant himself is imagined as a representative of the Western Christian imperial conquest and colonization of other cultures. Aldridge's reading here reveals the assumptions implicit in centuries of Western Christian contact with other cultures: the act of conversion is viewed as a death and rebirth, a violent vanquishing of the old, allowing the new—Western—Christian self to emerge.[6]

Aldridge's paradoxical use of biblical typology anticipates Marrant's own practice, though Marrant ultimately reflects a decidedly more complex theology than Aldridge. Like his editor, he repeatedly invokes the biblical text to make his startling experience both comprehensible and familiar. As he draws readers near to his experience, he sets the terms for the interpretive work they must do as they encounter his text. For example, they are to see him, first, as a biblical hero responding to dramatic adversity with extraordinary faith and, second, as a messianic servant suffering for the redemption of others: he is one of the biblical Daniel's three friends facing death in the fiery furnace (Dan. 3), Daniel himself in the lion's den (Dan. 6), and Jonah cast out to sea (Jon. 1, 2). By styling himself as various biblical figures persecuted by powerful forces, Marrant proclaims his outsider status, claims authority for that status by way of important scriptural texts, and provides a biblical framework for the oppression he experiences (85, 94). At the same time, he lays the groundwork for the critique of racism and violence that emerges as a powerful subtext in the *Narrative*.

Marrant uses biblical texts as defining paradigms for his own experience in his early and repeated references to reenactments of the experiences of Jesus described in Christian scripture and of the suffering messiah in prophetic Hebrew scriptures—including his account of his near execution (the reference point for Aldridge's allusion to the story of David and Goliath), the dramatic center of Marrant's *Narrative* and clearly a significant source of the popular appeal of the text. He encourages his audience to identify him and his plight with the suffering savior of Matthew 26 and Isaiah 53, biblical texts that invite readers to imagine a messianic Jesus as a black man encountering, appreciating, and then adapting to Cherokee culture. Marrant heightens the sensationalism of the dramatic account by disrupting readers' assumptions and stereotypes about race, at the same time appropriating a significant level of authority and importance for himself. The particular passages he identifies with as he faces his own execution situate him in a biblical tradition that allows readers to conceive of him as a righteous victim of injustice, a conception that becomes crucial throughout the *Narrative*. As he relates his experience:

> I prayed in English a considerable time, and about the middle of my prayer, the Lord impressed a strong desire upon my mind to turn into their language, and pray in their tongue. I did so, and with remarkable liberty, which wonderfully affected the people. One circumstance was very singular, and strikingly displays the power and grace of God. I believe the executioner was savingly converted to God. He rose from his knees, and embracing me round the middle was unable to speak for about five minutes; the first words he expressed, when he had utterance, were, "No man shall hurt thee till thou hast been to see the king." (85)

In the interview that follows, the "king" asks Marrant how he has sustained himself:

> I answered, by the Lord Jesus Christ, which seemed to confound him. He turned round, and asked me if he lived where I came from? I answered, yes, and here also. He looked about the room, and said he did not see him; but I told him I felt him. The executioner fell upon his knees and intreated the king in my behalf, and told him what he had felt of the same Lord. At this instant the king's eldest daughter came into the chamber, a person about nineteen years of age, and stood at

my right hand. I had a Bible in my hand, which she took out of it, and having opened it, she kissed it, and seemed much delighted with it. When she had put it into my hand again, the king asked me what it was? And I told him the name of my God was recorded there; and after several questions, he bid me read it, which I did, particularly the fifty-third chapter of Isaiah, in the most solemn manner I was able; and also the twenty-sixth chapter of Matthew's gospel; and when I pronounced the name of Jesus, the particular effect it had on me was observed by the king. (86)

In this dramatic center of the narrative, Marrant saves himself by speaking Cherokee, signaling his attempt at identification with the Cherokee people and emphasizing his cultural hybridity. Representing the religious dominance of English Christianity in his message and marginalized Africans in his person, his linguistic foray into Cherokee via prayer confronts the reader with a decidedly complex autobiographical subject. He transforms his circumstances—unnerving his executioner and leading, first, to a consultation with the king, then to a plea for his life by the king's daughter, and ultimately not only to Marrant's survival but also to his entry into the Cherokee community, which effectively replaces the family that rejected him. Christianity signals both his loss of the original family and his entry into a new family. Further, the fact that he speaks Cherokee not to the Indians but to God in front of the Indians underscores both the performative element of his encounter and his conception of God: multicultural, multiply identified, assumed to be present in all cultures, all languages. Challenging the hierarchies he has experienced firsthand in his original culture, reported on in his account of Indian/white encounters, and knows of from the Countess's unhappy history with David Margate, Marrant imagines a vision of commonality and multiplicity, of shared ground on divine turf. It is important that he deemphasizes his own agency here, stressing divine direction. In contrast to hundreds of accounts where language is presented as simply one aspect of the heathen barbarism of a band of non-English-speaking others, Marrrant's account portrays God as directing him to speak, specifically to *pray*, in a language foreign to English settlers, his readers.

Furthermore, the particular biblical text and the specific figure that he identifies himself with are as significant as his linguistic identification with the Cherokee. Marrant refers to biblical texts known in Christian hermeneutic traditions as "suffering servant" passages, so named because they describe one who suffers for others, redemptively. The servant's experience is paradoxical in that he endures suffering and humiliation and then, as a consequence, exaltation or reward because his sufferings provide tremendous benefit—rescue, survival, redemption—for others. Most often the passages refer to the messianic sufferings of a spiritual savior, although Moses, Joseph, and even Israel in the Hebrew Bible have been seen within this interpretive paradigm.[7] Marrant's selection of this particular biblical image allows him to be seen both as sufferer and as triumphant redeemer, thus negotiating multiple spiritual and emotional narrative identities (drawing simultaneously on paradigms of humility and authority) just as deftly as he negotiates his literal multiple cultural and racial identities. The paradoxical images associated with these passages would have situated readers to see him in a fairly complex way without his issuing them a straightforward challenge.

The suffering servant passage of Isaiah 53 for instance, which Marrant chooses to read in his encounter with the Cherokee, describes the "man of sorrows" as a lamb led to the slaughter, one despised and rejected, who takes on himself the burden of punishment for others. The passage and the larger motif it invokes provide a way of reading the violence that is a substantial part of his *Narrative*. His appeals to the Christian story suggest this violence as both necessary and redemptive, as divinely ordered, both real and symbolic, a ritual act signifying punishment and redemption—all traditional ways within biblical traditions of reading the meaning and nuance of the suffering servant passages. Marrant performs the function of redemption that the biblical text refers to even though the actual violence within the narrative is averted.[8] Moreover, he invites his audience—presumably, first, the Indians who witnessed his performance of the Isaiah passage as he read it, he says, "in the most solemn manner [he] was able," and, second, his contemporaries who read the published autobiography—to see *him* as the man of sorrows, the one whose sufferings will benefit others. His emphasis is not on the survival of the sufferer but on the sufferer's innocence and his redemptive action for others. By displacing himself and his concerns here, Marrant again asserts himself in a paradoxical way, becoming not mainly a survivor but a savior, a Christ figure whose actions transform an entire community.

The biblical contexts and parallels would have been crucial to readers' sense of the story Marrant tells, but there is a nonbiblical narrative that further establishes its rich intertextual appeal. By the time Marrant's *Narrative* was published, the story of John Smith and Pocahontas had become legend (notwithstanding its questionable veracity) on both sides of the Atlantic. Both Marrant and his readers would thus likely have been familiar with Smith's iconic story of his own rescue from execution by an Indian chief's daughter. The enduring appeal of the story is easy to understand, even up to the most recent iterations in Disney's animated *Pocahontas* and Terrence Malik's *The New World*. Smith's account reinforced for American and British audiences crucial hierarchies of race and culture: the Indian princess, in her remarkable cultural epiphany, overcomes allegiance to her original culture in order to recognize the virtue of the Englishman's culture and self, not only rescuing the individual John Smith but also subordinating herself and her band to the larger—decidedly hostile—colonial project.

The crucial differences between Marrant's popular captivity account and the even more popular story of Pocahontas and John Smith allow rich insights into Marrant's unusual vision of culture and religion in his own tale. Marrant as John Smith simply does not work. Rather, Marrant problematizes much of what Smith typifies in his narrative of Indian captivity and rescue. The (now infamously) arrogant narrator Smith memorably represents England, imperialism, Western culture, and, of course, Christianity. Pocahontas's intervention, then, serves to validate those forces. In contrast, Marrant presents himself as representing a different, perhaps more specific, Christianity. Though he is a native-born, English-speaking American, he is at best a highly complex, even problematic representative of English settlement culture, first, because he is African American and, second, because he has been tormented by and is in exile from not only settlement culture but his own family of origin. His rescue, then, seems to represent not so much acquiescence or vanquishment in the way Pocahontas's story has been remembered, or even, perhaps, the way Aldridge sets the audience up to read Marrant, but a significantly messier vision. Marrant cannot accurately be seen as a vanquisher because, in contrast to John Smith, he represents no colonizing civil or political power. Moreover, by choosing to remain with and adopt the cultural practices of the Cherokee after the chief's daughter saves him, he presents a very different model of freedom from that of Smith's tale, where Pocahontas herself is "freed" from her Native bonds; indeed, Pocahontas becomes an emblem for the colonial assault on Native cultures, not only by her adoption of English culture—dramatically memorialized by her famous portrait—but by her death in England of smallpox. Marrant's *Narrative* inverts the Pocahontas story.

The autobiographer's description of his own near execution in this central story can be understood further in the context of two other memorable scenes of specific violence within the *Narrative*: his reunion with his family, where his younger sister is beaten for claiming to recognize him; and a later incident in which a plantation owner's wife initiates the brutal punishment of slaves with whom Marrant has had a deep affiliation. The inclusion of the latter account (the most important distinctive feature of the undated fourth edition) deepens the sense of Marrant's racial critique. Moreover, reading Marrant's account of this incident as a return to or even commentary on his description of his own near execution further complicates an understanding of his treatment of race, specifically his own racially inflected theology. Both scenes may be understood as reenactments of the crucifixion of Jesus, especially since Marrant frames his own near execution in terms of the Isaiah passage, with himself in the role of the suffering redeemer. Within this interpretive framework, which would have been familiar to his readers, Marrant's faith saves not only his own life but the souls of the Cherokee as well: the "savages" ready to do violence to the "Christian" stop on the brink, repent, and embrace the Christianity offered by the surprising racial other who partakes of their culture by speaking their language, by voicing a connection between himself and his captors. Within the conventions of the Protestant spiritual autobiography, the sacrifice, though averted, nonetheless provides salvation for both Marrant and the Cherokee. Marrant's life is spared; the Indians are converted to Christianity; Marrant adopts Cherokee culture. This incident and the consequences for the actors within it provide a stark contrast with the account near the end of the narrative of occurrences at the plantation, where violence is not averted and where the redemptive action occurs by an altogether different means: as the white plantation owner's wife, a representative of European civilization and, by extension, Christianity, causes the brutalization of slaves whose primary crimes are race and piety, it is they who live out a more sincere figuration of the religion the plantation owners represent.

The incident at the plantation initially seems to mirror Marrant's encounter with the Cherokee leader. Like the Cherokee who questions young Marrant concerning his faith in God, though with different intent and results, Mrs. Jenkins brings slave children before her to interrogate them concerning their religious knowledge:

> She had two of the children brought before her to examine and made them say the Lord's prayer to her, she then asked who taught them? and they told her the free Carpenter. She also enquired, how many he had instructed, and at what time he taught them; and they told her, it was in the Evening after they had done work. She then stirred up her husband against us, who before had several times come in while I was instructing the children and did not appear displeased with it: she told him it was the ready way to have all his negroes ruin'd, and made him promise to examine further into the matter, and break up our meeting; which he then very soon did, for a short space; for he, his overseer and negro-driver, and some of his neighbors, beset the place wherein we met, while we were at prayers; and as the poor creatures came out they caught them, and tied them together with cords, till the next morning, when all they caught, men, women, and children were strip'd naked and tied, their feet to a stake, their hands to the arm of a tree, and so severely flogg'd that the blood ran from their backs and sides to the floor, to make them promise they would leave off praying, &c. though several of them fainted away with the pain and loss of blood, and lay upon the ground as dead for a considerable time after they were untied. I did not hear that she obtained her end of any of them. She endeavoured to perswade her husband to flog me also, but he told her he did not dare to do it because I was free. (91–92)

Juxtaposing the two tales reveals their striking connections and contrasts. Marrant depicts both the Cherokee leader and Mrs. Jenkins asking questions that are rooted in concerns with their own power as each one confronts the religious reality and alternative authority of a cultural outsider. Mrs. Jenkins and the Cherokee chief represent the power and authority of their separate traditions. Marrant (who has the children refer to him as the "free Carpenter," making an unsubtle though still indirect connection between himself and Jesus) is positioned as an outsider, an unwitting interloper rather than an invader, interested in survival (his own, in the first story) and assistance (to the slave children, in the second). His prayers with the Cherokee stop the movement toward violence at every turn: first with the examiner and judge (84), then with the executioner (85), and finally with the chief (86–87). Marrant describes God's divine intervention in these conversations as invoked by the Indians' curiosity about his religion. He relates that the Indians wonder to whom he prays, remark on the invisibility of the audience for these prayers, and observe Marrant's earnest faith and youth. The resulting responses culminate in the staying of his execution and in the conversions that follow. Prayer, coupled with Marrant's linguistic foray into Cherokee, serves as a bridge. From Marrant's and his Christian readers' perspectives, that prayer provides a moment of transformation that leads both to the tribe's conversion and to Marrant's adoption of Cherokee culture.

In dramatic contrast, the whites in the later narrative respond to the act of prayer with increasingly intense acts of violence. Mrs. Jenkins's curiosity initially centers on the slave children's knowledge of the Lord's Prayer, and she initiates the first action against the plantation slaves at the scene of a prayer meeting. Rather than the miraculous averting of violence in the execution incident, here the threatened violence is brutally enacted and graphically described. In further contrast, whereas Marrant in both cases presents prayer as an expression of personal piety and religious conversion (his own and others'), Mrs. Jenkins, representing white slaveholding Christianity, interprets prayer not as an act of piety but as a dangerous political activity, one that leads to "ruin'd Negroes" (91). Without commenting on it, Marrant presents the hypocrisy of the Christian slaveholder's position along with the potentially liberatory effects of Christianity by juxtaposing his own earnest response to the slave children's interest in Christianity with Mrs. Jenkins's entirely pragmatic view of the potentially negative consequences of inculcating piety in slaves. Further, it appears from the narrative overall that Mrs. Jenkins, ironically, is right: prayer is both dangerous and potent politically, leading to near-fatal violence in one case, averting the same in the other.

For Marrant's contemporary readers the scene of violence would have been unmistakably reminiscent of the suffering of Jesus in the Christian passion story: the slaves are stripped, tied to a tree, brutally flogged, mirroring the familiar gospel account. In Marrant's presentation of the Jenkinses' reenactment of the crucifixion of Christ, (and again in contrast to the scene of averted suffering with the Cherokee), redemptive effects are limited but nonetheless present. Mrs. Jenkins is punished; she dies a terrible death without experiencing the mercy that is at the heart of this narrative: "It pleased God to lay his hand upon" her with a violent fever which no medicine could cure, causing her to die soon after "in a very dreadful manner" (92). Furthermore, Marrant notes that she "fails to attain her end": the slaves continue to meet "to this day, by which it appears that the work was of God; therefore neither the devil nor his servants could overthrow it" (92). And finally, Marrant notes, after his wife's death Mr. Jenkins not only allows the slaves on his plantation to meet once again unopposed but attends those meetings with them. To his own spiritual benefit, he joins his own slaves in the once forbidden act of prayer for which he previously brutalized them.

Marrant, though not offering a clear abolitionist argument, nonetheless embeds an effective, even if oblique, antislavery argument in his *Narrative*, which by the end has presented "conversion" narratives not only of John Marrant but of his family, the Cherokee band, the slaveholding Mr. Jenkins, and his slaves. Marrant presents multiple models of conversion and its opposite, suggesting that spiritual receptivity (of which, of course, he himself is the ultimate model in this spiritual autobiography) occurs in surprising places. Such a theological assertion would have reinforced readers' beliefs about evangelical religion even as it secured the narrative authority of Marrant himself.

Furthermore, the plantation owners' original refusal to become agents of the Christian mercy Marrant urges them toward, and their retrenchment into racialized ideas about the virtues and vices of good and bad Negroes, surfaces the hierarchies that the rest of Marrant's text and his own complex identities resist: "[Mr. Jenkins] told me afterwards that I had spoiled all his Negroes, but could not help acknowledging, that they did their tasks sooner than the others who were not instructed. . . . He then said, I should make them so wise that he should not be able to keep them in subjection. I asked him whether he did not think they had Souls to be saved?" (92). Historian Albert Raboteau, among others, has examined in detail the dynamic that Marrant figures here: the opposition between slave masters, who are interested in the particular teachings of Christianity that would result in compliant slaves, and the slaves themselves, who are interested in the fundamental theological proclamations of their personhood and freedom assumed in Christian concepts of salvation and liberation. Marrant's accounts of these two incidents—his own near execution by the Cherokee and the brutalization of slaves by whites—identify that same dynamic as they simultaneously dismantle readers' categories for understanding the drama of captivity that he presents.

Beyond the lesson of personal piety for readers of captivity stories, his didactic religious text carried a critical edge: a lesson concerning spiritual receptivity and cultural encounter. In Marrant's story, Indians—distant from himself and white readers by virtue of race, culture, language, and religion—are immediately willing to redefine their own assumptions about an outsider when he crosses their border. In contrast, whites—representing the authority of the religious and cultural system that Marrant himself endorses—react with brutality when invited into a system of belief both familiar, because it is a version of English Christianity, and distant, because it is intensified (in evangelistic zeal) and represented by a black "other" who reforms a nonthreatening set of beliefs by inflecting them with issues of compassion and justice. These, like most of the writers discussed here, he places at the core of the tradition.

In the end, the scenes of averted and enacted violence provide a counterpoint to the multicultural, multilingual religious vision with which Marrant concludes his *Narrative*. As he prepares for his next spiritual and cultural sojourn, this time to preach to black Loyalists in Nova Scotia, he refigures a passage from Revelation into his theological imagination, drawing on specific images of the races, cultures, and languages of his own experience. He takes leave of his readers by asking for their prayers for his safety and for the fuller realization of his vision of the Christian gospel, expressing his hopes in a way that typifies the religious imagination throughout his text, both challenging and reinforcing the traditional Christianity of his era and region: "That strangers may hear of and run to Christ; that Indian tribes may stretch out their hands to God; that the black nations may be made white in the blood of the Lamb; that vast multitudes of hard tongues, and of a strange speech, may learn the language of Canaan, and sing the song of Moses, and of the Lamb" (95).

Noting that in the earlier editions (those, as Potkay and Burr argue, more fully controlled by Aldridge), this concluding passage and the title page are the only references to Marrant's race, Zafar says that relying solely on these passages would cause a reader to "set down Marrant as a kind of Black Puritan captive, a Christianizer whose contact with the 'other' is not defined by color but by an imperial, western religion" (61). This conventional use of images of color, the hope that "black nations" may be "made white"—which fit readers' expectations (images familiar from the Book of Revelation) and resonate in the works of writers who record conflicts similar to those discussed here, including Phillis Wheatley, Olaudah Equiano, and William Apess—must, however, be read in the context of the plantation experiences Marrant records in his own edition of the *Narrative*, where he demonstrates a more complex and profoundly more critical race consciousness. Further, as I and others demonstrate here and elsewhere, these references—to race and to conventional views of morality and religion in the context of an analogical color code—are never facile, just as surely not for the writer then, as they are not for the reader now.

Even as we note the conventional metaphoric alignment of blackness with evil and whiteness with Christianity, we must also note that the linguistic transformation Marrant imagines here (and language has been crucially important in his account) refers to "the language of Canaan" and "the Song of Moses" and "the Lamb." His final heavenly vision seems to depict a more complex world than his readers might have done. He imagines "multitudes" singing in languages that maintain an important biblical referential relationship to the foreigner and outsider—the Canaanite, the outsider in the land of promise. Further, Marrant imagines a church that crosses racial lines. His Christian audience would have been ready to call to mind the passages from Revelation that anticipate a global apocalyptic vision, but Marrant contemporizes and specifies that vision. The tongues, tribes, and nations (referred to in the Bible) are no metaphors here but, rather, actual contemporaries—the races that encounter each other in North America in the violent terms established by the religious colonizing visions of European settlers. Marrant uses a biblical text to imagine what Christianity allowed theoretically and theologically but refused to practice: a faith community where a spiritualized notion of equality in, say, salvation—extended to cultural and social practices.

Readers today may readily interrogate Marrant's ironically imperialist drive to impose his religion on the Cherokee and his representation of them as immediate, eager converts; his own adoption of "white" Christianity makes him suspect; we regard with suspicion his proselytizing efforts with Indians, slaves, and readers. At the same time, we must recognize how surprising Marrant's racial and religious imagination is and how he reforms, alters, the Christianty he has adopted. The *Narrative* emphatically disrupts many presuppositions of his contemporary white Christian readers.

Furthermore, dismissing African American conversion to Christianity as acculturation without exploring the dynamics of such a conversion gives us a facile but less than insightful view of the complexities involved. As Katherine Bassard has argued in her work on African American women's writing, characterizing Christian conversion as a process that erased the culturally specific subjectivity of African American converts is too easy an analysis and may prevent us from understanding why so many African Americans made use of the discourse of conversion: "For individuals socially 'cursed' with a racialized and othered subjectivity, conversion represented one of the few discourses, and certainly the most prominent, holding the promise of a radical change in subjectivity" (*Spiritual* 23). Easy dismissals have been all too common a part of discussions of Native and African American writers, as critics have issued problematic and often ahistorical tests of authenticity; facile distinctions concerning identity and culture seem to have become less common, however, as critics have attended to the subtleties and complexities of experience and self-definition for writers of color in the early period. Careful reading of Marrant's work demonstrates the possible results of roomier, informed analyses, just as Marrant himself theorizes about God and race in ways profoundly more capacious than the belief system of the culture from which he inherited his religion. His theology informs and empowers the cultural transgressions that occur in this text. In the end his enlarged religious vision is in keeping with the requirements of the genre of spiritual autobiography that he presents to readers—a vision of religion that would question the assumptions at the heart of their traditions.

4

MOSES AND THE EGYPTIAN

Religious Authority in Olaudah Equiano's *Interesting Narrative*

☦

> Without any crime committed . . . without judge or jury . . . I could not by the law get any redress from a white person.
> Olaudah Equiano

FROM THE first image that greeted readers of his book, Olaudah Equiano presented the self of his 1789 autobiographical narrative as a pious Christian, one whose religious conversion meant a kind of freedom as significant as his manumission from slavery. In the striking frontispiece portrait Equiano sits with Bible in hand, insisting—in his visual as in his textual presentations of himself—that the Christianity he embraces is the defining feature of his life story. He responds, as Susan Marren has suggested, to two paradoxical imperatives: one, to write himself into creation as a speaking subject and, two, to write an antislavery polemic (94). At the same time, the text speaks straightforwardly of a third authorial imperative: within the religious tradition of Protestant Christianity, Equiano seeks to tell the story of his soul's spiritual journey, to testify to God's actions in his life. Readers today have sometimes seen the author's piety as something of a maneuver: the savvy African, knowing what his British and American audiences need in order to accept him as a credible narrator, uses religion as a mask for social critique. Others see him as wholly devoured (just as he feared he would literally be devoured when he saw the slave ship) by Western culture, losing his voice and himself to Christianity.[1] Attempts to analyze the formidable forces of imperialism, culture, slavery, and race—of which religion is a profoundly important component—that take place over the course of Equiano's *Narrative*, have oversimplified and occasionally dismissed Equiano's Christianity. If we take the facile view that he is simply using religion to manipulate readers, or if we see him as simply manipulated by religion, we ignore the earnest and consistent piety that sets the tone and establishes the purpose of the narrative.

To be sure, the self presented in *The Interesting Narrative of the Life of Olaudah Equiano* is a complicated one, as almost all the literature on this text suggests. Contemporary readers are disposed to appreciate the complications of his racial identity but also to see his own race awareness and social critique as most probably at odds with his religious piety—not an entirely new problem. Readers who dismiss the religiosity of this text today follow the argumentative course and esthetic sensibilities established by earlier respected readers, including Mary Wollstonecraft, who, in a 1789 review, admired many of the qualities of Equiano's text—most particularly his gripping account of his enslavement and his journey toward freedom—but ultimately judged the text inferior, primarily because of the author's piety and his "tiresome" account of his religious conversion.[2] Yet sidestepping the religious meaning and purpose—central for the autobiographer himself, a source of discomfort for some critics—causes one to overlook some of the most intriguing conflicts in the text. As William Andrews (*To Tell*); Susan Marren; Angelo Costanzo; Vincent Carretta (*Equiano*); Adam Potkay ("Olaudah"); and Helen Thomas have argued, Equiano's *Narrative* ought to be understood in the context of several genres, including, notably, the tradition of eighteenth-century spiritual autobiography. Moreover, reading his religious perspective as an earnest expression of his self leads to an appreciation of the complexities of his text, specifically, to the way piety informs, empowers, and limits his social criticism.

Certainly, the *Narrative* presents problems. Like many historical texts that directly address issues of race, Equiano's reveals its author's shifting, occasionally paradoxical self-presentation and ideology. Despite, for instance, his progressive polemical intentions, his apparent desire to have the autobiography provide a vehicle for a moral argument against slavery (seen most obviously in repeated, straightforward appeals to the reader), the *Narrative* is not, as many critics have noted, unequivocally antislavery. Rather, Equiano expresses specific opposition to the violence of slave masters. And although textual evidence suggests that he has written his way into a more sweeping antislavery position by the end of the text, the uncertainty of his response to slavery, noted repeatedly in scholarly discussion, remains. On the one hand, Equiano repeatedly and directly confronts the racism of his readers by arguing against the racial violence at the heart of the practice of slavery, identifying the profound contradiction between religious values of compassion, mercy, and justice—which he believes his readers, and all true Christians, share with him—and slavery. But on the other hand, the antislavery argument is severely compromised by his description in the *Narrative* of his own participation in the "Peculiar Institution" as an overseer and trader of slaves *after* his manumission. At least in the context of his own immediate experience, he condemns not slavery but certain kinds of slavery (Carretta, Introduction xxi). He certainly opposes all forms of physical abuse as he witnesses it, but only long after his return to England, and perhaps as a result of his writing the *Narrative*, does he come to the consistently antislavery position that impels him to seek an appearance before Parliament.[3]

Religion may be viewed as at the heart of the matter in Equiano's shifting, conflicted perspective, as the shaping force in his now acquiescent, now critical stance. More specifically, his engagement with the scriptures, read through the lens of his own experience, informs the voice of social criticism that appears in the *Narrative*, the voice that emerges out of Equiano's growing sense of the liberatory power of the biblical text. At the same time, his Christian piety and his admiration for the Christian colonizing work of the West placed limits on that critical stance, causing him to espouse viewpoints that now seem to us patently contradictory, viewpoints that, ironically, empowered him with a sense of both integrity and survival. My discussion focuses on Equiano's presentation of himself and his text to readers, and on a number of the most potent interpretive moments in the autobiography, notably the catalogue of violence in his chapter 5. I am most interested, finally, in examining the voice of social criticism that emerges and the way that voice seems valenced by the author's experiences of the biblical texts he uses.

Equiano's Christianity is shaped not only by his personal piety and spiritual experience but also by a range of material experiences with Christians. In order to gain the conversion experience he seeks, the experience that seems to give him the authority to tell his story, Equiano must account for the consistent hypocrisy that he has seen and experienced at the hands of actual Christians.[4] His experience of racial violence requires him either to find a way to condemn those actions within a framework of Christian authority or to abandon Protestantism altogether as a source of meaning and power. He chooses the former path and then, by way of the authority of biblical texts, establishes a set of touchstones that allow him to condemn the Christianity of his experience and to affirm in its stead an idealized Christianity, a biblical reality in which justice and compassion triumph.[5]

Christianity is central to Equiano's conception and presentation of himself; he takes pains throughout his story to establish his credentials as a true Christian. Indeed, the *Narrative* may accurately be viewed not only as a spiritual autobiography but as a conversion narrative as well. He cites his credentials variously: he is, for instance, a sea captain and then a British gentleman. But he returns throughout the text to his religious self, the bedrock of his authorial voice. By telling his spiritual autobiography he establishes a bond of common humanity and religious belief with his largely Christian audience, assuming, as would most of his readers, that any individual life story has meaning within a larger, supernatural paradigm (Carretta, Introduction xx). As he establishes the authority of his Christian self, so too he establishes the authority of a particular kind of Christianity, distinguishing that "true" Christianity from the Christianity of slaveholders and requiring readers to make that same distinction.

Equiano's authority as a narrator, as a Christian, and as a former slave making an antislavery argument resides firmly, he insists, in the Bible. Throughout the narrative he uses strategic appeals to his audience on the basis of scriptural text and metaphor. What emerges from careful readings of those appeals clarifies the personal power and the rhetorical usefulness of Christianity and the Bible for Equiano. Key, of course, to his condemnation of slavery (and to many other antislavery texts from the eighteenth and nineteenth centuries) is the Golden Rule.[6] Repeatedly accusing readers of failing to enact a bottom-line Christianity, Equiano shames them for their refusal to "do unto others," to exercise the most basic human compassion. His reliance on the argumentative appeal of the biblical Golden Rule, his insistence on its obvious incompatibility with slavery, is a cornerstone of his work. Without minimizing the power of this aspect of his religiosity, however, I want to point out that he uses other, perhaps less benign, strategies of appeal to biblical authority to condemn the actions of slave masters and to articulate his own, rather more complex, theological location.

Profoundly self-aware in this text, Equiano carefully schematizes the narrative of his experience via the biblical texts so that the reader is compelled to experience his perspective, including, quite centrally, his own outsider status. By presenting himself as being in line with a biblical tradition of outsiders, he requires the reader to take on that outsider perspective as well. As William Andrews has argued, the reader of Equiano's narrative must "undergo a de-culturation process through which he divests himself of his insider's cultural myopia and accepts the complementary value of the African outsider's perspective. . . . [T]he reader is recreated in the image of Equiano instead of the other way around" (*To Tell* 57–58). Integral to this process is his use of scripture, as he requires the reader to recreate herself or himself in his image by way of the biblical outsiders with whom he identifies and to whom he refers. A reader encountering this text could not have maintained the religious tradition to which text and reader belong without this kind of identification and recreation. Thus the decentering and reflection inherent in any autobiographical reading—more acute, perhaps, for religious readers of religious texts—is radically intensified here, as the author provides a set of selves for the reader to try on, selves both new and familiar (and, certainly, religiously authoritative).

The negotiation is accomplished primarily as a result of Equiano's careful and cumulative use of biblical texts and references, each of which deepens the reader's identification with outsiders (like the author) who have been victimized by people in positions of power—such people, precisely, as Equiano's imagined reader: white, Christian, literate, privileged. Always writing through the lens of the converted believer, Equiano presents a life ordered and interpreted by way of religion. And he assumes religiosity on the part of his readers, assumes that they too will derive meaning from the religious framework of his text. As Katalin Orban has noted, all other moral arguments are embedded in the fundamentally religious argument that structures the entire narrative. And it is a particular kind of religious argument, based almost exclusively on specifically biblical authority. Equiano finds the moral and ethical weight he needs to make his case against Christian complicity with slavery and, even more broadly, with racism in a subtle and carefully employed presentation of himself within a biblical framework.

In a general way, he does so in describing Africa and in his recurring use of the present tense, by which descriptions of Africa and Africans become immediate, specific, and recognizable. The strong likelihood (recently established in Carretta's biography) that Equiano was not, in fact, born in Africa underscores the significance of his authorial choices, particularly his arrangement of the material on Africa. His lengthy description of cultural origins (whether these were experientially substantiated or not) speaks to his understanding of himself vis-à-vis his racial identity, his identity as a former slave, his European cultural orientation, and his biblical interpretive paradigm for himself and his experience. Such understanding occurs in the introductory material but also later in the text: in chapter 4, when he becomes a Bible reader, Equiano is immediately struck by the proximity of biblical culture and the African culture of his origins. Though writing as a converted Christian and thoroughly Europeanized gentleman, he honors "Ebo" culture, arguing that readers should do the same, specifically on the basis of the proximity of Ebo and Hebrew biblical culture.[7] He draws repeated parallels between the two: "We practiced circumcision like the Jews, and made offerings and feasts on that occasion in the same manner as they did. Like them also, our children were named from some event, some circumstance, or fancied foreboding at the time of their birth. . . . [W]e had many purifications and washings; indeed almost as many, and used on the same occasions, if my recollection does not fail me, as the Jews." He is, he says, "struck . . . very forcibly" by the "strong analogy [that] . . . appears to prevail in the manners and customs of my countrymen, and those of the Jews, before they reached the Land of Promise." He goes on to suggest, with the help of the speculations of a number of scholars, that perhaps "the one people had sprung from the other," which then leads him to an extended, fascinating reflection on possible meanings and origins of skin color (41, 43, 44).

His strategy in his description of the Ebo is consistent with the biblical hermeneutics employed throughout the *Narrative*. By detailing the proximities of Ebo and biblical Hebrew culture, he challenges Westerners' assumptions about "primitive" behavior, asking them, in effect, to recast their favorite Bible stories in a specific, African setting. Moreover, he presents Ebo culture, by way of the biblical text, within a paradigm that sets it at the very heart of the dominant religious tradition of his British and American readers, for whom Equiano's Bible becomes a bridge to understanding and appreciating a specific African culture. Building on the way the Christians' sacred text had already situated one particular distant culture—that is, early Judaism—he requires readers to reframe their eighteenth-century understandings of African culture in the context of their own traditional Christian worldview. In Equiano's figuring of things, Africans, specifically the Ebo, must be viewed not the way various racist versions of Christianity would have viewed them—the fallen sons of Ham, descendants of Cain, a lost tribe of Israel—but rather as a parallel to Christian interpretations of Old Testament Israel, a biblical people chosen and favored by God. By drawing specifically and occasionally elaborate parallels between Ebo and the early Jewish culture referred to in the Bible, he challenges readers to resituate race and culture. In his refiguring of things, Africa remains in need of the colonizing and missionizing efforts of the Western Christians with whom he identifies himself, but with a difference: here, Africans are imaged as the center of Christian sacred history, the bearers of God's promises, the recipients of God's favor.

Equiano's particular introduction of himself is as markedly biblical as is his presentation of the context for his cultural origins and racial identity. In the visual and textual images that accumulate at the outset of the narrative, he presents himself most centrally as a Bible reader. Furthermore, the passages he selects allow him to attend to and identify with narrative situations and characters that speak, occasionally quite directly, to issues of oppression and justice. Equiano's interpretive experience becomes emphatically relevant here, as we imagine and reconstruct his readerly encounter with the texts he presents.

The striking frontispiece of the *Narrative* is a portrait of the author holding an open book, where clearly visible are the words "Acts Chap. iv, V. 12." And on the title page, under the author's name is an epigraph composed of two verses from the book of Isaiah. These two biblical reference points remain constant in each edition of Equiano's text even as the physical representation of the writer himself undergoes some changes.[8] The textual citations form a fundamental part of the authorial portrait, announcing the writer's piety as well as his purpose to show readers the meaning of the text of Acts 4.12: "Neither is there salvation in any other [than Jesus Christ]: for there is none other name under heaven given among men, whereby we must be saved."[9] This life narrative, like other spiritual autobiographies produced in this period, is to be religiously instructive as well as self-reflective in nature: Equiano means to evangelize his readers. The epigraph presents texts related to the first, verses 2 and 4 from Isaiah 12, which declare God's

Olaudah Equiano, frontispiece portrait and title page, *The Interesting Narrative.* Courtesy Schomburg Center, New York Public Library.

power to strengthen and save the faithful: "Behold, God is my salvation; I will trust, and not be afraid: for the Lord Jehovah is my strength and my song; he also is become my salvation. . . . And in that day shall ye say, Praise the Lord, call upon his name, declare his doings among the people."

All three Bible verses attest in straightforward fashion to Equiano's piety (he has relied on the truth of these passages) and his primary religious purpose (he sets out to convince others of this truth). By linking his authorial purpose with what the prophet Isaiah commands as a faithful response on the part of God's people, he establishes an unquestionable framework for his text: like the prophet, and in response to that imperative, he will "declare God's doings" to the reader. Further, his use of the Acts passage, with its emphasis on the saving power of the *name* of Jesus, carries out the ongoing concern with naming throughout the *Narrative*, for its author has been called Olaudah, then Jacob, then Michael, then Gustavus Vassa, and now Olaudah Equiano again. Potkay argues that the Acts text "signif[ies] that the chain of nominal substitutions that constitutes his earlier career might now come to a close." He notes further that the verse was a favorite of George Whitefield's (whose preaching Equiano experienced)[10] and that the use of this text in the visual representation of Equiano links him to the Evangelical tradition and Pauline theology of salvation that Whitefield represents ("Olaudah" 687). Certainly, it illustrates the centrality of Equiano's Christian identity as well as his relationship to a tradition of similarly minded people of faith. Moreover, the earnest piety it represents is consistent throughout the narrative.

At the same time, the references to Acts and to the book of Isaiah suggest meanings that, without countering his evangelistic intentions, further complicate and deepen his stance as an antislavery writer. Equiano's sense of the possible implications of biblical passages that speak to and about oppression and injustice is forcefully highlighted by the context of the passage in the Acts of the Apostles, suggesting that his piety is informed by an awareness of political realities, and that his rendering of his life narrative is certainly more than that of a pious Evangelical who sheds an African identity simply to gain a conventional British Christian one, complete with laudable but finally fairly tame abolitionist tendencies.[11]

Equiano reads his scriptures through a lens of the literal and spiritual focal point of his life: liberation. Many texts could be used to announce the straightforward religious meaning he insists he wants to convey: that is, the Christian message of the salvific power of Jesus; in describing his actual conversion in chapter 10, for instance, he makes references to more than fifteen biblical passages in approximately two pages of narrative (190–92). As a practiced and knowledgeable Bible reader he had a range of texts at hand, dozens of which would have conveyed the message of salvation. His portrait connects him to the verse in Acts, however: the passage spoken by a *captive* narrator engaged in the act of opposing the power of those who imprison him reveals a religious agenda that complicates the more obvious (and acceptable) piety of Equiano's selections. The account from the Book of the Acts of the Apostles occurs after Peter and John have been imprisoned for healing a lame beggar. When asked to speak on their own behalf, Peter preaches the words that Equiano cites, silencing the religious elite, who marvel both at the miraculous healing and at the eloquence and authority of Peter and John, "unlearned and ignorant men" (Acts 4.13–14).

The specific context for the quotation seems important both because it shows Equiano attending to a passage where words of authority and power, words that have resonance for his evangelical tradition, are spoken by captives and also because the passage depicts first-century Christianity as a radical force counter to and outside of the mainstream, one that invites in, heals, and restores those who have been disenfranchised by their communities: in this case, a lame beggar is healed by uneducated, common men. Further, in this passage the voices of authority that speak from the biblical canon are themselves captive and oppressed by a political system that is revealed to be both unjust and arbitrary. Peter and John are imprisoned precisely because their religion challenges established, elite religious authority and because they use supernatural healing power to identify with and aid another outsider, even further removed than they are from privileges of power and public acceptance. By tapping the biblical and historical traditions represented by the words of the apostles at a moment when those narrators themselves are actually oppressed and imprisoned, Equiano provides readers with a reminder of their own tradition's profound identification with the disenfranchised, highlighting a feature of Christianity that respectable religious readers might otherwise have ignored: the historical legacy of Christianity that features those outside of, and profoundly opposed to, established systems of religious and political authority. And Equiano underscores the centrality of this particular text and the circumstances of its narrator for his own sense of the meaning of his life when he uses the same passage as the culmination of his poetic rendering of his conversion (197). Furthermore, these imprisoned narrators speak about witnessing the power of God in the context of a situation of oppression that remains unchanged. The larger reality faced by Peter and John, who in the narrative they present are marginalized by their faith, is not transformed. No political or social overturning calls the forces that imprison them to account, a fact that must surely have been noted by Equiano and may well have shaped his own conflicted political stance regarding slavery. Here he adds his own testimony to biblical textual presentations of narrators like himself, who seek to speak about their experience of God in the context of oppression that remains unchanged.

The other passages that Equiano uses to introduce himself to his readers, the two verses from Isaiah, function in somewhat similar ways. Both texts point to the saving and comforting power of God; both also provide ostensive biblical legitimization for Equiano's autobiography. As Isaiah directs, he will "praise the Lord, call upon his name, [and] declare his doings among the people." At the same time, and like the reference to the passage from the Acts of the Apostles, the context for these verses from Isaiah enrich a reader's sense of appreciation for Equiano's choices, as they emphasize his strategic attention to scripture that speaks directly to issues of oppression and justice. Again, he might have chosen from a myriad of biblical texts that assert the saving power of God as well as a command that the faithful proclaim God's power. His particular selection, however—the twelfth chapter of Isaiah—occurs between two chapters of dramatic descriptions of God's judgment against injustice, particularly God's destruction of the wicked. In them, God shows mercy to the poor and meek (Isa. 11.4) but destroys the wicked, whose vice is specifically defined by their oppression of the poor and meek (11.4; 13.11). These passages depict God as a righteous judge who overturns the injustice of cruel political situations, and Equiano's attention to them underscores his concern for justice, just as surely as his piety. If readers are to believe the implications of his use of scriptural literature throughout his narrative, they must understand him as a Bible reader and, therefore, one quite aware of the contexts of the passages he chooses, and of the implications of those texts and contexts for the circumstances of his specific experience and for the reality faced by all enslaved Africans.

Equiano's identification with biblical narrators, particularly captives, becomes especially prominent in his account of his manumission, where he can tell of his experience only with the aid of biblical texts, only by appealing to scriptural narratives of liberation. He recalls, first, words of thanksgiving he attributes to Psalm 126: "I glorified God in my heart, in whom I trusted."[12] These words, he claims, have been "fulfilled and verified" by his own specific experience of liberation. In a typological interpretive move—typical of spiritual autobiographies in the Protestant tradition—he imagines himself and his experience as reenacting the truth of the biblical text. In a similar fashion he moves to the New Testament, likening himself to Peter: "My imagination was all rapture as I flew to the Register Office: and, in this respect, like the Apostle Peter, (whose deliverance from prison was so sudden and extraordinary, that he thought he was in a vision), I could scarcely believe I was awake" (136). No matter that Equiano had already presented himself as striving toward and being duped out of his freedom for most of his life. He declares a need for the Apostle Peter's story here to convey a sense of "suddenness," nonetheless. Given his repeated attempts at freedom and the lens through which he consistently reads his experience, Equiano's narrative need for a biblical account of literal bondage and freedom is understandable. But his rhetorical need for Peter as exemplar has little to do with the feature of suddenness, as he straightforwardly asserts. By way of the biblical reference Equiano insists that like him, Peter was a captive: Peter, the central apostle, the figurehead for early Christianity. Equiano relies on Peter to explain his experience of freedom and, by forceful implication, of captivity as well. He brings his outsider experience forcefully into the mainstream of the religious tradition of his readers and claims an apostolic authority by his identification with Peter.

Moreover, the profundity of his experience of achieving liberation, as well as the biblical parallel for that experience, is underscored by a beautiful and moving passage that adumbrates this notion that he cannot, finally, express his emotional response to the experience of freedom:

> Who could do justice to my feelings at this moment? Not conquering heroes themselves, in the midst of a triumph—Not the tender mother who has just regained her long-lost infant, and presses it to her heart—Not the weary hungry mariner, at the sight of the desired friendly port—Not the lover, when he once more embraces his beloved mistress, after she had been ravished from his arms!—All within my breast was tumult, wildness and delirium! My feet scarcely touched the ground, for they were winged with joy, and, like Elijah, as he rose to Heaven, they "were with lightning sped as I went on." (136)[13]

All four examples, says Equiano, are inadequate to the intensity of emotion that he experienced in response to manumission. Each metaphor, descriptive of circumstances conjuring extreme human emotion, works only by negation. The answer, clearly, to his rhetorical question of who can "do justice" to his feelings at this moment is emphatic: no one, save the biblical narrator describing the great prophet's gaining not earthly liberation but liberation from earth and entrance into heaven. He seeks the most extraordinary metaphor possible here, choosing to equate his experience of the end of his enslavement with Elijah's magnificent entrance into heaven in a supernatural whirlwind (2 Kings 2.11). He dismantles the familiar line of Christian conciliation in the face of slavery, which would counsel slaves to wait for heavenly justice to end earthly troubles. Here his earthly deliverance must, he says to readers, be viewed in the context of heavenly liberation. He reverses the familiar terms here as he equates his earthly deliverance with the heavenly liberation of Elijah. Further, his use of the figure of Elijah affirms the centrality of biblical meaning and story for Equiano. But the assertion underlying the image—that earthly liberation has no adequate analogue other than the gaining of heaven—entirely undercuts the line of argument so familiar to Christian slaves and their masters, that freedom would come "by and by" in heaven for those who would wait for it.

By linking his release from slavery with the spiritual and dramatically supernatural events of the Elijah story, Equiano asks readers to conflate spiritual liberation with liberation from slavery in order to understand the latter. He is released, he says, "suddenly," surprisingly, dramatically. Those readers who have had dramatic conversions may call upon those spiritual experiences in order to understand his actual liberation from actual bondage, which they must see here, he insists, in a biblical context.

Furthermore, even the form of his rhetorical question—posed, ostensibly, to convey the inexpressibility, the extraordinary quality of the emotional rapture corresponding to freedom—asserts Equiano's voice of protest as well as his profound connection with biblical texts as essential both to the narrative of his experience and to his antislavery argument. By asking "who could do justice," he raises for readers multiple issues. First, he identifies their distance from his experience, which is, he says, emphatically not like what readers (here imagined as conquering heroes, tender mothers, weary mariners, and bereft lovers) know about deprivation or the excesses of joy. Rather, he insists, his experience exceeds readers' paradigms of the pain of loss and the ecstasy of reunion. Second, he provides a familiar biblical story, an alternative context, to make his alien experience meaningful despite the inhering unfamiliarity that he argues for. The argument, then, is that readers both can and cannot approach this experience. The only way into his story, he says, is to look beyond personal experiences to a textual one: the supernatural event of Elijah in the heavenly whirlwind. Here, as elsewhere in the text, the Bible provides a familiarized other. In this context a known (and thus familiar) story of extraordinary (and thus other) events provides a paradigm for Equiano's account.

And finally, the text suggests the political protest that is woven into these biblical parallels throughout the narrative. By forming his question in terms of "justice," Equiano asserts that, in fact, the reader cannot do justice to his feelings or, by implication, to him, to his identity, to his experience. The accumulated negations provide a framework for an argument that he stops short of fully developing: that readers must reach the limits of Christian sympathy; they cannot, in fact, adequately appreciate the complexities of Equiano's identity and experience.

At another moment Equiano appeals to the power and authority of scripture by interpreting in the immediate context of slavery Jesus's own declaration of his mission in the Old Testament prophetic tradition: "[Jesus] tells us, the oppressor and the oppressed are both in his hands; and if these are not the poor, the broken-hearted, the blind, the captive, the bruised, which our Saviour speaks of, who are they?" (108). Here Equiano taps the biblical literature of social justice at one of its most rhetorically potent moments. To appreciate fully his vision of biblical justice and the way that vision has empowered his own sense of his position and authority as a religious person who is both faithful to the tenets of conventional Christianity and aware of the contradictions presented by practicing Christians around him, one must consider the specific and immediate provocation (that is, within the *Narrative* itself) for Equiano's interpretive move, as well as the context of the biblical passage to which he appeals. Equiano cites this passage as he reflects not only on his own horrific experience but also on the sexual violence inflicted on female slaves. Obliquely referring to rape, he asks, "Is not this one common and crying sin, enough to bring down God's judgment on the islands?" (108). In line with the prophets of the Hebrew Bible, he imagines God as judge and liberator, envisioning a moment when he will witness a final, dramatic putting-to-rights of all the horrors he has experienced and witnessed. And he records his hope for such a vision in chapter 5, where a kind of catalogue of violence structures the other events of the narrative.

In the passage he thinks of, from the Gospel of Luke, Jesus quotes from Isaih (61.1–2) to address the situation of the oppressed and abused, those whose experiences have dominated this section of Equiano's narrative: "The Spirit of the Lord is upon me, because he hath anointed me to preach the gospel to the poor; he hath sent me to heal the brokenhearted, to preach deliverance to the captives, and recovering of sight to the blind, to set at liberty them that are bruised, to preach the acceptable year of the Lord" (Luke 4.18–19). At the same time he recalls the more extensive declaration from Isaiah 61 in which the prophet describes a complete overturning of reality for those who have been oppressed by established systems of power. This, says Isaiah, will be the day of God's retribution and punishment. Jesus' identification with this prophetic vision of a God of justice who will right wrongs and reverse fortunes clearly inspires hope in Equiano for earthly justice, despite all that he sees and experiences.

Equiano continues in chapter 5 to chronicle the regular, horrific exploitation he has witnessed, from systematic sexual violence to discrete acts of personal humiliation: a French planter who regularly rapes his female slaves in order to procure more slaves (his own children) without incurring further financial costs; slaves sold by the pound and the lump; children torn from their mothers; a slave who tries to gain a small bit of independence by fishing, only to have his fish stolen by whites. As he describes this final incident, Equiano records the injured fisherman's philosophy, the familiar strain of heavenly—and only heavenly—hope for those with earthly injuries: the response to injustice in this world must be to cast one's hope on heavenly authority; when he is injured, says the slave, he must "look up [for justice] to God Mighty in the top." Equiano recounts that he is moved by his fellow's "artless tale," vaguely suggesting that he endorses the theological perspective that reinforces the way Christianity has frequently worked in concert with political systems that enslave and oppress by urging earthly patience and heavenly hope as a response to immediate injustice (110).

Despite this model of and even reflection upon acquiescence as a Christian virtue, however, Equiano's encounter with the fisherman leads him to contemplate religious justification for an altogether different course of action: "I could not help feeling the just cause Moses had in redressing his brother against the Egyptian" (110). Rather than consider the score of biblical examples of individuals who silently or otherwise suffered political and personal oppression, Equiano thinks of one who did the opposite—of Moses, the great biblical liberator of slaves. And the biblical story he refers to challenges the terms by which his readers would have understood racial hierarchies in general and slavery in particular. By recalling a biblical narrative in which Africans enslaved Israelites, Equiano challenges the sympathies of white readers. First, they must identify themselves with slaves and with the situation of enslavement. More, they must image Egyptians (rather than whites) as enslavers. Such a reference interrogates readers' assumptions about power and race, underscoring the fundamental concern of social justice at the heart of Equiano's emerging argument with slavery.

Even more important is the particular biblical moment he refers to in the Moses story, an instance of biblical violence in the context of his response to the catalogue of violence against enslaved Africans. He recalls the story in Exodus 2: Moses, raised under the protection of Egyptians, walks among his enslaved Hebrew fellows and witnesses an Egyptian beating a Hebrew.[14] He responds with immediate, violent revenge, quickly murdering the Egyptian and hiding his body. When others, including Pharaoh, learn of his act, he flees. Equiano's use of the Bible here entirely contradicts his halfhearted endorsement of his friend's philosophy to look for justice only in spiritual terms, suggesting instead the rightness, perhaps the necessity, of personal agency, even when it means engaging in acts of violent resistance or retribution. Equiano does not choose the certainly more well-known, dramatic, and religiously appropriate account of Moses's central role in the supernatural Passover and Exodus, where humans participate in God's liberatory action; rather, he selects a story featuring human agency, an individual act of violent retribution. His comment on the account of Moses as murderer—that he had "just cause"—underscores his interpretive work and personal connection with the potentialities of the passage, potentialities that subvert the most facile notions of long-suffering Christian mercy and patience in the face of terrible distress. Later in the *Narrative*, Equiano shows the same impulse for a theology of retributive violence when he longs for God to strike his captors dead (118). What is important here is that he attends to a biblical passage where the oppressor is struck down by a human, rather than a divine, hand of judgment.

Equiano's appreciation for the action of Moses sets up his use at the end of the chapter of Milton's Satan, who voices justification for violent revolt. In attending to this observation, Potkay assumes Equiano's disavowal of the young Moses: "[He] knows that he cannot be Moses, because the Christian dispensation has no room for the violent retaliation imagined by his younger self" (688). But in fact, the mature self of the autobiographer offers no censure, no hint of criticism of the urge for justice here. Further, he does not provide readers with an explanation of the full meaning of his admiration for Moses's act of violence, nor does he examine the paradox that such a reference presents in light of his overall acquiescence in the *Narrative* to the system of slavery. His emphatic affirmation here of Moses's violent rebellion is consistent with his inclinations in other places in the *Narrative*, both in the reliance upon a biblical text or model and in the undeveloped quality of the reference. For instance, Equiano articulates his Christian piety and submission even as he plans to escape from his master. Expressing his abject repentance at the outset of chapter 5, he weeps; expressing his certainty that God is punishing him for his behavior, he begs God to forgive him, and prays for wisdom and resignation (95). And yet in the subsequent paragraph, he attempts to escape. His radical submission to God does not hinder his active rebellion against his master and against the identity conveyed upon him by other Christians.

This particular section of the *Narrative* is quite troubling for other reasons as well. Equiano voices his earnest piety here in response to his reenslavement at a moment when, trusting in his master's promises, he had expected to be freed. Rather than cursing his master for betraying his word, Equiano sees his reenslavement as God's punishment for a momentary lapse of personal piety, when, anticipating his freedom, he had sworn to celebrate by carousing. He seems at this point to affirm the religious perspective of his enslavers: he condemns himself and assumes that he is unworthy, even as he prays for divine deliverance. The passage is perplexing, both because of the internal contradiction between a plan to escape and an intention to submit and because of the larger context in which this contradiction occurs: Equiano condemns himself for the imperfections of his piety at the same time as he records the horrific violence of slave masters. His religious piety, even his self-critique, seems sincere here. But Equiano's expression of those concerns accomplishes other rhetorical tasks as well, reinforcing for readers his own religious credentials, about which he is utterly in earnest, and, at the same time, casting severe judgment on slave masters and traders whose violence dominates the rest of the chapter. Surely he intended readers to note the very problem that my students consistently observe here—the absurd and distressing contrast between one Christian who earnestly strives toward an absolute (and to many readers, peculiarly personal) virtue, castigating himself for a momentary lapse in a narrowly defined piety, and other Christians who consistently enact brutal violence without any sense of shame or self-consciousness.

The piety exemplified in this passage has been seen as a problem, as part of the equivocal self that recurs in the *Narrative*. Rather than simply noting the equivocation or registering my disappointment, I want to examine an instance of that equivocation, again with the aim of understanding Equiano's in fact rather remarkable sense of his own authority vis-à-vis the Bible and Christianity. Perhaps the most startling example of his equivocal voice in this text, what readers have come to see as his failure to come fully to terms with his own experience as a slave and his own relationship with the institution of slavery, is his decision after his manumission to remain with his master and then subsequently to act as a purchaser and overseer of slaves himself. Throughout the last section of the *Narrative*, one can see examples of the complex self-perception that allows him to make these decisions.

Perhaps one of the most intriguing instances is Equiano's return to the trope of the Talking Book, which he used at the beginning of the *Narrative* in describing his own encounter as a young African boy with Western culture. Called the "ur-trope" of the Anglo-African tradition by Henry Louis Gates, the Talking Book motif features an encounter between a nonliterate observer and a text, very often the Bible or a prayer book (*Signifying* 131).[15] The motif recurs variously in African American texts with consistently rich results—suggesting myriad meanings for pivotal moments of contact between an African narrator and European culture, between orality and textuality, and all the accompanying assumed hierarchies. It occurs first in 1772 in Gronniosaw's *Narrative*, and then in four other slave narratives before 1815 (Gates, *Signifying*, 130).[16] Throughout the African American tradition, as Gates argues, the trope is a site of revision and repetition that demonstrates the extraordinary intertextuality of the tradition. Many readers have commented on Equiano's initial use of this trope—which occurs in the context of his encounters with other icons that indicate his own foreignness and the power of the cultural forces that confront him as a newly kidnapped slave—but fewer have discussed his return to the trope when he describes his own role as a representative of Western power, civilization, religion, and literacy.[17]

The latter instance occurs in chapter 11, after his account of his religious conversion in the preceding chapter, and after repeated, extensive reflection concerning the injustice of the enslavement and racial violence he has survived, he provides an account of his own attempt to act as a Christian colonizer, the likes of which originally enslaved him. In the company of Mosquito and Ulua (Equiano knows them as "wool-wow" or "flat-headed") Indians in what is now Nicaragua, he makes a number of observations concerning cultural practices and traits, including, most notably, both the honesty of the Indians and their inclination to get drunk on the liquor of Europeans. At one point Equiano is charged by his employer with "managing" a large band of drunken Indians who are engaged in a dispute and becoming increasingly violent. In order to gain control of the group, Equiano recalls his reading of Columbus and models his own response after the manipulations of the explorer:

> I therefore thought of a stratagem to appease the riot. Recollecting a passage I had read in the life of Columbus, when he was amongst the Indians in Jamaica, where, on some occasion, he frightened them, by telling them of certain events in the heavens, I had recourse to the same expedient, and it succeeded beyond my most sanguine expectations. When I had formed my determination, I went in the midst of them, and taking hold of the governor, I pointed up to the heavens. I menaced him and the rest: I told them God lived there, and that he was angry with them, and they must not quarrel so; that they were all brothers, and if they did not leave off, and go away quietly, I would take them to the book (pointing to the bible), read, and *tell* God to make them dead. This was something like magic. The clamour immediately ceased, and I gave them some rum and a few other things; after which they went away peaceably. (208)

This instance and the chapter from which it emerges are enormously revealing of Equiano's complex sense of his own identity, speaking as they do to his cultural hybridity, his profoundly ambivalent relationships to Western culture and religion, and his own identity as an enslaved African.[18] He participates—without accompanying comment that would alert us to his self-consciousness about his participation—in the same cultural game that resulted in his long enslavement, exploiting the distinctions between notions of "savage" and "civilized," the very categories he alerts readers to in his account of his own enslavement as a boy, when he holds a book to his ear in an attempt to hear it speak to him, when he sees snow and thinks it the result of magic, when he believes his white captors seek to eat him. Furthermore, in the context of the descriptions that make up this entire chapter of the *Narrative*, he positions himself as a civilized Western Christian (which of course he assuredly is), describing Indian culture with a sense of disdain and disgust and exploiting the power of his cultural resources (including rum) to manipulate and subdue these "Natives"; he is alarmed at what the Indians eat and drink; he thinks their music unpleasant, their dancing curious. Yet at the same time as he records his sense of ethnic and cultural distance from and superiority to the Indians he observes (sounding frequently like any other colonizing European), he consistently reminds his civilized, Christian readers of his cultural distance from *them* (his readers), as well, and of his consequent proximity to the less "civilized" people of his *Narrative*. He notes that the Indians' musical instruments resemble those of "other sable people" like his own, and that they dance not as couples but in single-sex groups "as with us" (209).

His narrative perspective, conflicted in his account of interactions with the Indians, becomes even more complex in the context of the entire chapter. Just after presenting his observations about the Indians, he relates his subsequent seizure, reenslavement, and torture by the owner of a sloop who intends to compel him to serve on his vessel no matter his resistance, and to sell him if he will not cease resisting. After narrowly escaping this situation, he confronts other similar circumstances, all the while protesting that he cannot rightly be enslaved, since he has successfully purchased his freedom. The whites who seek to reenslave him, however, see other facts that conflict with Equiano's sense of reality and identity. Because of his remarkable competence and experience, he is a tremendously attractive potential member of any crew, made even more valuable by his sense of responsibility and his personal virtue (which again and again in the *Narrative* so dramatically separates him from those around him, frequently Europeans, who carouse, drink, lie, and steal from their employers). But most important, the whites see that he is an African, enslavable by the obvious fact of his race and consequently just as exploitable as the Central American Indians.

Equiano's resistance to the realities he encounters here is both vigorous and ineffective, speaking to the hierarchies that inform his view of himself and others, the hierarchies he frequently notes but never fully examines. He argues, for instance, that the barbarous behavior of his captors is worse than that of the Turks (among whom he has traveled), even though his captors are Christian (211). He explains that the Indians (to whom, ironically, he goes after the escape noted above) are "more like Christians than those whites," despite the fact that the Indians are unbaptized (214). He is tortured "without any crime committed, and without judge or jury, merely because I was a freeman, and could not by the law get any redress from a white person in those parts of the world" (212).

In some ways it is not at all surprising that Equiano models himself after the legendary conqueror Columbus. Clearly, he sees both the Indians and himself through what Mary Louise Pratt calls "imperial eyes," assuming his own superiority in education, cultural refinement, and spiritual enlightenment. Still, it is difficult to read of his encounter with the Indians without thinking of this presentation of his experience as a commentary on his earlier account of Western Christian slavers on the coast of Africa. His references to his own race, to the skin color of the Indians, and to African culture remind readers of the complexity of his identity, positioning him as distinct, as an outsider, able to comment on the deficiencies of his Christian British fellows even as he participates in the same exploitive system.

The events of the end of Equiano's *Narrative* reveal the limits and contradictions of his identity as it is constructed for him by those around him, and as he himself imagines it. Free or slave, Christian or not—these distinctions become, in the end, irrelevant. Equiano at the end of his story is a free, well-educated, Afro-British seaman with an impressive résumé and a list of well-connected references. Nonetheless, he is still subject to the violent whim of slaveholders who act on the basis of racial hierarchies. His self and his experience have been predetermined not by the predestinarian God he fervently worships but by those around him who continue to perceive him as enslavable.[19] Even his own proficiency in Western ways, including the appropriation of power and of a colonizer's mind and tricks, does not alter the way others see him. He may, in the course of this narrative, have written himself into existence as a subject; he exists in it, for himself, as an actor and, perhaps most importantly for his own view of things, as a Christian who has received God's grace and experienced God's transforming power, just as surely as he experienced his own transformation from slave to free. But his identity for his immediate reading audience was determined entirely by race, remaining unaffected by the transforming religious experience he sees as central to his story.

As with the other writers examined in this book, material realities trump both the ideal and the spiritual. Equiano achieves remarkable success, unusual authority, a public persona bordering on celebrity. Like Occom, Marrant, Bailey, Lee, and Apess, he could have been imagined as the exceptional representative—an attractive, even compelling public testimony to the transforming power of Christianity in an imperial package. But he is stopped by the brutal experiential realities, the material limits, of that transforming power. And so his narrative, like the others', tells another story as well: the story of those restrictions and boundaries. The limits both of Equiano's sense of his own identity and of his argumentative position—in which he asserts a protest against the brutal aspects of slavery without wholly objecting to all forms of the practice—are underscored further by the news he receives regarding those slaves he had formerly overseen, those with whom he had been so careful and compassionate, those for whom he had been such a conscientiously "good" master: in this chapter he learns that their new master treated them brutally, and they are all dead.

Although Equiano himself does not fully articulate a sweeping antislavery position, the arrangement of the narrative, whether purposeful or not, certainly indicates the need for such a position, as it reveals that a merciful slave master's compassionate behavior is, finally, inconsequential for the lives of the slaves: in the context of the slave system, one master's virtue or, at least, restraint is immediately subject to overturning by the next master. Moreover, Equiano's own experience of being unjustly and illegally reenslaved, by being juxtaposed with the fate of his former charges here, underscores the fact that the slave system did not accommodate restraint, did not accommodate even its own compromised vision of appropriate limits on brutal behavior. And this argument—as it surfaces in the events, if not in Equiano's comment on those events—resonates with the suggestion made throughout the *Narrative* that, finally, Christianity is utterly incompatible with slavery. Hence, as Equiano repeatedly asserts, the Christian exemplars that he meets are entirely inadequate, indeed, vicious models of the transforming theology he has come to believe, a theology focused on an overturning of power, on placing the outsider in the center.

His engagement with larger issues—most notably with the racism upon which any kind of justification of that slave system was founded—

begins to emerge here, but it remains emergent rather than fully formed. He stakes out a claim on the edge of a religious ideology stretched to the limits by his experience, looking for a model of justice and compassion as powerful as the ones he has encountered in the biblical text, models far more powerful than those he cobbles together from the momentary breaks in the brutality of his own experience. Equiano glimpses and moves toward a religious vision eclipsing that of many of his Christian contemporaries, a vision rooted in particular moments and readings in the scriptures, a vision fully informed by his own specific experience of slavery. And the contradictory strains evident in his encounter with Christianity and even in his own articulation of it are part of an old, conflicted conversation about what it means to be a person of faith in a biblical tradition.

5

GENDER, CHRISTIAN SUFFERING, AND THE MINISTER'S VOICE

Submission and Agency in Abigail Abbot Bailey's *Memoirs*

☦

> . . . sometimes those who pretend to be our best friends cruelly oppress.
> Abigail Bailey

ABIGAIL ABBOTT BAILEY'S 1815 *Memoirs* recount years of brutal domestic abuse. Like the other narratives of suffering examined here, her account is embedded in interpretive attempts to determine the spiritual meaning of her experiences. Originally published after her death by her minister, Ethan Smith, *The Memoirs of Abigail Abbot Bailey* were republished in 1989 under the title *Religion and Domestic Violence in Early New England*, edited and introduced by Ann Taves.[1] As far as we currently know, it is the only text of its kind from this period, describing domestic violence in a detailed personal account and offering vivid, though frustratingly incomplete and somewhat uneven, portraits of both abuser and survivors.[2]

Bailey's frankness provides a window into one early American writer's interpretive quagmire as she tries to make sense of a particular kind of suffering and violence within the context of American Protestant Christianity. Readers of earlier American literature are familiar with the attempts of Thomas Shepard or Anne Bradstreet, for instance, to make spiritual sense of the deaths of family members who have died too soon, their struggle to accept the theological paradox of untimely death at the direct hand of a God believed to be both sovereign and loving. Further, writers of captivity narratives (a genre discussed in chapter 3) try to make sense of the violence they both perform and see in their encounters with frequently demonized Indians. In both cases the genre conventions include a normative feature of American religious writing: an interpretive privileging of the text's didactic function for both writer and reader. The writer engages in reflective work within the text toward the end of understanding the dilemma presented by a sovereign God; reflecting on experience, including sensational experiences of physical abuse, torture, and murder, he or she simultaneously invites readers into the process of sanctification afforded by the suffering or trauma described in the text. In tone and rhetorical style Bailey's narrative is somewhat similar to the best-selling Mary Rowlandson narrative of Indian captivity and can be meaningfully read within that tradition and genre. At the same time, Bailey presents readers with an altogether different interpretive dilemma: she must account for intimate, rather than racially othered, human evil—the violence of her husband, her children's father. Her effort to create meaning out of her circumstances constitutes a significant interpretive challenge, and her experiential and rhetorical response to that charge constitutes the rather complex purpose of the *Memoirs* as emphatically as, say, Jarena Lee's announced purpose to argue for women's rights to preach (the subject of chapter 6).

For much of the narrative, Bailey asserts her belief that her husband (like the rest of the circumstances of her life), remains under the sovereign control of God, repeatedly indicating that she watches and waits to see how God will change him. The theological paradoxes reflected on by writers wrestling with experiences of untimely deaths of family members or of violent conflicts with racial and cultural others in the context of conquest and colonization become differently complicated here. Bailey's initial theological paradigms fail entirely in the face of intimate violence and a familiar, yet ultimately unredeemable, perpetrator.

Bailey's text is, finally, about her attempt to make religious sense of the violence of her experience, or, rather, about her coming to terms with her own inability to resolve the religious meaning of her experience in ways that she and her readers would have found satisfactory (that is, within an acceptable biblical paradigm and with a suitably didactic resolution). In the end, the transformation she expects and longs for, an evangelical awakening or rebirth of sorts, does in fact occur—not for Asa (presumed, for much of the text, to be the main character in the drama she lives) but for Abigail herself, who turns out to become the surprising center of her own story. Once she is able to see the violence in her home in a human rather than exclusively divine context, she discovers an unexpected sense of agency, an authoritative voice, biblical rhetoric, and a specifically ministerial persona with which she speaks not only of her own but to others' experiences as well.

Bailey provides two important contrasts with the other writers I discuss. A white New England Protestant in a white New England Protestant community, she neither brings the experience of racial and cultural difference to her life narrative nor manifests any apparent self-consciousness concerning her own exclusion from traditional sources and sites of power within her religious tradition. Unlike the writers here who register and then examine as sources of power their own outsider identities, Bailey seems unaware either of injustice or of corollary platforms for dissent. She is probably most obviously understood as a representative neither of a departure from nor a disruption of the pattern of Anglo-American Protestant life-writing but rather as an extreme exemplar of the theological and literary features we might expect to find from, say, Daniel Shea's discussion in *Spiritual Autobiography in Early America*. In fact, her piety, self-preoccupation, radical commitment to a theological construct of divine sovereignty, and use of biblical typology make her seem remarkably like some of the earliest and specifically Puritan English American autobiographers. In contrast to Occom, Marrant, Equiano, Lee, and Apess, though, Bailey did not experience the official, institutionalized racist or sexist exclusion that informs and frames the other autobiographies examined here. The mistreatment, violence, slavery, prohibitions, and constraints that lead each of those writers to a position of simultaneous dissent and piety seems, both literally and imaginatively, never to have occurred to Abigail Bailey. She apparently experienced her concerns as she articulates them—as intensely private, spiritual.

Bailey's interpretive conclusions present a fairly dramatic contrast to the other writers, all of whom to some degree come to understand their own oppressive circumstances in the context of biblical notions of justice. Because she identifies the oppressive force in her life as divine, rather than institutional, societal, or even personal, she cannot appropriate the potential meaningfulness of a biblical tradition of resistance. In contrast to Jarena Lee, for example, whose call to preach positions her to see up close the actual limits of any conceptual or theological commitment to dismantle hierarchies, Abigail Bailey maintains a commitment throughout most of the *Memoirs* to understand her life exclusively in private, pietistic, devotional terms. So whereas the other writers not only see but in fact expose the connection between the suffering and restrictions of their immediate circumstances and the religious structures that helped, implicitly and explicitly, to cause them, Bailey fails to suggest such a connection, though it is crucial and inescapably obvious to readers interested in female subjectivity in the context of patriarchal authority.

Her identification is, of course, gendered and as biblically inspired as the other writers' sense of Christian social justice. Her response was largely scripted for her by her inculcation of a religious tradition of female submission, which is part of what makes the immediate experience of reading Bailey's *Memoirs* profoundly distressing for twenty-first-century readers aware of widespread and frequently unreported domestic abuse and of the social, religious, and cultural forces that help perpetuate intimate violence. The question now most emphatically brought to her narrative is the same question that observers bring to current accounts of domestic abuse. My students, for instance, want to know one thing and only one thing about this text: What made her stay and prevented her from taking action earlier and more effectively? The answer to that question is complex, inextricable from overarching questions about how Bailey understood her self, her husband, and her religious experience. Furthermore, part of examining identity, agency, and religion in this text means attempting to understand what allowed Bailey to survive, as well as what prevented her from taking action sooner and more resolutely than she did. A careful reading must include an examination both of her inaction, her endurance of years of brutal physical and psychic abuse, and also of her action, her ultimate decision to divorce her husband and protect herself and her children from further harm.

There are moments, for instance, when she comes close to imagining herself as a kind of martyr, ready to be slain to demonstrate her willingness to submit to the violent hand of the Calvinist God in whom she believes. Ultimately, she rejects such an image of herself, however, and I argue that there is an implied or intimated dissident self in Bailey's *Memoirs*. She effectively breaks free of the private theology that conceptually imprisoned her, just as she literally breaks free from her husband's brutality. Over the course of the text she develops an altered vision of her circumstances, of herself, and of God, a vision that allows her to resist her husband and take a decisive course of action against him. That vision takes shape in opposition to official, institutional religious culture, specifically represented by ministerial voices in the text, as well as in response to her own primarily private readings in scripture about suffering and oppression. The text begins with Bailey in a radically submissive posture, subordinate not only to God but also to those she imagines as God's agents—including and particularly her husband and her ministers. The text ends, however, with Bailey not only interacting with but appropriating the voice and role of the minister for herself, and taking the place of a husband and father within a family not her own. In so doing she achieves a contextually extraordinary level of agency and personal authority, qualities that illuminate her survival and resistance. Moreover, she also produces this text, which, in contrast to the official counsel given to her in her ordeal, neither offers facile lessons nor advises patience and endurance in the face of hardship. My reading of certain elements in this complex memoir include its intertextuality—the overlay of scripture, Bailey's account of her ministers' counsel, and her own textual production and agency: her move from being a *reader* (of God's text, of her own perplexing experience) to becoming a *writer* about the same.

Bailey's profoundly religious perspective must be situated in its historical context of Great Awakening Christianity. As Ann Taves explains (Introduction), Bailey was a Congregationalist from a traditionally religious family who (along with many members of her community) experienced an evangelical conversion that initiated her into an emotional strain of New England Calvinism. Such a shift is consistent with much of the culture in her historical moment and region, where "Old Light" and "New Light" Protestants were competing for ideological supremacy and congregations. "Old Light" Christians opposed the emotional revivalism of the Great Awakening and, specifically, the preaching of George Whitefield and his legacy, affirming rather the authority of established clergy against that of lay and itinerant preachers (such as Samson Occom, Jarena Lee, and William Apess). "New Lights," represented strongly among rural and frontier churches, insisted on the authenticity of the emotional experiences that characterized religious revival and criticized Old Lights as overly intellectual, spiritually detached, and lifeless. Bailey was formally admitted to church membership in an Old Light congregation in what is now Concord, New Hampshire. Two months later she moved with her parents to an area known as Coos—the frontier towns of Newbury (now in Vermont) and

Haverhill (now in New Hampshire)—where she was converted by the revival preaching of a minister named Peter Powers to a New Light religious experience (Taves, Introduction 3–11).

Despite her own earnest evangelical piety, Bailey married a man significantly less religious than herself, though one who at the time of their marriage appears to have been a reputable member of the community. Her *Memoirs* consist primarily of an account of the results of that marriage, along with her own religious reflections on her experience. A vicious abuser, Asa Bailey habitually beat Abigail and their children, attempted to rape one of their servants, and repeatedly had sexual encounters with other women. Punctuated by moments of extreme contrition and emotional vulnerability (now widely recognized as a typical pattern of behavior for domestic abusers), Asa's violence escalated over the course of several years, resulting finally in the repeated rape of his own adolescent daughter, Phebe.[3] When Abigail at last resolved to divorce him and to procure a property settlement that would protect the interests of her large family, Asa abducted his wife and hired a kidnapper to seize his infant daughter. Subsequently, he had several of his children kidnapped. This domestic struggle, with Abigail seeking a divorce and settlement and Asa opposing (sometimes violently) those attempts, lasted two years. In the end the family escaped his control: Phebe left home on her eighteenth birthday; Abigail obtained a divorce and property settlement; and Asa was exposed, though not legally prosecuted, and then resettled in another town.[4]

Bailey's *Memoirs* resulted from her self-conscious reworking of the private prayer diaries in which she initially recorded her experiences as they occurred. The manuscript for the *Memoirs* was found with Abigail's papers after her death; unfortunately, the original source, her prayer diary manuscripts, have not survived, although the minister who edited the *Memoirs* manuscripts included some materials from them. Taves notes that an examination of the excerpted passages suggests that whereas the *Memoirs* provided explicit details of factual events, the diaries were primarily a reflective, devotional record. Although it seems unlikely that Bailey planned for widespread publication of the *Memoirs*, neither does the text seem to have been intended to be entirely private (as her diaries almost certainly were) but rather to address and assume readers. She begins her narrative, for example, in this way:

> I Abigail Bailey (daughter of Deacon James Abbot of Newbury, Coos, who moved thither from Concord, N.H. A.D. 1763) do now undertake to record some of the dealings of the allwise God with me, in events, which I am sure I ought to remember, as long as I live.
>
> I shall first, in few words, record the merciful dealings of my heavenly Father, in casting my lot, not only under the gospel, but in a family, where I was ever treated with the greatest kindness by my tender parents. (56)

She goes on to recall both the events of and her spiritual journey through her ordeal: that is, her attempt to present (presumably to some imagined reader, most likely her children and grandchildren, perhaps her immediate community as well) her sense—uncertain and qualified as it was—of God's role in her experiences.

In the "advertisement" originally published with the *Memoirs* (and included in Tave's edition), editor Ethan Smith, who was Bailey's minister during the 1790s (after Asa's Bailey's abuse had been exposed but during the time of his repeated returns and attempts to block a property settlement) explains that after Bailey's death the manuscript had been found by friends who, with his (Smith's) help, then pursued publication. Taves notes that it is impossible to determine how close the published version is to the original manuscript, which did not survive. While we have some of the details of the violence that occurred for years in the Bailey home, we clearly do not have Bailey's full account here.[5] As the editor himself announces:

> In transcribing these memoirs, I have taken liberty to abridge some pages—to shorten some sentences—, and to adopt a better word, where the sense designed would evidently be more perspicuous, and more forcibly expressed. But I have taken care to preserve *entire* the sentiment of the manuscripts. I have been careful to give no stronger expressions of the wickedness, or cruelties of Major Bailey, than those found in the manuscripts. But in various instances, expressions of his wickedness and cruelty, found in the manuscripts, are here omitted; not from the least apprehension of their incorrectness; but to spare the feelings of the reader (52).

The minister's reluctance to preserve Bailey's full record of her husband's brutality may parallel the "sentiment" he insists he preserves in the manuscript: that is, it may reflect Bailey's own resistance to acknowledging the violence she survives. Author and editor seem agreed in their emphasis on the religious meaning of the experiences and in their hesitation to record the full detail of what Smith calls Asa's "expressions of viciousness and cruelty."

Furthermore, the narrative is packed with references to biblical texts as Bailey struggles to understand and respond to her circumstances in an exclusively scriptural framework. She interprets her husband's violations and scripts her own responses within her religious paradigm of a sovereign God, specifically a God with a history of visiting trouble on the faithful and of a radically submissive people who must seek to understand and cooperate with (that is, not resist) the hand of God in their lives. The more specific context for submission operative for Bailey, of course, was the tradition of female, particularly wifely, submission, an integral part of New England Protestant culture.[6]

Bailey's religious consciousness, as alien as it seems today, in fact resonates with contemporary mind-sets in some ways. Ann Taves describes it as "strikingly modern": "Insofar as interpretive presuppositions rooted in the religious culture of colonial New England have shaped and continue to shape, albeit unconsciously, the way that even secularized Americans interpret their experience today, the memoirs provide us with an opportunity to view those presuppositions in bold relief" (Introduction 2). Even if one rejects the notion of New England Protestant culture as a kind of monolithic influence, the particular legacy of the religious ideology of Bailey's text—at least within certain communities—is no mere residual (or "unconscious") effect. Women within some conservative evangelical Christian communities today (the inheritors of Bailey's religious tradition) share Bailey's sense of piety as well as her commitment to patriarchal authority. A recent examination of the relationship, for instance, between a vigorous commitment to an unsubtle, aggressively patriarchal theology and violence against women shows not terribly surprising parallels between Bailey's domestic experience and those of contemporary conservative evangelical women.[7] Feminist historians of religion view this overarching problem as resulting from the fundamentally patriarchal nature of Christianity. As Anne Braude explains: "The theme of many stories of American religion is a strong association of lay piety with femininity and of clerical roles with masculinity. As Mary Maples Dunn puts it, 'passive females, ruled over by ministers . . . personify Christian virtue.' . . . Church structures reified gender hierarchies. . . . The conceit of male dominance has been essential to the logic of American religion" (91). American Protestantism's endorsement of a specifically female virtue of submission, and its sacralization of not only suffering in general but of gendered masculine violence in particular, comes into play in dramatic ways in Bailey's narrative.

The initial commentary on Bailey's narrative provided by historians of religion Ann Taves and Catherine Albanese makes note of the way she seems to conflate the two authority figures of God and Asa as she struggles—even at the outset of her marriage, before the abuse begins—to behave as an idealized, submissive religious wife, an interpretive paradigm established for her by other women (and men) writers within Christianity in general and Puritanism more particularly. David Leverenz has examined seventeenth-century Puritan language and metaphor, paying particular attention to representations of femininity and sexuality in masculine sermonic discourse. Puritans, who were especially taken with the biblical poetic text of the *Song of Songs* with its erotic language about two lovers' desire for one another, frequently analogized their own relationships with God in terms of bride and bridegroom in the larger context of covenant theology. The church (and by extension the individual Christian) figured as the bride in this covenant between two unequal parties. Her role was to yearn and wait for her husband, her lover. The analogically feminine role seems to have been a particular preoccupation, as it recurs not only in sermons but in diaries and in public and private poetry as well. And although the metaphor suggests a rich emotional and spiritual potency for men, it created an especially fraught psychic and spiritual terrain for women, inculcated as they already were with messages of their own unequal status within religious and social spaces. The yearning, submissive bride figure may have been less appealing and certainly a differently complex metaphor for Puritan women who experienced that prescribed role in their everyday, nonsymbolic worlds. But it would have been profoundly problematic in circumstances such as Bailey's, where the idealized loving power of the bridegroom was enacted instead as brutalization; and there were no alternative models, no biblical texts addressing what the bride—whose approved virtues were devotion, innocence, submission, and absolute faith in the bridegroom—was to do under such unimaginable circumstances. Further, Bailey's preoccupations—so evident in her *Memoirs*—with the sovereignty of God, a Calvinist emphasis on God's absolute control, and a denigration or even denial of human will, helped shape the nearly fatal problem with agency that she recorded and reflected on.

Evidence of the complexities of Bailey's conflation between God and Asa occurs throughout the *Memoirs*. It is possible, for instance, that Abigail's exclamation when she regards the horrific results of a child's accidental injury that her husband did *not* cause reveals this link in a fairly specific way. Her crying out that "it is the Lord has done it" (109) seems almost a proclamation of relief that, happily—and, in the context of his overall violence to the family over the course of the *Memoirs*, for once—Asa has *not* done it; God must be the unambiguous source of this particular trouble. In this instance, she calls attention to the fact that she sees God as dramatically separate from the person of her husband, while also acknowledging that she expects to experience and will submit to violence at the hands of both.

Abigail's conception of her husband's behavior as analogous to God's actions on her behalf leads to the passivity that she exhibits in much of the account. She resists seeing Asa—even in his most violent moments—in any terms other than as an agent of God. Both are sovereign, inscrutable, and frequently cruel. Compelled by her religious ideology, she sees Asa as a vehicle for her own sanctification: God is the author of the trials that will strengthen and purify her faith; hence she concerns herself not with Asa's destructive effects on her children or herself but with what God may be teaching her through this suffering. She longs, therefore, not merely that Asa (whose transformation she anticipates) may do the right thing but that she will. At times manifesting what seems a peculiar kind of egocentrism, she thinks of her own spiritual journey as the primary story. Further, her preoccupation with her own spiritual development seems to prevent her from seeing the full earthly horror of her own and her children's actual experiences.

One may more fully understand Bailey's attitudes toward divine and earthly religious authority, as well as her retreat into a private religious world, by examining the presence and voice of the minister in her narrative, the voice that in the end she comes to acquire as her own. Her responses to the ministerial presence reveal her experience of the strong appeal of a highly authoritative religious system and the paradoxical quality of her own relationship with religious authority. Her fairly complex response to official ministerial voices allows insight into the way her sense of agency and authority shifts over the course of the text.

The ministers in Bailey's *Memoirs* repeatedly issue calls to wifely patience and restraint, reinforcing the prevailing religious cultural ideology and practice, affirming Bailey's own inclinations toward inaction and submission. Indeed, ministerial counsel features prominently in the autobiography. In one instance, after Abigail and her family have endured Asa's cruelty for some years, but before he begins his sexual abuse of Phebe, Abigail recounts her response to a message a minister preaches at their home: "He treated, in a clear and wonderful manner, upon the trials and sufferings of the followers of Christ. I truly thought God had prepared this sermon peculiarly for me; and sent his servant, the present preacher, to teach and strengthen me, relative to whatever trials he might be preparing for me, that I might not faint in the day of adversity, but learn patiently to endure affliction" (67). She recalls that she understood the minister's words about suffering as counsel preparatory to her later, more horrific trials. The minister's words establish for her both an expectation that the abuse will worsen and a vision of that abuse as a spiritual trial designed by God.

Subsequently, when Asa intensifies his violent attacks on the family, and after Abigail confronts him with his sexual abuse of Phebe, she is again influenced by a ministerial perspective and, again, that influence leads her to strengthen her resolve for patience and submission in response to Asa's increasing violence. After attending a Sabbath meeting in a neighboring town during a period of religious revival, she seeks guidance from that minister:

> I had a delightful opportunity with a minister of Christ there. Without letting him know my particular trials, I asked him many questions which had a relation to them. My desire was, that God would direct him to give answers suitable to my case, which I think he was led to do. He remarked upon the trials of Joseph; and of various of the ancient people of God, and he was led to give me a most lively view of the duty of casting my burdens on the Lord and waiting patiently for him. I felt great consolation in my soul. For I was conscious that I had been thus waiting on the Lord, and trusting in him. (84–85)

The reference to Joseph's "trials" would have spoken to her specific (though not, apparently, specified to the minister) experience of violence. In the book of Genesis Joseph's brothers plot to kill him, then sell him into slavery and fake his death instead. Years later, when his brothers need his help and forgiveness, Joseph refers to their abuse and abandonment in ways that Bailey echoes in her own figuration of Asa's brutality: "But as for you, ye thought evil against me; but God meant it unto good" (Gen. 50.20). Confirmed by the minister in her course of action, then, Bailey continues to protect her husband, assuming that her greatest responsibility is to exercise patience and trust in God—activities she understands as essentially spiritual and necessarily in opposition to action she might otherwise have taken to protect herself and her children. Her intentional withholding of the "particular trials" from the minister underscores the compelling pressures both internal and external to keep silent about the violence occurring in her home—violence she may have understood in profoundly symbolic ways, despite its literal consequences—and the way her commitment to a fundamental religious value of female submission works in concert with these pressures.

In response to this minister's preaching, and in this section of the text where she deliberates on how to respond to her knowledge of Phebe's abuse, Bailey records experiences of religious ecstasy that for a time completely obliterate her concern with her husband's violence. Her description of that experience of spiritual ecstasy allows further insight into the way her faith functions for her. The intensely personal, insular quality of her piety determines Bailey's sense of focus (as well as the thoroughly gendered notion of authority in her account), which contributed in significant ways to her response to her husband throughout her marriage. No matter the depth of horror, her first concern is to understand the religious meaning in it all. She describes Asa's control and abuse in terrible specifics, including a moment when she believes he will kill her. She recounts his infidelity. She details his bizarre, frustrated attempt to seduce his own daughter, then witnesses his violent response to that daughter's resistance, including one instance in which he beats Phebe nearly to death. Further, she describes her feelings of helplessness, intensified by her well-progressed pregnancy and by her daughter's refusal to expose her own distress by bringing accusations against her father. Since she cannot induce Phebe to testify, she believes she cannot yet bring accusations against her husband: "I hence saw, that in relation to commencing a legal process, God's time seemed not yet to have arrived" (82–83).

After Phebe, overwhelmed with grief and shame, leaves home, Abigail describes in detail her new religious experiences. Her daughter's misery, survival, and departure from her father's abuse become a backdrop for the experience the narrative privileges, which is Abigail's account of her own religious ecstasy: "For sometime I was so swallowed up in God, that I seemed to lose a view of all creatures. I do not know that I had a thought of myself. I seemed hid from a sight of the world in an ocean of bliss" (85). In fact, in referencing the turmoil in her family, she goes as far as to assert that her present religious experience of "spiritual blessings far more than . . . overbalance all [her] outward calamities" (86). In this section of the narrative Abigail's concern for Phebe seems mostly mitigated by her ongoing, almost obsessive interest in her own religious experiences and in her husband's spiritual state.

Bailey's religious retreat, seemingly unthinkable in the context of her circumstances, can be partly understood as an unconscious yet strategic mode of survival, an imaginative response to real events she would have found unimaginable. If we acknowledge the tremendous difficulty for Bailey of conceiving of actual escape or resistance, we can imagine her retreat into a private spiritual world as a means of survival. Enduring actual experiences she finds too horrible to comprehend fully or acknowledge to others, she seems at times to live analogically, emphasizing the potential figurative meaning of her experience, which nearly eclipses actual consequences in reality for herself and her children. Shifting to another realm allows her, at least temporarily, to obliterate the self caught in horrible circumstances and to be, instead, "swallowed up in God," thus—spiritually at least—transcending any struggle over how to survive, how to protect her children, how to end her marriage, and how to proceed with questions of law, property, and financial support.

Bailey's ecstatic experience makes historical sense as well. Her movement in the narrative from her victimization by Asa into a mystical spiritual union with God may be understood as part of a tradition of mysticism, often erotic and frequently literally and/or metaphorically female. Christian mysticism's most famous (and frequently represented) practitioner, Teresa of Avila (1515–1582), recorded mystical experiences that linked pain and pleasure in an overwhelming ecstatic experience of union with the divine which, like Bailey's, then transformed her this-worldly experience as well. Closer historical contexts suggest that Bailey's experience would not have been at all unusual in her region and religious community. Religious "enthusiasm," even to the point of the ecstatic experience that Bailey describes, is consistent with the phenomenon of religious revival in this region and era. As both Taves and Albanese explain, she would have been in a populous company; her ecstatic reality would have been shared and reaffirmed by members of the community, many of whom were manifesting responses to a minister's preaching that included extraordinary physical and emotional experiences. Influential ministers such as Charles Chauncy may have disapproved and done his best to explain away what he and other "Old Lights" saw as the excesses and abuses of religious enthusiasm, but the faithful continued to share such experiences in some communities to the point that fainting and other physical manifestations became expected.[8] Bailey experiences the spiritual state of self-loss normative for evangelical revival in her community, the experience called for and expected of the faithful.

Just as historical contexts for Bailey's religious ecstasy illuminate her narrative perspective and experience, so does a discussion of the meaning of incest. Whereas any sexual relationship between a father and underage daughter would today almost certainly be framed in terms of sexual violence and incest, such a framework was not readily accessible in the eighteenth century. Abigail would likely have been prepared to understand incest as a particularly offensive form of adultery; at first, however, she may not have connected her sense of Asa's cruelty and violence to his sexual relationship with their daughter. "As a form of adultery rather than child abuse, incest was seen primarily as a threat to the wife, the marriage, and the social order," writes Taves. "In this view, the wife rather than the child was assumed to be the primary victim of father-daughter incest." This sense of contextual meaning, distant from ours, helps to illuminate Abigail's initially limited expressions of concern for the effects of Asa's actions on Phebe. Taves argues that we understand incest in a fundamentally different way than Abigail Bailey and her peers would have. We now see it as an abuse of power within a dependent relationship, as family violence, as child abuse; however, "the identification of father-daughter incest as a form of sexual abuse creates a theoretical link, not present for Abigail, between the incest and Asa's physical and emotional violence" (Introduction 26). And Bailey does evade acknowledging such a connection for some time in the narrative. But, Taves's informed contextualizing notwithstanding, some sort of shift in perspective does, in fact, occur for Abigail in her view of her husband's relationship with Phebe, and it seems quite likely that the shift occurs precisely because she comes to see the violence at the heart of it (just as in his relationship with Abigail herself). That realization prompts her to recognize Phebe more clearly as a victim of her father's evil, an understanding crucial to the interpretive transformation Abigail undergoes, which provides the foundation for her eventual resistance to Asa and leads to her writing the text she produces.

Bailey's initial perception of the violence in her home as part of a sacred process of sanctification fits her religious ideology, which honors passivity and, quite particularly, female passivity. But even more to the heart of the matter, an examination of Bailey's own reading of scripture suggests that she internalized a part of the Christian tradition that sacralizes violence, further problematizing for her what readers see as the obvious and necessary response of resistance. What we may now regard as her startling passivity may also be understood as her reenactment of the central truth of her religious life—the crucifixion of Jesus—or as an adumbration (to choose merely one example from the score of suffering biblical figures she calls to mind in her text) of the story of Job. Sanctified violence—meaningful in an immediate way for the sufferer in conferring spiritual benefits, but also deriving larger significance from the overall pattern of theological meanings for violence within the Christian tradition—form part of the context for Bailey's narrative.

Feminist theologians have critiqued the problem of Christian interpretations of violence, specifically the relationship to the inescapable patriarchalism of Christianity, and the way that sacralized violence—particularly emphasized in many Christian traditions—contributes to a religious culture that not only fails to see but allows for violence against women and that authorizes or even prescribes a passive response. Womanist theologians, especially concerned with the profound problem for African American women of centering religious meaning in sacrifice and suffering, have posited alternative frameworks for the Christian concept of redemption, specifically rejecting the notion of a sacrificial atonement—and of sacred and/or substitutionary suffering, or what theologian Dolores Williams terms "surrogacy." According to Williams, "The image of Jesus on the cross is the image of human sin in its most desecrated form, . . . an image of defilement, a gross manifestation of collective human sin" (166). Such theological revisioning of violence as a manifestation of sin rather than sacred sacrifice illuminates Bailey's interpretive (and therefore experiential) challenges.

Rene Girard's career-long exploration of violence and the sacred further informs the dynamic of violence at work in Bailey's narrative, particularly in the matter of her relationship to Phebe and her suffering.[9] Girard's work in interpreting violence and the sacred in literature and culture is complex and, ultimately, invested in an overarching argument about universal patterns and meaning. What I am most interested in here, however, is Girard's specific concern (shared by contemporary theological movements concerned with social justice and compassion for the world's suffering and poor) with the voice of the victim, an insistence that violence within Jewish and Christian traditions ought to be understood in ways that emphasize the ultimate revelation at the heart of suffering for its witnesses, which must be understood as a rejection of human violence. For Girard, structures of violence are embedded in the social order, and the experience of witnessing the innocence of victims of violence unmasks those structures; God is emphatically a God of and for victims. Such a construction of violence, which emphasizes the transformative power of suffering for the witness, who then condemns the violence and chooses solidarity or identification with the sufferer, illuminates Bailey's transformation in the *Memoirs*.

One of the turning points in her gradual move from passive victim to agent occurs as she realizes the effects of Asa's violence, not on herself but on her daughter. Once Abigail begins to understand Phebe as a victim and identifies the girl's suffering, that truth compels her to come to terms with her husband's acts in new ways. When she gains a fuller understanding (from two other daughters, and then from a personal visit to the self-exiled Phebe) of the extent of her husband's abuse, she is initially horrified. Bailey's reaction is intriguing and not fully expounded; she seemed, earlier, to have known much of Phebe's abuse, identifying her husband's conduct as "abominable" and urging Phebe to move toward legal prosecution, to "become an evidence against him" (81). But her reaction to the consultation with her daughters reveals that she has acquired new information or gained new insight, perhaps learning of further physical abuse of other children, or of new details concerning his abuse of Phebe. Perhaps she has been given a clearer understanding that Phebe was not seduced but raped by her father. Perhaps it is simply the new context—her daughters' discussion of their father's abuse—that has constituted revelation.

Whatever the new information or insight, her children's narratives allow her to see their suffering, particularly Phebe's, in new ways. Bailey conveys a dramatically intensified reaction to her husband's offenses, and she repeatedly records her daughters' horror as several of them sequentially hear and then tell what their younger sister (described by Bailey as "too young to be a legal witness, but old enough to tell the truth") "saw and heard, more than a year before, on a certain Sabbath." The (unspoken to the reader) details cause the oldest sister (the one who finally relays the account to her mother) to faint. Though the reader does not learn of the specific offenses here, Bailey does, and she conveys her reaction in the strongest possible terms: "I had long before had full evidence to my mind of Mr. B's great wickedness in this matter; and I thought I was prepared to hear the worst. But verily the worst was dreadful! The last great day will unfold it. I truly at this time had a new lesson added, to all that ever I before heard, or conceived, of human depravity" (87).

Consequently, she moves to a more considered response to Phebe and toward a more specific legal action against Asa. Phebe's reaction now becomes an important, even primary consideration. It seems likely that at this point Abigail begins to recognize the sexual violence at the heart of her husband's actions against Phebe, that her sense of Asa's offenses is intensified by the necessary, now unavoidable, acknowledgment of her children's suffering, setting off a transformation of her view of her husband and, in fact, of herself as well. She begins to gain agency as she finds that she must, finally, take action on behalf of her children and herself. The feeling language in which she records her view of Phebe reveals that her new empathy with her daughter's pain transforms her view of suffering, effectively despiritualizing it, converting it from meaningful metaphor to a stark reality requiring a swift response. And whereas earlier in the narrative God's and her husband's' agency had been blurred, she now distinguishes between them in order to see and make judgments about the suffering her husband has caused. She may have been willing to sacrifice herself on an altar of sanctification, but she determines here that she cannot sacrifice her children, whom she now differentiates from herself. The ecstatic abstraction of the previous section gives way at this point to subsequent narratives revealing Abigail's transformed sense of power, manifested both in her rhetoric as a narrator and in her actions in response to Asa. Abigail's identification of and with Phebe's suffering compels her to agency, which includes a critical judgment of Asa's actions and a crucial distinction between Asa's culpability and God's sovereignty.

At the outset of the *Memoirs,* Bailey announces that her story, at least in part, is an extended reflection on the meaning of suffering. Demonstrating that her experience of perplexity results from a simultaneous belief in a good and sovereign God and her experience of violence, she makes a theological assertion, then cites examples of suffering biblical characters whose experiences may provide parallels to hers. By placing her own suffering in the context of biblical suffering, she makes it both less and more extraordinary—sanctified, biblically precedented, but not necessarily understood. After noting that it had always been her hope to marry a good and peaceful man, she says:

> But the all wise God, who has made all things for himself, has a right, and knows how, to govern all things for his own glory; and often to disappoint the purposes of his creatures. God often suffers mankind sorely to afflict and oppress one another; and not only those who appear as open enemies;—but sometimes those who pretend to be our best friends, cruelly oppress. Cain slew his brother. And the brethren of Joseph hated him, and sold him into Egypt.
>
> It is happy when cruel treatment is overruled to promote a greater good. Job's afflictions did thus. The trials of Joseph but prepared the way for his greater exaltation. David, by being hunted and distressed by Saul, was prepared for the crown of Israel. Daniel in the lion's den, and the three children of God in the raging furnace, were prepared for deliverance, honor and salvation. (57)

She refrains from commenting, however, on the conclusive meaning of her own experience—specifically on the absence of any "happy" sense that her experience of cruelty has been "overruled to promote a greater good" as were those of Job, Joseph, David, and Daniel.

Later, when she notes that she has learned that trust in God requires her to use what she terms "means," (174) she implies that this lesson is perhaps the only greater good produced by the suffering she has recorded. Her dramatic spiritual journey, at least up to her final departure and divorce from Asa, is a pilgrimage toward a sense of agency and self, founded upon a commitment to "means" within her radically passive religious sense of herself in a world controlled by divine agency. Her theology of suffering here implies that persecution may be part of a divine process in the life of an individual, but the violence in the narratives she records, biblical and her own, is caused by humans, whom God "suffers" to "afflict and oppress one another." Even our "best friends" may "cruelly oppress" (57). Moreover, the introductory comment, along with the narrative of her experiences, emphasizes a particular dimension: that the incomprehensibility of suffering, the idea that the "greater good" sought by the victims (including reflective autobiographers such as Bailey) may or may not become apparent.

In much of the narrative, Bailey maintains a posture of submission, refusing agency in order to enact her faithfulness to the work of God in her life circumstances. In keeping with her religious tradition, she assumes that faithfulness to God leads directly to obedience to her husband: "I think God gave me a heart to resolve never to be obstinate, or disobedient to my husband; but to be always kind, obedient, and obliging in all things not contrary to the word of God. I thought if Mr. B. were sometimes unreasonable, I would be reasonable, and would rather suffer wrong than do wrong" (57). That proclamation reveals at least two things. First, initially she views even her personal disposition (which readers today might say is the cause of so much of her troubling response to Asa's brutality) as a dynamic synthesis of what God "gives" and what she "thinks" (forms of the latter verb occur twice); thus, in announcing the beginning of her experiences with her husband, she indicates that her own theological starting point is a Calvinist preoccupation with the absolute sovereignty of God. Second, in keeping with this theological commitment, perhaps, and informed by gendered assumptions about her role as a wife, she sees agency as more dangerous than passivity. Her announced preference to "suffer" rather than "do" wrong specifically indicates that she perceives victimization as less dangerous than inappropriate behavior. Spiritual safety, then, is to be preferred over literal safety (absence of suffering).

She interprets all experiences primarily in terms of the sovereignty of God, who orders and allows events. The first time she learns of her husband's sexual infidelity, for instance, she recalls the Bible's teaching that "in the world ye shall have tribulations" and that "all things shall work together for good" (59–60). When Asa attempts to rape a servant, she cites the stories of the Exodus, Daniel, and Jonah—noting in each story the act of supernatural deliverance for the sufferers—and counsels herself, "Cast thy burden upon the Lord, then" (62). She seems in these instances consistently to view herself as the sufferer (ignoring, for instance, the servant). Further, these initial revelations of Asa's unfaithfulness and violence do not seem to mitigate her view of him, which is shaped by both theology and sentiment:

> For though he had made so high pretenses to religion many years before, as has been mentioned, yet he had evidently turned back to the world; and he daily shewed himself to be destitute of saving grace. But he had a good knowledge of the sacred scriptures; and I took great satisfaction in conversing with him upon them. I felt the tenderest affection for him as my head and husband. I ever rejoiced when he returned from abroad. Nor did I see him come in from his daily business, without sensible delight. Much pleasure I took in waiting upon him, and in doing all in my power to make him happy (66).

But as she takes pleasure in her husband, her "head"—a reference to a New Testament text, (Eph. 5.23) traditionally interpreted to require the submission of wives to the authoritarian rule of their husbands—so she chastises herself for loving him and other earthly relations too much, for being "too closely tied to my friends, and my earthly blessings" (66).[10]

Indeed, she expects, apparently as a result of her guilt over her unrestrained love for her family, that God will punish her by visiting her with calamity, and she aims to prepare herself to meet whatever trials may come her way. She prays that when God "should see fit to take from me my dearest worldly comforts, I might humbly submit, and say, 'it is the Lord; let him do what seemeth him good.' . . . I hence did earnestly attempt to look to God for strength, and to cast my burden on him; till I was brought to be able to say, not as I will, but as thou wilt. Thy will, O Lord, be done" (67). In the biblical reading she provides here, Bailey follows the interpretive practices of her tradition: although her submission seems overwhelmingly gendered throughout the memoir, her biblical paradigm for suffering and humility is specifically male and a central part of her religious tradition. The verses she quotes in the passage above, for example, refer first to the story of Eli and Samuel in 1 Samuel 3, where the child and prophet Samuel is called upon to warn of God's imminent, punitive wrath, and then to the central story of Christianity, that of the suffering and crucifixion of Jesus. Bailey's biblical citations here and elsewhere underscore the earlier discussion concerning the way she developed a theological framework that ascribed profoundly divine meaning to her own struggles, making her particularly ready to envision her own suffering in a context of redemption, similar even to that of Christ, anticipating redemptive effects (perhaps for herself or perhaps for her husband or children) from submitting to a divine sentence of violence, delivered to her by the hand of her husband.

When Asa verbally abuses her, she reminds herself to find refuge in God, "that [she] might learn [her] duty, find consolation, and have [her] faith, patience, and submission strengthened" (68). She reads her scripture with a single-minded focus on submission, sometimes, as in the examples above, ignoring concomitant issues raised by the same passage, story, or character. So rather than understanding the Exodus narrative, for instance, as a story first of resistance against oppression and then of divine deliverance and triumph over evil, she sees submission, patience, and long-suffering as the point. (Recall, in contrast, Equiano's revealing reading of the same drama, where he attends primarily to Moses's aggression: his murder of a slave driver.) Similarly, in citing Daniel, Bailey emphasizes his waiting for and trusting in God's deliverance, omitting reference to the act of political and religious resistance that caused a ruler to slate Daniel's execution in the first place. So rather than the defiant Daniel who refused to bow to a royal edict he deemed capricious and unjust, she focuses on the subsequently patient Daniel, waiting for the deliverance that does come, in a dramatic and miraculous fashion.

Her selective use of the Daniel story is particularly intriguing in its additional corollary interpretive possibilities. Like Daniel, Abigail is in a subordinate position to an established authority figure who derives power from established, socially recognized, and apparently theologically justified powers. But unlike him, she fails until long after she and her children have endured extreme abuse to resist this power, despite a recognition of its gross injustice. Failing to see the biblical alternatives, the authoritative foundations that the other writers discussed in this book make such dramatic use of, Abigail remains focused in much of the narrative on radical submission, abject humility, as the required posture for all spiritual growth. Moreover, the external religious world represented in her narrative seems to reinforce that. In the midst of her struggles when she records her reaction to a sermon, the topic is patience and long-suffering. And when she does finally muster the courage to speak in very veiled terms about her domestic trauma, the minister counsels patience and courage to bear difficult trials. She is consequently reassured, confident that she has been following just that advice.

Bailey's response to the ministerial voices in her *Memoirs* helps explain her near self-annihilation, her retreat into a private religious reality, and her passivity in response to the physical and psychological suffering of herself and her children. At the same time, however, that response reveals other aspects of the self she constructs via prayer and memory in this text. Bailey's articulation of abject self-loathing (which might accurately be understood as specifically Christian and gendered female) is not surprising, given what we know of her tradition and experience, but her sense of agency and authority, revealed most fully near the end of the text, contradicts it. Just as her recognition of Phebe's victimization transforms her view of Asa's violence, so her emerging sense of herself as a minister for others enables her to gain a sense of authority that her religious tradition might have precluded.

The editor of the *Memoirs* and author of the "Advertisement" and the "Introduction" interjects substantial commentary, providing another significant ministerial voice in this text and allowing readers a window into the religious sensibility informing the assumptions and practices of Bailey and her original, immediate readers. Designed primarily to persuade readers of the authenticity of the author's piety, and to explain his role in bringing her *Memoirs* to publication, Ethan Smith's introduction illuminates the religious contexts for Bailey and her original readers, whose favor Smith hopes to gain. Recounting her conversion, he quotes at length from her prayer diary, emphasizing the role of a particular preacher in convincing her of her own complete depravity, noting approvingly that she described herself as a "guilty and very filthy creature . . . of all things the most corrupt and abominable" (Bailey 53), a demonstration of the sensibilities that seem to lead her to distrust—in fact, to discount altogether—her own judgment and agency, the sensibilities that resonate throughout the *Memoirs*. Bailey's description of herself here demonstrates the way this strain of religion disposed adherents to a sense of powerlessness and a fixation on their own personal states to the exclusion of wider concerns and questions, thus providing some context for the obsessively personal spiritual sensibility in the *Memoirs* that distresses contemporary readers, and, almost certainly, allowed Bailey to ignore for a time the very real effects of her disastrous marriage. Ethan Smith's affirmation of Bailey's spiritual self-concept, his citation of it as evidence of her credibility and authority for early nineteenth-century readers, suggests it as a norm, even an ideal.

Ethan Smith's voice, however, and his appropriation of Bailey's own voice does more than establish the context for the *Memoirs*. Smith's presence in Bailey's text reveals the difficult lines of authority and self that she negotiated. The same minister who approvingly repeats her description of herself as a filthy creature (indicating that she was consequently prepared to join the church) later interrupts Bailey's narrative to issue a judgment concerning her lack of action, her failure to prosecute her husband. After Abigail has described Asa's abuse of Phebe, Smith interjects a footnote providing readers with a commentary on Abigail's inaction: "The discreet reader will repeatedly wonder that this pious sufferer did not look abroad for help against so vile a son of Beliel, and avail herself of the law of the land, by swearing the peace against him. Her forbearance does indeed seem to have been carried to excess" (72). Smith then suggests several possible ways of understanding Bailey's inaction—all of them rooted in his sense of her individual identity, her personality, her piety: he remains silent on the larger causes of her sensibility—on the theology, the preaching, and the domestic practices characterizing the religious tradition that both he and Bailey represent. In commenting on her excessive "forbearance," he sees only the way she "erred," not the relationship between his own notion of Christian virtue, particularly feminine virtue, and that same forbearance.

Smith ends his interjection with a final judgment on Bailey, which he assumes readers will share: "After all, it will be difficult to resist the conviction which will be excited in the course of these memoirs that Mrs. B. did truly err, in not having her husband brought to justice. The law is made for the lawless and disobedient" (72). Paradoxically, he chastises her for her inaction within a religious system that discouraged her from understanding that she could take any legitimate action, a tradition that seemed at times by its very design to inspire self-loathing—particularly female self-loathing—and suffering. Further, his judgments of viciousness, rooted as they are in a Calvinist sense of total human depravity, have a leveling effect on the reader: he envisions Asa as unequivocally demonic, a "son of Beliel," in the same religious context as Abigail's religious credentials, citing with approval her self-conception as a filthy creature. In castigating her for her inaction, Smith himself surely perceived significant, crucial differences in Abigail Bailey's self-expression of humility, via a Calvinist spiritual metaphor for her unworthiness before the sovereign God, and his own identification of her husband with the devil. But the reader encountering his judgments and Abigail's near fatal inaction is struck by the starkness of the psychological and theological trap in which she was caught and by the (inadvertent but nonetheless effective) ministerial hand in its design.

The minister's voice, representing the official perspective here and elsewhere records but fails to comprehend the crucial experience of the less powerful, those victimized by the doctrines, metaphors, and biblical analogues he tenders. Indeed, Ethan Smith's particular judgments of Abigail Bailey notwithstanding, it is his ministerial peers' official counsel that fuels her inaction throughout the text. When she finds a way to begin to speak about her suffering (which she does only in the most abstract, guarded terms), the church's official advice, delivered through a trusted minister, urges her toward an even more profound passivity than that which she has so far practiced; patience, silence, and inaction, she is assured, will lead to greater spiritual benefits, the goal she consistently seeks and the appropriate goal according to the sense of piety that her tradition reinforced.

Despite ministerial voices and counsel, however, Bailey does progress into a stronger sense of selfhood. The irony of the ministerial editor's response to her narrative is underscored by the fact that although he admonishingly comments on the limits of her actions against Asa, he does not comment on the progression toward action and resistance in the text. Bailey's developing agency is visible in the way she becomes her own character after her identification with Phebe. Though she continues to echo biblical narratives, she also becomes, finally, a central character in an immediate drama with material rather than metaphoric or exclusively spiritual consequences. The concrete world, such an important feature of the other narratives examined in this book becomes decidedly more central in the second half of Bailey's text, where she acknowledges the myriad decisions and actions now under her control. She divorces her husband (despite his resistance), gains a property settlement (notwithstanding Asa's multiple attempts to deprive her of this), and successfully resists his efforts to regain control of the family.

Throughout, she records her reflections about her progress in making decisions concerning the material circumstances she and her children face as she acts out her resistance to Asa's control. In striking contrast to her self-portrayal early in the *Memoirs*, Abigail now presents herself as having a strong sense of agency, exercised in resistance not only to Asa's repeated moves for control but also to the various other individuals he introduces into their circumstances, individuals hired or otherwise controlled by him. In one example, a Mr. Ludlow, who has been fooled by Asa into believing false stories about his domestic troubles, pressures Abigail to trade the farm for unseen land in New York and to reconcile with her husband for the sake of her own and her children's interests:

> Mr. Ludlow . . . had studied law, and practiced some as an attorney; and he thought if I did not become reconciled to Mr. B I was in considerable danger of losing my part of the interest. I told him, he could talk very fast, and make things seem smooth, and fair:—but his talk was in vain. I told him I had no necessity of informing him on what I had made up my judgment and determination. But my mind was fixed. And he could neither flatter nor terrify me to alter it. I should not do what I deemed wrong, whatever the consequences might be. And I did not believe, (I informed him,) that God would suffer Mr. B. to take away the part of the property, which justly belonged to me and my children. (113)

Although the struggle (over property, children, divorce) between Asa and Abigail continues, her proclamations of resistance here and elsewhere are in notable contrast with the radical passivity at the outset of the narrative.

Like many other eighteenth-century autobiographical texts, Bailey's includes regular reevaluations of her behavior and spirituality; she presents herself as a pilgrim, one who is journeying toward an ever deepening sense of religious commitment. The judgments reflective of her most recent spiritual state consistently supersede her previous spiritual states; she regularly reiterates her hope that in the future she will be still further along her path. This feature—characteristic of spiritual autobiographies within Puritan and neo-Puritan traditions, and a fairly predictable feature of captivity narratives—makes some life-writing within this tradition seem somewhat nonlinear; major events blur together, and turning points seem difficult to determine. But in contrast to, say, Jonathan Edwards's "Personal Narrative," a revealing point of comparison for Samson Occom's text, Abigail Bailey's narrative relates clearly delineated and significant turning points in her journey toward her own survival. In fact, one major turning point, presented almost as a moment of supernatural revelation, occurs when she arrives at what is to her a startlingly new conclusion concerning her own response to Asa. When, after escaping his abduction and returning home, she begins to take action toward divorce and property settlement, her husband responds by having their children kidnapped in an attempt to distract her from her new resolve and to establish control over her in their negotiations about property. At this point, Abigail acts with uncharacteristic resolve. In contrast to the many moments in which she has resisted or condemned her husband, only subsequently to forgive him in the name of Christian charity and to acquiesce to his continued control, her resolve in this instance results in firm action, which then in fact does persist for the rest of the narrative:

> I told Mr. B. I had important business, on which I must now attend; and I did not mean to be diverted from it. I told him I had long viewed it a great privilege to cast all my cares upon God. And I believed God would give me firmness to pursue my object with him; and also, that God would take those children out of his cruel hands, and restore them to me. Mr. B. appeared to feel mortified and in some measure defeated.
>
> I then and ever understood that trusting in God implies the due use of proper means. In the present distressing case therefore, I was determined to have all done that was possible, to recover my children. (174)

In presenting this turning point, Bailey leads the reader to evaluate her previous and subsequent behavior by way of this moment, both her hesitation to oppose Asa earlier in the marriage and then, finally, her resolution and follow-through in ultimately doing so.

The sense of agency Bailey develops within her religious sensibility empowers her to oppose Asa. She has come to a new theological truth, one she did not know at the outset of these experiences. She articulates the new spiritual lesson she has learned: trust in God "implies the due use of proper means." Her fascinating word choice suggests legal nuances from contractual law that would be consistent with Calvinist covenantal theology. Further, her "implies" conveys the idea of this truth as unspoken or perhaps not straightforwardly asserted but nonetheless true. The immediate effect of this new truth is revelatory: no divine edict calls Bailey to wait and watch for the resolution of her husband's violence; on the contrary, she must take action ("means") against him as a result of her trust in God. In other words, she has a theological revelation about the legitimacy, even for a pious Christian woman, of agency.

Importantly, the actual turning point here consists as much in revelation or reflection as in action. Indeed, the revelation seems to *follow* the actions she has increasingly taken. The emphasis throughout the narrative has been on Abigail's interpretive work, her state of mind concerning her ordeal. Here, she comes to a new conclusion about her position in relationship to events: she must demonstrate her trust in God not by waiting and forbearing, as she has done, but by acting on behalf of herself and her children to resist Asa. The transforming effect of this theological revelation is evident even stylistically in the relentless "I" of the passage, coupled with active, specific verbs: "I told," "I believed," "I . . . understood," "I was determined."

Although the revelation concerning "means" for Abigail Bailey is fleshed out in the consistent action she takes against Asa, despite his continued acts of aggression, her sense of agency is seen in perhaps fuller ways once Asa is effectively and permanently separated from the family.[11] The Abigail Bailey who survives, who resists the spiritualized self-annihilation that she has inclined toward during her experience of violence, overcomes her own marginalization by way of appropriating a ministerial voice of authority, power, and agency: the masculine discourse of public religious speech. Once Asa Bailey ceases to be a subject in Abigail Bailey's story, readers see another view of the self she has gained over the course of the narrative. Text appended to the end of the *Memoirs* by her minister/editor not only shows her agency and authority but also complicates her relationship to the ministerial and biblical voices and texts that have shaped her narrative proper. The editor concludes the *Memoirs* with additional materials in which he describes Bailey's later life and death as well as the circumstances of her children. He provides a fuller picture of her character and, most important for this study, her "ministry."

The portrait that emerges, both from editorial description and then from appended primary texts by Bailey herself, shows the once radically passive Abigail now acting as a minister herself. Smith relates, for example, that after her marriage ended, she visited different families and "ably" assumed the role of spiritual leader in these households: "If the man were absent, and the family were willing, she failed not to read God's holy word, and to pray night and morning, in the family. This was to her a delightsome employment, which long and pious practice had rendered most familiar, and in which she was very able" (180). The editor's example, presented with the apparent intent to persuade readers of Bailey's continued piety after her marriage ended, also allows readers to see her authority and leadership, qualities that differentiate her from the self that emerges in the *Memoirs* proper. Within the closely circumscribed gender roles of her religious community, she finds a space in which she can perform that function so disastrously enacted by her own husband—that of father and, more, of minister to the household. Just as Jarena Lee so effectively does in her ministerial memoir, Bailey exploits the opportunity afforded by the absence of an authoritative male to assume the role of father, head of the family, and—in a limited domestic sense—minister, as she takes responsibility for the spiritual leadership of families not her own.

More compelling evidence of Bailey's transformed and now ministerial self occurs in the texts Smith includes from Bailey's prayer diary. In addition, a letter she wrote to one congregation assumes an authority that, again, presents a strong contrast to the uncertain sense of self in the memoir. In what may seem a paradox, Bailey articulates her discovered authoritative self in rhetorical echoes of the Christian scriptures—in her tone, the authority she establishes for herself, the apparent relationship she assumes with her readers, and even the turns of phrase from various biblical texts: "I feel as though I had you by the hand, or rather by the heart, and cannot let you go. My tender love for you, and for the cause which I plead seems to demand a few words more.... Think not that I have lost confidence in you; and this animates me to attempt to stir up your minds by way of remembrance, in hopes that you will become more engaged and heavenly" (183). The repeated use of the personal pronoun, as well as the consequent presumption of personal authority, contrasts with the tone of the narrative persona in much of the text of the *Memoirs*. Unlike the private and predominantly perplexed self in that more interior text, the letter shows Bailey's public, authoritative self, an alternative, perhaps, to the forms of authority enacted in the *Memoirs* proper. In contrast to the ministerial advice she received, Bailey seems to exercise her authority in the context of tenderness and love, revisioning the authority of an uninformed minister as well as the authority she endured at the hands of her husband. Perhaps, as in some captivity narratives, in Bailey's text a strong self emerges from having survived the events recounted in the *Memoirs*, from having ultimately resolved to take action on behalf of herself and her children, and from having recorded her own life narrative.[12]

Outside of the knot of her own trauma, she speaks with frank and apparently unselfconscious confidence, pastorally commanding her readers. Just as Occom, Marrant, Equiano, Lee, and Apess do, Bailey takes on the pulpit and a biblical voice of authority—quite specifically the voice of the Apostle Paul in the New Testament, delivering personal appeals in letters to the early church communities. Abigail, like Paul, chastises faithful readers, simultaneously upholding her love for them, which she describes in specifically pastoral terms as she calls the congregation to adhere to higher spiritual standards. Paul talks, for example, about having the Philippians in his heart (Phil. 1.7), and he frequently speaks of having confidence in his readers (2 Cor. 2.3, 7.16, 8.22, Gal. 5.10). Bailey's letter employs both the phrases and the tone of the apostle. Accustomed as her readers were to hearing formal ministerial discourse and biblical exposition, they would have recognized the sermonic and epistolary form here, as well as Bailey's repetition and variation, her repeated use of questions (the dominant rhetorical feature in Apess's polemic use of sermonic rhetoric), her constant allusions to biblical texts by way of turns of phrase, motif, and narrative: "We are assured that those who love God will keep his commandments. . . . Shall we not then, dearly beloved, give evidence to ourselves, and to others. . . . Shall we not hold fast our profession without wavering? Shall we not consider one another to provoke unto love and to good works . . . Are we not as a city set on a hill? Are we not under peculiar obligations to let our light shine before men, to the glory of God?" (182). The effect of biblical language and sermonic style would have rendered Bailey's discourse familiar to her readers, even though it is in marked contrast to the victimized and uncertain persona that dominates the text of the *Memoirs.*

Bailey's "dissent," then, and her link to the other writers in this discussion, occur in her rejection of the script written by her religious tradition. And while she fails to draw the crucial connecting line (identified by feminist theologians) between her tradition's concept of God and the abusive authority of her husband, she does, finally, resist that authority. Breaking out of the role circumscribed for her, she uncovers a nightmare version of the requisite piety and domesticity and presents an autobiographical self fashioned in opposition to that ideal—not only in the preacherly materials appended to the *Memoirs* but also in the didactic text of the *Memoirs* itself, which will instruct readers not only in the acts of spiritual self-reflection but also in the dangerous waters of patriarchal marriage.

The vigorous interrogation of authority that fueled the resistance of these other writers was dramatically circumscribed in Bailey's congregational experience. Personal piety and individual emotional experience were expected in her religious culture; dissent from institutional authority was not—in contrast to the experience of Jarena Lee, who witnessed dissenting men organize a new religious community and, eventually, a denomination. Indeed, one of the many interesting facts we learn of Bailey is from her comment that she despises the "impertinence" of Methodism, which, she says, may or may not lead to Christianity but certainly not to the kind of Christianity she herself wished to practice (180). That comment, though not surprising in light of her lifelong affiliation with congregationalism, as well as her disgust at her husband's becoming a Methodist minister, reveals another aspect of the dynamic interplay of authority and religion. She places herself on a continuum, and her location is significant: although familiar with revivalist strains within her own established Congregational denomination, she does not approve of the emerging unaffiliated or newly affiliated revivalist congregations with looser forms of governance and theology. If those looser structures and the biblically sanctioned antihierarchicalism of some strains of Protestant Christianity led in some cases to the public dissent expressed in the other narratives, here one can see, at least in part, the results of condemning them.

The *Memoirs* can leave contemporary readers with an overall impression that Bailey failed, for the most part, to gain a sense of authority or agency throughout her experience. Her preoccupation with submission, patience, and restraint in the face of the violence that she and her children endured threatens to overwhelm any other observations readers might make. Indeed, her apparent inability to comprehend the *nonspiritual* meaning of her experience sets her apart from the other writers discussed here. And although it takes her nearly a lifetime to develop the sense of agency that does enable her to survive, she fails altogether to engage in a social critique of her experience, the critique that is both self-conscious and central to the other writers. Like them, Bailey sees herself as part of a religious tradition characterized by deep piety and biblical adherence. Like them, she presents her own identity as profoundly religious. But whereas Occom, Marrant, Equiano, Lee, and Apess understand their experiences of victimization in the context of a biblical view of oppression and injustice—that is, as an enactment of the evil described in biblical texts—Bailey does not, for much of her narrative, view the violence in her family in this way. Like the other writers she does find her voice, at least in part, by way of the tradition that has authored her oppression. The biblical texts she has memorized and meditated on fuel her victimization and her passivity, as well as her dramatically circumscribed "dissent." Like the other writers examined here, she imagines and then enacts her authority by way of scripture.

The crucial differences between Bailey and the more clearly dissident writers, however, may emerge from her discomfort with the less respectable (and more radically democratic) incarnations of revival religion. Still more important is her ideological and personal isolation, her failure to see herself and her circumstances as shaped by her religious tradition and a flawed social institution rather than by, say, God, on the one hand, or Asa's personal evil, on the other. When Samson Occom, in contrast, at the end of his narrative, identifies the dynamic of his relationship with New England missionaries in terms of the story of the beating of the "poor Indian boy," he accesses his and his audience's awareness of the larger story of two distinct communities and the unequal power dynamics constantly at work between them. He also identifies, implicitly, the way those dynamics are affecting other Christian Natives, and he later acts on that sense of identification at Brothertown. Marrant chooses to see a relationship between himself, a freeborn black, and the plantation slaves who endure persecution both despite and because of their Christianity. Equiano acknowledges the effects of a failed Christian vision in the inescapable violence of an unredeemable slave system. When Jarena Lee interrogates the gendered terms of the religious tradition she endorses, she does so, first, informed by the immediate experience of resistance and dissent of her African American male counterparts. Her awareness of her own victimization by those same men is an extension of the argument that both they and she understand on the basis of their shared experience of race. And Apess's entire narrative may be read as the account of coming to an awareness of a collective sensibility and seizing its power, as he reidentifies with his original culture and then becomes an activist for another Native American community.

In juxtaposition with these writers, Bailey's isolation becomes especially striking. She understands both her religion and her suffering as private affairs. No dynamics in her particular circumstances allow her to see her connection to other women. Whereas Jarena Lee travels and preaches with other women, Bailey, alone, wonders how much of her circumstance to reveal to her male minister. Indeed, other women, like the rest of the community, are almost nonexistent in Bailey's story. Her very limited experience of collectivity occurs only as her daughters reveal their suffering to her. She never gains ideological access to a collective rather than an entirely personal framework for both suffering and identity. All the other writers here saw and understood their religious tradition's effects on them in both personal and collective terms. Bailey's sensibility remained, for the most part, personal, isolated, unconscious.

6

DEVOTION AND DISSENT
Jarena Lee's Rhetoric of Conversion and Call

☦

Let the woman learn in silence with all subjection. But I suffer not a woman to teach, nor to usurp authority over the man, but to be in silence.
  1 Timothy 2.11–12

Denied vision. Excluded, excluded, excluded from council, ritual, activity, learning, language.... Religion. When all believed ... silence in holy places.
  Tillie Olsen, *Silences*

JARENA LEE'S 1836 autobiography records parallel concerns: her earnest desire to exhort readers toward Christian conversion and consequent religious sanctification, and her equally earnest account of her own resistance to masculine prohibitions that hindered the true workings of the holy spirit, workings that seemed most frequently to take a feminine form. Lee enacted a call to preach in a Christian religious tradition that (like most in her era and since) prohibited women's public speech and barred women from the pulpit and ordination. Like the other writers discussed here, she composed her autobiography in response to the spiritual requirements of her religious tradition—a revivalist strain of early nineteenth-century evangelical Protestantism, a legacy of Great Awakening Christianity. And also like the other writers, Lee may be understood, in Françoise Lionnet's terms, as a "divergent" individual, "living on borderlines," using "linguistic and rhetorical structures that allow [her] plural selves to speak from within the straightjackets of borrowed discourses" (19). Lee anticipates Lionnet's notion of *metissage*, speaking from a place of indeterminacy, speaking against the traditions and practices of a dominant culture that might have defined her quite differently from the way she determines and presents her own complex version of her life.

Within the form of the spiritual autobiography, Lee makes a powerful proclamation on behalf of women's rights to public speech, including a quite specific call for recognition of women's divine speech via the pulpit, which was being denied them. As a part of her revivalist Christian vision and experience, Lee sees human speech as the realm of the Holy Spirit. Just as the Bible is inspired, so (at least sometimes) is human speech in the everyday world she describes in her autobiography. In this context, she argues—directly, polemically—for the necessity of women's public religious speech despite traditional prohibitions. Further, Lee's narrative enacts the same rhetorical argument by consistently contrasting efficacious female religious discourse with the frequently ineffectual (and thus obviously uninspired) speech of male ministers. She must preach, she must speak her story of faith, because God has inspired and ordained it and because God's people need her to do so.

Born to free black parents in New Jersey in 1783, Jarena Lee had a Christian conversion experience as a young woman in response to the preaching of Richard Allen, of Philadelphia's African Methodist Episcopal church, and informed him that she had received her own call to preach. Allen had founded the AME church in reaction to the racist separatism that he, Absalom Jones, and other African American Christians had met with in the Methodist Episcopal Church in Philadelphia. Allen and Jones, in one of the most famous acts of defiance against institutionalized Christian racial hierarchies in U.S. religious history, formed the renowned (and still vital) Bethel Church in Philadelphia, first as an "African" offshoot of the Methodist denomination, still under that church's authority, and subsequently as a distinct denomination with its own governance and ministers. "Mother Bethel," as the Philadelphia congregation of the AME is still known, remains the official cradle of the African Methodist Episcopal church, and, arguably, of African American institutional Christianity.[1]

Despite his rejection of racist prohibitions and separatism in Christianity, Richard Allen initially reinforced the very religious hierarchies that he himself had suffered under and publicly defied, telling Lee (in response to her announcement of a calling to preach) that even this particular church, founded though it was on an assertion of the liberatory effects of Christianity, could not allow women to preach or to function in any official ministerial capacity. He urged her to fulfill her calling in the less formal (and certainly less powerful, less public) ancillary roles typically assigned to women: speaking at prayer meetings, exhorting the congregation after the preacher's official sermon had ended, and the like. After more than a decade of struggle with white Methodism in Philadelphia, Allen was "determined that blacks should have the power to incorporate themselves into individual churches. [But] he was, nevertheless, no schismatic in areas of Methodist doctrine," which prohibited women preachers (Andrews, Introduction 5).

Initially, Jarena Lee complied; she also fulfilled social expectations for a conventional middle-class woman by marrying and having children, but by her own account she continued to chafe against religious prohibitions. Eventually, according to her narrative, she interrupted a sermon in Bethel Church to preach extemporaneously on the same biblical text as the minister (not Richard Allen in this case). Allen then recanted and subsequently sponsored her efforts to become an itinerant preacher under the official authority of the denomination. Allen and Lee remained lifelong friends; he supported her preaching and ministry to the extent of caring for her children for extended periods of time as she itinerated. She preached to white and black audiences and enjoyed fairly wide acceptance among Methodists. She traveled hundreds of miles and preached hundreds of sermons. Audiences found her remarkably effective, and she had a particularly compelling appeal for African American listeners; her own memoir indicates that slaves often traveled great distances and took extraordinary risks to hear her preach at Methodist camp meetings.[2]

In 1833, Lee hired an anonymous editor to have a portion of her personal journal prepared for publication. She subsequently published and sold a thousand copies of her *Life and Experience*, in 1836, and then printed another thousand in 1839. Ten years later she prepared an expanded version of her life account for publication and sought approval, as was required of Methodist preachers, from the AME's Book Concern—which rejected the manuscript of the second edition. Catherine Brekus suggests that the decision was shaped by the shifting historical circumstances of Methodism: by midcentury "few African Methodist clergymen wanted to memorialize a woman who so perfectly symbolized the uneducated, visionary enthusiasm of their early history" (296). It is likely that the Book Concern understood the subversive quality of Lee's narrative, her vision of personal conversion embedded in social and cultural transformations. Whatever the reason for the Book Concern's rejection, Lee responded by publishing the edition without its approval and support.[3]

Lee constructs her own religious authority in her autobiographies and argues for the same rights for other women in ways that anticipate the work of feminist theologians in the last several decades. In line with the arguments of womanist theologians such as Katie Cannon and Delores Williams, and *mujerista* theologians such as Ada María Isasi-Díaz and María Pilar Aquino, Lee makes use of and insists on the authority of an experiential hermeneutic. She reads biblical texts through a lens of her own experience of exclusion and anger to insist on her rights to full personhood and full religious authority and agency, all defined on her own terms. She calls attention, further, to her own alternative self-construction by transgressing the boundaries set by African American preachers such as Richard Allen, who understood the liberatory power of a biblical tradition to break down hierarchies of race, even as he initially reinscribed hierarchies of gender. He may have missed the irony of his preliminary hermeneutical limitations, but Jarena Lee did not. Through Lee, Allen came to recognize a new site for the liberatory values he had already justified via the scriptures and the successful formation of the Bethel congregation in Philadelphia. Together, Lee and Allen lived out alternative gender roles as they enacted the consequences of what they ultimately perceived as a divine call to equality.

Like Olaudah Equiano's, Lee's narrative is preceded by a pictorial representation of the writer. And like Equiano's visual presentation of himself, Lee's rendering shows readers, first of all, a pious Christian: her arm rests on the biblical text. Further, she is conventionally feminine, modestly, even demurely attired. Her covered head and white shawl may have called to readers' minds apostolic injunctions concerning female authority, particularly Pauline texts that instructed women to cover their heads in deference to masculine authority (1 Cor. 11) and to refrain from teaching men (1 Tim. 2, the text quoted in the epigraph to this chapter.) Her shawl and simple bonnet suggest a domestic rather than the public sphere, and she looks decidedly middle class, with no hint of finery—perhaps the intention is a revivalist Christian version of the Quaker principle of simple dress. She is not in step with the fashion of the day; her dress suggests an eighteenth- rather than a

Jarena Lee, frontispiece portrait, *The Life and Religious Experience*.
Courtesy Schomburg Center, New York Public Library.

nineteenth-century portrait. At the same time and in implicit contradiction, however, she is also portrayed as a writer: her right hand holds her pen, her inkstand is at the ready, her left hand seems almost to be in motion, suggesting potentiality, agency. Lee's attire suggests conventionality, even as the actual rendering—a picture of a female writer and preacher in a public text—records her subversion of convention, her entrance into male tradition and masculine discourse.[4]

Lee's portrait may also have recalled readers' memories of another female writer's frontispiece portrait, that of the poet Phillis Wheatley, who became known for the qualities Lee was interested in establishing in her own visual and textual self-portraits: piety, disruptions of preconceived notions of identity concerning both race and gender, and rhetorical skill. Like Wheatley, Lee hoped to accomplish multiple purposes. To begin with, each writer had a literary production, a text, that she needed to convey to readers. Beyond that, the work itself, the means of presentation, needed to initiate an argument concerning the authenticity of the writer (and, by extension, the community she represented). Wheatley's pious neoclassical verse asserts her humanity, her literacy, and her intellectual skill. Lee's life narrative, making the argument for women's right to preach, demonstrates her spiritual credentials, her preacherly skill, and her oratorical power. In the case of each writer the visual presentation initiates that rhetorical purpose as it establishes her relationship with her readers.

The self-presentation emphasizing Lee as a writer or speaker—pen in hand she takes up her story—continues on the title page, where she amplifies her particular relationship to the religious tradition of her readers in the title of the 1836 spiritual autobiography—*The Life and Religious Experience of Jarena Lee, a Coloured Lady, Giving an Account of Her Call to Preach the Gospel*—and also in the epigraph that follows, where she quotes the biblical prophet Joel's announcement that "it shall come to pass ... that I will pour out my spirit upon all flesh; and your sons and your *daughters* shall prophesy" (2.28; Lee's emphasis).[5] In the preliminary lines of her text she announces, first, that the central concern in this life story will be her call to preach and, further, that the central features of her identity—which she distinguishes, interestingly, not specifically by religious conversion here but by race and gender—determine her move into a tradition in which she both *is* and *is not* welcome. She seems to construct her autobiographical self simultaneously in what Mae Henderson has identified as two means of discourse:

"testimonial/familial" and "competitive/public": she positions herself to speak in multiple and overlapping constituencies, attaining insider, familial authority with some and asserting a competitive authority with others. She invites women—African, Native, and European American— to identify with her on the basis of sex (and her proclamation of her own gendered status) and the prohibitions she has experienced as a result. She invites African American men, especially those in this newly formed tradition, to see (as Richard Allen came to do) a link from their experience of exclusion to her own. And all her readers—presumably earnest Christians—are invited to see her authority within a biblical tradition, even (or especially) a prophetic authority that would correct and call for judgment on the prohibitions she condemns.

In contrast to the male writers of color I discuss here, Lee understands and critiques the male authorial narrative prerogative. The men's sense of linguistic tradition, including hymn language, biblical narrative, and ministerial oratory—further strengthened perhaps by their sense of their Christian readers' expectations—may have allowed them to identify with masculine authorial personae even to the extent of using that tradition to envision racial alliance and to challenge readers' unexamined presumptions about race in their own sacred texts. Equiano, for instance, realigns readers' assumptions about color by comparing Jews and Africans; Apess presents images of a dark-skinned Jesus to his white readers.[6] Such rhetorical moves show not only what these writers sought to achieve with white Christian readers but also what they themselves had achieved in interpreting the European religious tradition they received. They image the presence of the divine—the historical Jesus and the Christian savior—in a semblance of themselves, the practice European Christians had engaged in for centuries. Male authorial privilege may be further highlighted in some of these texts by contrasts with Lee. John Marrant and other African American male narrators (Jupiter Hammon, for instance) do not (or barely) make mention of their race in their life narratives. Jarena Lee, in the absence of such strategies of shared masculine authorial privilege, emphasizes her doubled outsider credentials, the oppressions of race and sex, in her title's reference to herself as a "Coloured Lady," accompanied by her picture.

Further, her scriptural epigraph presents an immediate argument via the authority of a biblical text: rhetorically, the prophet Joel presents Lee's case to readers by both foretelling her existence and providing divine legitimation of her call to preach. From the beginning, Lee's text is specifically *about* preaching, about her claim to authority, and, more specifically, it is an argumentative response to those who would silence her. The rich intertextuality of the epigraph serves obliquely to highlight the lineage of both narrative and speaker. Lee quotes a passage from the prophet Joel, which is, in turn, repeated by Luke (quoting Peter) in the Book of Acts in the frequently retold story of the incidents at Pentecost, a watershed moment in the Christian scripture's historical narrative of early Christianity. In the Pentecost story the Holy Spirit miraculously descends to earth and ushers in a new era; the encounter features supernatural signs and wonders, including—quite centrally—remarkable manifestations of men and women speaking in languages unknown to them. Lee then calls to mind all of these earlier accounts—the prediction or anticipation in Joel, the realization or fulfillment in Acts, and the way those narratives have since functioned in Christian communities, particularly those (including the newly formed African Methodist Episcopal) that emphasize experience and expression in the life of the congregation, especially during organized, official gatherings for worship. The important idea emerging from the Pentecost narrative is that the arrival of the Holy Spirit would be characterized by manifestations of divine power that would dismantle or at least disrupt established hierarchies and their prescriptions concerning gender and speech.

Joel's text foretells extraordinary events that indicate the dramatic and historically disruptive arrival of the presence of God. In the Acts of the Apostles the biblical writer, in a tradition that Jarena Lee then appropriates, quotes that prophetic text about the overturning of gender hierarchies as a mark, a visible sign, of the presence of God. The text calls readers to understand the extraordinary signs and wonders as manifestations of God's power: a woman preaching (along with dreams, visions, blood, smoke, and fire) signifies the presence and activity of God. All the events are disruptive, out of the ordinary; all signal God's entrance into and activity in the world. In that rhetorical context, Jarena Lee calls her biblically literate readers to understand her own preaching, announced and documented in her life narrative as not merely a legitimate or acceptable procedure but a harbinger of the power and presence of God, a demonstration or, perhaps even more authoritatively, a reenactment of the supernatural events of the day of Pentecost.[7]

This biblical text has been especially important to Christian communities that emphasize experience and emotion in private and communal worship, congregations with a radically decentered notion of authority and church hierarchy which rely on both individual authority in the lives of the believers and also the tangible presence of the Holy Spirit, often manifested in supernatural signs and wonders calling to mind those described in the Book of Acts. This stream of Christianity, a legacy of revival religion that includes the African Methodist Episcopal tradition, focuses on experience. From its inception in the late 1780s, the AME was characterized as a revivalist congregation that viewed extraordinary experience as evidence of the presence of the Holy Spirit. Indeed, John Fanning Watson, in his 1819 anonymously published *Methodist Error; or, Friendly Christian Advice to those Methodists who indulge in extravagant emotions and bodily exercises,* decries the senseless "shouting Methodists" at Bethel Church, specifically noting the schism initially provoked by race, telling his readers that the Bethel Christians "have now parted from us [the Methodist Episcopal Church] and we are not sorry" (qtd. in Taves, *Fits* 77). As Ann Taves notes further in her study of experiential religion in the United States, Watson's detailed rebuke, full of firsthand description as well as commentary, has proved useful to contemporary scholars: "His descriptions of worship at the Bethel Church in Philadelphia and of singing and dancing at camp meetings in the area by blacks and whites provide some of the earliest Protestant accounts of the call-and-response style in worship, the spirituals, and the ring shout. In his discussions of exegesis, we have clues as to the biblical typologies that informed the emergent camp-meeting tradition and the later interracial Holiness and Pentecostal movements" (*Fits* 78). The Bethel community, according to its observers, was one among many where involuntary shouts, leaping, and dancing were understood as an ordinary part of worship, the presence of the Holy Spirit being made manifest in these physical, supernatural expressions.

Lee's selection of the epigraph from the Book of Joel significantly aligns her specific experience with what revivalist Methodists—black and white—would have understood already as a tradition in which upheaval, peculiar and extraordinary events, signal God's activity. Hence Lee suggests that a particular, peculiar spiritual event has been her own religious call to the pulpit. Moreover, she regards her call to speak despite traditional prohibitions as a direct consequence of the workings of the spirit. Both the Joel text and her own acknowledge the prohibiting hierarchies as well as their liberatory, God-authored overturning.

The immediate experience that Lee proceeds to narrate bears a complicated relationship to the prophetic text, however, chronicling as it does the religious community's or, certainly, the religious hierarchy's resistance to the author's appropriation of Joel's egalitarian vision. Much of the narrative records her difficulty in realizing her call. Lee's entire spiritual autobiography, even the account of her conversion—which might be expected to be the central feature—is presented as a part of her journey toward legitimizing her call to preach. She acknowledges as much in her title, which indicates that the subject will be not only her "life and religious experience" but also, more specifically, an "account of her call to preach the gospel" (25).

Initially, Lee envisions herself as both inside and outside the traditions she claims. Earnest piety guarantees her insider status; insistent proclamations of her call to preach despite prohibitions establish her outsider role. Moreover, she presents herself alternately as a novice on a spiritual journey—in need of both God's transforming power and the approval of the more experienced community—and as a prophet, the voice of God correcting the faithful and their mistaken leaders for their failure to apprehend divine truth. Lee establishes her theological views, intertwined as they are with her own sense of authority and mission, in a number of critical moments in the narrative. Early in her story, before her conversion, for example, when she describes herself as "extremely ignorant" of religious matters, she seeks wisdom from the Bible in a spiritual journey that involves disturbing voices and distressing illnesses. But she is thwarted: a Roman Catholic woman discourages her from reading the scriptures, hiding her Bible and replacing it with a novel instead (28). The account fits into Lee's construction of her own identity and her argument against those who would silence her: despite their opposition, she earnestly seeks God. More important, it serves as an introduction to how the Bible comes to function for her and suggests, further, that women readers can find power and agency not in fictions that arguably reinscribed for them positions of powerlessness and sentimental subjectivity but in alternative identities, divinely authored and discovered via careful and strategic readings such as those she demonstrates in her narrative.

Popular novels of the period regularly featured explicit tales of female powerlessness. Stories of "fallen" women, seduced and then left bereft of their "virtue," lovers, illegitimate children, families, friends, and their own lives served as didactic and thus acceptable fictions—

allowing readers (occasionally, as in Susanna Rowson's *Charlotte Temple*, identified specifically by the narrator as young girls and their guardians) to encounter sensational stories in the approved context of religious and moral instruction. Such novels regularly featured heavy-handed indictments of novels and novel reading, usually making an explicit connection between seduction by books and seduction by men. The textual agendas of such novels as Rowson's, Hannah Smith Foster's *The Coquette*, and Tabitha Tenney's *Female Quixotism* (to name a few of the most popular) have now been complicated by both historians and literary critics interested in the subtexts and contradictions of seduction novels.[8] But Lee's anecdote about the novel-pushing Catholic would have played into readers' fears and judgments of fictional narratives and female virtue.

The anecdote would have fanned other fears as well. The figure of the Roman Catholic woman as a villainous, Bible-hiding obstructionist to religious piety would have stoked white Protestant American readers' anti-Catholic sensibilities, already a vigorous force by the time of the publication of Lee's autobiography. Samuel Morse had suggested in 1834 the formation of a political organization to be known as the "Anti-Popery Union," the same year that anti-Catholic mobs burned a Catholic convent in Charleston, Massachusetts.[9] By the 1850s, Irish Catholics had become lynching victims, and a new political party, the infamous "Know-Nothings," sworn to defend the United States from Catholicism, would sweep Congress and state legislative houses. Lee's figuring of the antibiblical Roman Catholic woman would thus have appealed to readers fearful of the burgeoning numbers of foreign-born Roman Catholics in their midst, perhaps suggesting to zealous Protestant readers that there were those further outside their tradition than this earnestly evangelical, U.S.-born, African American woman preacher. Indeed, the incident suggests a host of hierarchies inviting readers to select the most objectionable kinds of outsiders.

Just as important, the incident would have called to readers' minds Lee's larger theological project (and, to varying degrees, that of the other writers discussed). She reminds her Protestant readers that she and they adhere to a religious system wherein authority is grounded in individual conscience and scripture, in opposition to a Roman Catholic sensibility that (at least in a nineteenth-century Protestant reading) would honor tradition, institutional and papal authority, and priestly hierarchy. The implicit message is theologically life affirming and, clearly, liberatory for Lee, but it is also quite cleverly situated theologically: being a good Protestant reader in the nineteenth century meant being also vigorously anti-Catholic. At the same time as she appeals to religious (and cultural, since resistance to Catholicism in nineteenth-century America was rooted in unashamed nativism) hostilities, she aligns readers with a protofeminist and progressive racial ideology, versus the forces of racism, misogyny, and papistry that all align against the spirit-infused Lee.

The structure of the text underscores the argument that the rest of the narrative makes plain: the main topic is Lee's preaching, presented as (and ultimately, after much travail, understood by the church to be) a manifestation of God's power and presence. The narrative is divided into four parts: in the initial section Lee describes her conversion and "sanctification"; the second, titled "My Call to Preach the Gospel," recounts her call and the church's prohibition that prevents her from acting on it; a third, very brief section is titled "My Marriage"; and finally, in "The Subject of My Call to Preach Renewed," she records the church's eventual coming to terms with her preaching. Furthermore, after the autobiographical subject Jarena Lee encounters the opposing aspects of Bible and sentimental novel, her own text presents a forceful rejection of the experiences that such novels frequently romanticized. Her personal life, the details of marriage, children, and domesticity that constitute a woman's conventional story, is referred to only briefly. Indeed, the section "My Marriage" with its terse (about a page) account appears both in the organization of her text and in her overall story as a disruption, a difficult but brief aside on the way to the substantive story announced in her title.

Lee's presentation of her life story, then, opposes not only the form of the sentimental female novel but the gendered social expectations that made it a best seller: the assumption that the central story of a woman's life consisted of marriage and motherhood. Lee discusses her marriage only as it relates to the difficulty of realizing her call to preach, presenting it primarily as crisis and loss. She marries a preacher and is then obligated to leave her community and make a home with him at some distance from her intimate friends and partners in ministry:

> In the year 1811, I changed my situation in life, having married Mr. Joseph Lee, pastor of a Society at Snow Hill, about six miles from the city of Philadelphia. It became necessary therefore for me to remove.

> This was a great trial at first, as I knew no person at Snow Hill, except my husband, and to leave my associates in the society, and especially those who composed the band of which I was one. None but those who have been in sweet fellowship with such as really love God, and have together drank bliss and happiness from the same fountain, can tell how dear such company is, and how hard it is to part from them.
> At Snow Hill, as was feared, I never found that agreement and closeness in communion and fellowship, that I had in Philadelphia, among my young companions, nor ought I to have expected it. (39)

Happiness, love, intimacy, and personal fulfillment occur for Lee not in the context of marriage but in ministry.

Indeed, marriage presents her with difficulty, hinders her from enacting her call, and blocks her from the "bliss and happiness" she had experienced with her religious community. She describes ensuing sorrow, illness, and resignation (in contrast to her former "agreement and closeness"). Once she resigns herself to her circumstances, including illness, she resumes her religious work in a very limited way: "the Lord would send sinners" to her house to see her, and she would preach to them. She recounts her struggles with illness, sorrows, and the corollary worry that as a result she will not be able to preach. Then, as quickly as it began, the marriage section ends—with the news of family deaths, including her husband's: "About that time I was called to suffer in my family, by death—five, in the course of about six years, fell by his hand; my husband being one of the number, which was the greatest affliction of all." The management of detail is quite interesting here; her husband, of whom readers have learned almost nothing except that his ministry hinders Lee's, is simply "one of the number" of her losses. The other deaths are of persons not named, and her experience of her husband's death as the "greatest affliction of all," after an affliction-filled marriage, is not developed further. What follows, however, is a pretty dramatic reversal of the difficulties that characterized her marriage. Though she is left "alone in the world with two infants," she recalls biblical promises of divine provision and protection, and then she moves toward a return to her old community, her old life, and her call to preach. Illness ceases to be a topic.

Lee's Christian conversion, which might have been the main story, serves mainly as a precursor to her work as a preacher. Notably, her conversion results from another's preaching: "My soul was gloriously converted to God, under preaching, at the very outset of the sermon" (29). First she responds positively to a sermon by Richard Allen. Three weeks later, according to her own account, she experiences a conversion to Christianity as she listens to (presumably) another preacher, whose words work to transform Lee's concept of herself. In that moment she describes herself as quite literally and dramatically transformed by the power of the preacher's words. But even as she describes her conversion—a requisite feature of conventional Christian autobiography—she also presents the context, or perhaps the cause, of her own ministerial vocation: effective preachers who produce powerful results. Furthermore, the transformation wrought by the preaching here immediately compels Lee toward her own preaching, which she presents as an inevitable, specific consequence:

> That moment, though hundreds were present, I did leap to my feet, and declare that God, for Christ's sake, had pardoned the sins of my soul. Great was the ecstasy of my mind, for I felt that not only the sin of *malice* was pardoned, but all other sins were swept away together. That day was the first when my heart had believed, and my tongue had made confession unto salvation—the first words uttered, a part of that song, which shall fill eternity with its sound, was *glory to God.* For a few moments I had power to exhort sinners, and to tell of the wonders and of the goodness of him who had clothed me with *his* salvation. During this, the minister was silent, until my soul felt its duty had been performed, when he declared another witness of the power of Christ to forgive sins on earth, was manifest in my conversion. (29)

Lee describes the moment of her conversion in terms of her encounter with the spoken word and her compulsion to reenact that spoken word with others. The passage richly demonstrates his sense of authority in relation to the established power of the institutional church as she emphasizes her agency and action, noting the minister's response as occurring only *after*, and apparently as a consequence of, her own achievement of satisfaction; she seems to suggest that she allows or releases him to speak. Furthermore, she focuses on the spiritual source of her speaking: her *soul* is actually the agent here; her soul performs "its duty." The intriguing double sensibility of her rhetoric provides a kind of cover for her own agency, otherwise so apparent. She both does and does not defy authority. By drawing on and altering a convention of the genre—the separation of autobiographical speaker and autobiographical subject—she presents her soul as a separate agent and deflects any direct claim to authority: it is specifically her spiritual or heavenly self, soul, that initiates action and claims responsibility, a self in apparent distinction from the human speaker Jarena Lee. The minister is speaking and doing; Jarena Lee's "soul" is speaking and doing. In a text about achieving liberation in the face of official and unofficial prohibitions, Lee locates her actual experience of freedom (her preaching) within a spiritual realm (soul, versus self). This rhetorical move invites her readers to shift focus from the actual breach of ecclesiastical law and social decorum that occurs in the human world to the spiritual realm—more important, quite likely, in the hierarchies assumed by her readers. The terrain for this event becomes uncertain: did the action occur in the church, between persons? Or did it occur in a spiritual realm, between "souls" (acting in accord with the divine)?

Her compulsion to speak, even at the moment of her conversion, juxtaposed with the minister's silence (which looms large here, and in a subsequent discussion turns to active disapproval and prohibition), establishes a pattern for the rest of the text, the tale of her attempt to overcome the human injunctions threatening to prevent her from realizing the call of God in her life. The injunctions eventually are overturned, and Lee's authority and authenticity are emphatically vindicated. Moreover, her account of the minister's silence, followed by his vague and ineffectual comment on her conversion, stands in stark contrast to the full and articulate account she provides of her own spiritual journey.

Throughout the narrative she establishes male ministerial failure or silence as the specific context and provocation for her own ministerial work. Although the argument she advances concerns the rights of all women inspired by the spirit to preach, her own preaching is configured first of all, specifically, as divinely ordained (a result of her personal, supernatural calling by God); next, as justified biblically by scripture passages that speak to the egalitarian quality of the work of the Holy Spirit (such as the verse she cites in her epigraph); and then, as practically or humanly necessary because of masculine failure or silence. Later in the narrative, when she addresses the subject of her call to preach, and after she has engaged in direct argument with those who oppose women preachers, she repeatedly notes her success in the context of male failures or limitations. She poses a rhetorical question to readers: if God has not indeed called her to preach, "how could he consistently bear testimony in favour of my poor labours, in awakening and converting sinners?" (37). That is, how could she experience success as a preacher (which, as the details of the narrative show, she undoubtedly does) if God was not empowering and approving of her work? Surely, she asserts, her success depends upon divine power and approval.

But she goes on to document in human terms the necessity of her preaching: she *must* preach, precisely because she can reach those who will not listen to others. Thus, her social and cultural marginalization, her dismissal by others, becomes further evidence of God's agency and is contrasted with the ineffectiveness of the predictable purveyors of spiritual truth: privileged white male preachers: "In my wanderings up and down among men, preaching according to my ability, I have frequently found families who told me that, they had not for several years been to a meeting, and yet, while listening to hear what God would say by his poor coloured female instrument, have believed with trembling—tears rolling down their cheeks, the signs of contrition and repentance to ward God" (37). Similarly, she records that a male minister was "labouring" unsuccessfully with a "very wicked young man" who was dying. Yet when Lee and another African American woman begin to speak to him in the minister's place, they share a supernatural vision, after which the young man converts (44). Lee thus compiles evidence for the efficacy and necessity of women in public ministry.

In her pivotal anecdote about her own preaching, she describes witnessing AME minister Richard Williams's failed attempt to preach at the Bethel church on the Book of Jonah. In the midst of his sermon he loses heart, explaining to the congregation that he senses he has lost the spirit; he cannot continue. Lee's response: "In the same instant I sprang, as by an altogether supernatural impulse, to my feet, when I was aided from above to give an exhortation on the very text which my brother Williams had taken" (44). Such extemporaneity in the midst of a meeting was not unusual in Lee's religious community or tradition, where preachers and believers alike assumed the immediacy and accessibility of God's presence. In that sense, Lee seems at first simply to be moving into the gap created by Williams, responding to a need created specifically by male failure, which is presented as the absence of the divine presence, the withdrawal of the spirit from male discourse.

Lee's actual sermon, however, offers a more complex, far-reaching, and subtle message—a social critique concerning women and religion.

Comparing her own experience with that of the biblical Jonah, she explains that like the famously recalcitrant biblical prophet, she too has been called by God to preach. In a fascinating rhetorical move she then relates how she "lingered like [Jonah], and delayed to go at the bidding of the Lord," obliquely referring to Richard Allen's and the denomination's refusal to recognize her call to preach on the basis of her sex (44). She inaccurately likens her own inability to preach to Jonah's reluctance; in the scriptural narrative, Jonah resists God's command and embarks on a diversionary sea voyage in the opposite direction from the city to which he has been divinely directed, whereas Lee's narrative (in which this brief summary of her sermon is embedded) has already recounted how she earnestly complied with God's call and eagerly attempted to preach but was prohibited by the traditions of her church.

Lee's apparent rhetorical savvy here, her understanding of her audience and context as she withholds these key details of her own story (well known, after all, by the actors in the drama who were present at this sermon but probably not familiar to the whole congregation), is further underscored by an appreciation of the interpretive traditions for the Jonah text. Jonah's reluctance has traditionally been interpreted as, at least in part, cultural arrogance: he wants to see the Assyrian city of Ninevah punished, not pardoned. But in response to his preaching—just as he has feared, he tells God later—the Ninevites turn to God, and God does pardon them. Jonah reacts to God's mercy by complaining angrily: "Was not this my saying when I was yet in my country? Therefore I fled before unto Tarshish: for I knew that thou art a gracious God, and merciful, slow to anger, and of great kindess, and repentest thee of the evil" (Jon. 4.2).

By presenting herself as an illustration of the Jonah text, Lee would have invited readers (including the more informed clergy, who would have known of her earlier attempts to preach as well as the church's refusal) to see the obvious, important differences between Jonah's narrative and her own. But a biblically literate audience would likely have recalled as well the cause of Jonah's resistance, its roots in cultural arrogance, manifested in presumptuousness about where and how the spirit of God should work. They would also likely have noted the cause of Lee's own compliant response to God's call, which in itself underscores a fundamental theoretical or theological tenet of the democratizing practices of the revivalist Christianity that resulted in the formation of the AME—the belief that God's spirit could be seen at work across the social spectrum and indeed in the most unlikely places, here configured not only as the undeserving Ninevites but as God's "poor coloured female instrument" (Lee's earlier reference to herself). Lee's sense of her violation of tradition is as clear as her sense that she is ordained by God to enact it: she notes that she fears she will be "expelled from the church" for "this indecorum." Instead—and, in her configuration of events, miraculously—Allen himself speaks up from the congregation, reversing his earlier position to announce that "he now as much believed that [she] was called to that work, as any of the preachers present" (45).

Lee might have offered this incident as the final justification for her preaching ministry; it seems instead to be a prominent moment in the larger whole, the story of her quest to do what she believed God had called her to do. Although this defiance and corollary defense might seem to sum up the ministry she has described all along in her narrative, Lee presents it instead as one more step, one more moment in a narrative most concerned with defending the speaker's divinely given authority. She goes on to describe more moments, more ministerial successes, in which she continues to enact her call, now validated by the church. Notably, enjoying more and more wide-ranging successes, she moves further and further outside her conventionally gendered sphere. She preaches to women, to women and men, and then to groups increasingly diverse not only in gender and race but in class as well: "There were lawyers, doctors, and magistrates present" (46). Eventually, she influences a white slaveholder "who was a deist, and who said he did not believe the coloured people had any souls—he was sure they had none" (46). And later, a Quaker magistrate and a "white lady of the first distinction" (47) credit her favorable effect on them. The message of these incidents concerns Lee's effectiveness as a preacher as well as the nature of the community; both give evidence of the antihierarchical Christianity she experiences and preaches.

Just as Lee's accounts of her conversion, her call to preach, and the effects of her preaching are inextricable, her subsequent descriptions of incidents in her spiritual journey emphasize the central issue of preaching and speaking, even as they reiterate a complex, deflected sense of agency. For example, in her account of her baptism she quotes a biblical text (Mark 16.15–16) that presents an injunction to preach just as strongly as it endorses baptism (presumably the relevant activity in the scriptural text and its most obvious context for writer and reader here): "I was baptized according to the direction of our Lord, who said, as he was about to ascend from the mount, to his disciples, "Go ye into all the world, and preach the gospel to every creature. He that believeth and is baptized shall be saved" (32).

Lee's sense of herself as a preacher is central to her conversion and call: just as she is converted *by* preaching, so she is converted *to* preaching; her vocational call seems fairly embedded in her religious conversion. Even God appears to be or to act as a preacher in Lee's narrative, often speaking audibly, as in "My Call To Preach the Gospel":

> On a certain time, an impressive silence fell upon me, and I stood as if some one was about to speak to me, yet I had no such thought in my heart. But to my utter surprise there seemed to sound a voice which I thought I distinctly heard, and most certainly understood, which said to me, "Go preach the Gospel!" I immediately replied aloud, "No one will believe me." Again I listened, and again the same voice seemed to say, "Preach the Gospel; I will put words in your mouth, and will turn your enemies to become your friends."
>
> At first I supposed that Satan had spoken to me, for I had read that he could transform himself into an angel of light, for the purpose of deception. Immediately I went into a secret place, and called upon the Lord to know if he had called me to preach, and whether I was deceived or not; when there appeared to my view the form and figure of a pulpit, with a Bible lying thereon, the back of which was presented to me as plainly as if it had been a literal fact.
>
> In consequence of this, my mind became so exercised that during the night following, I took a text, and preached in my sleep. I thought there stood before me a great multitude, while I expounded to them the things of religion. So violent were my exertions, and so loud were my exclamations, that I awoke from the sound of my own voice, which also woke the family of the house where I resided. (35)

As William L. Andrews notes in his edition of Lee's narrative, the context she establishes for her calling to preach echoes the calls of many biblical prophets and heroes (Introduction 238). Her readers would have recalled similar narratives of divine calling and human reluctance in the story of Moses (Exod. 4.1, 12), Jeremiah (Jer. 1.9), and others who encountered a divine promise to have words put in their mouths, overcoming their own inability or reluctance. Jesus's disciples

(Luke 21:15), too, were promised to be given speech, much as in Lee's narrative. Lee presents herself as in the same tradition as these biblical figures—prophets and apostles, all males—who have a mythic status and an unquestionable authority within Christian tradition. Each one's story would have been familiar to her biblically oriented reading audience.

In this context, then, her initial personal reluctance proves her authenticity; she is part of a long-standing tradition. Lee's insistent expressions of her hesitation to accept her call to preach, echoed elsewhere in the text, are a part of her overall, carefully constructed sense of agency, wherein she asserts herself only as she insists upon her own divine submission and deflects her own agency. Importantly, she does not articulate that reluctance as specifically gendered female but, in fact, presents reluctance as a characteristic of true biblical (male) heroes, further evidencing her credentials. Lee's preaching occurs in the foregoing passage as apparently beyond her control: she preaches in her sleep, involuntarily, and her own voice, accessed by the divine, awakens her. Far from willing these events, she resists them, becoming almost an observer of the divine action occurring in her own body. Her own voice, no longer under her control, awakens her and the rest of her household. Ironically, she can assert her authority by describing in detail her reluctance and continuing, ironically, to deemphasize her own agency.

Further, in her account of her call and throughout the narrative, Lee's emphasis on voices, actual sound, audibility, and even volume has special significance in the historical context of the evangelical communities of her era, especially as language was used to create cohesion among marginalized groups. Susan Juster has argued that "the evangelical community was largely a community of language rather than of people or space. If grace was not actually created by language (and Ann Kibbey, for one, suggests that it was), it was nonetheless cultivated, communicated, and celebrated by the words of preachers and converts" (*Disorderly* 33). In other instances, Lee writes of using a loud voice to pray (32) or to cry out in response to the voice of the divine (34). Loudness seems to have been characteristic of revivalist religious communities. Ann Taves notes in her discussion of "shaking Methodists" that revivalist Christians proudly referred to their own infamous loudness, for instance in a song, presenting the volubility mocked by their detractors as obvious evidence of their spiritual vitality (*Fits* 110–11).

Lee's narrative of conversion, sanctification, and divine call to preach features a series of dramatic conflicts, encounters that she interprets in straightforward, traditionally dualistic Christian terms—between good and evil. At the outset of the narrative the conflicts concern primarily internal and spiritual realities. So, for example, she hears voices, sees nightmarish visions, feels impelled by internal forces toward suicide. In some ways her description of these experiences is typical of Christian autobiography. Her tortured emotions, her belief in Satanic torment, her deep distress, even her struggle with inclinations of self-destruction over her own sense of guilt and sin, link her to the tradition of Western Christian autobiographers and mystics, including Augustine, Teresa of Avila, John of the Cross, Julian of Norwich, and the more regionally and historically proximate Jonathan Edwards. Further, Lee's connection to Edwards seems quite specific in her account of one of the many instances when she is suicidal:

> But notwithstanding the terror which seized upon me, when about to end my life, I had no view of the precipice on the edge of which I was tottering, until it was all over, and my eyes were opened. Then the awful gulf of hell seemed to be open beneath me, covered only, as it were, by a spider's web, on which I stood. I seemed to hear the howling of the damned, to see the smoke of the bottomless pit, and to hear the rattling of those chains, which hold the impenitent under clouds of darkness to the judgment of the great day. (30)

The image of hell as a gulf or pit into which one might fall is not unique to Edwards's now infamous sermon "Sinners in the Hands of an Angry God." The metaphors originate in the Bible and recur in other sermons by Edwards's contemporary preachers on both sides of the Atlantic. But the dramatically sensory language and the specific combination of images—the spider web over the pit of hell, providing the most precarious imaginable kind of foothold—makes the connection to the Edwards sermon (arguably the most famous in American literature) noticeable, at the very least. Though she does not mention the sermon or Edwards in the narrative, the reference seems likely. By 1833, the year Lee enlisted the assistance of an editor to reshape her spiritual journal into a memoir for publication and distribution at camp meetings, Edwards's writings, including "Sinners," had been republished and reissued to remarkably appreciative audiences who ensured their commercial success. Joseph Conforti, describing the

"Edwardsian cultural renaissance" of the first several decades of the nineteenth century, notes that "denominational, interdenominational, and commercial presses inundated the antebellum evangelical community with Edwardsian publications; the American Tract Society alone published over a million copies of Edwards's works. At the same time an ever-expanding religious periodical press created an Edwardsian journalistic industry which examined nearly every aspect of the eminent divine's life and thought" (37). Edwards was recognized as the authority on mass revivalism and on individual conversion. In fact, Conforti argues, to a certain extent he was not only revived but *created* in this period: "Antebellum evangelicals created an American religious tradition around Edwards's figure. They 'classicized' Edwards and his writings and in turn used his religious authority to 'traditionalize' nineteenth-century piety, revivalism, and theology" (37–38).

Edwards would have had particularly potent appeal for Jarena Lee. In *A Treatise concerning Religious Affections*, he became America's first (and perhaps, as Philip Gura's recent biography suggests, America's most enduring) apologist for the affective religiosity that Lee manifests so dramatically. Indeed, this particular role gave him special appeal to revivalists interested in shoring up any doubts about the authenticity of emotional expression or extraordinary manifestations of religious experience. Like all revivalist Christians, Lee shared Edwards's sense of the authentic role of human emotions in religious expression and a strong emphasis on individual conversion (which are both in evidence throughout her description of her ministry and her own personal spiritual journey). Further, Lee shared Edwards's experience of personal torment, depression, and doubt, which both writers, like many earlier Christian autobiographers, interpret in spiritual, specifically dualistic, terms. Lee's struggles with thoughts of suicide, which might otherwise have alarmed pious readers, would have been contextualized within Edwards's own emotional anguish as recorded both in his diary and in his "Personal Narrative."

In an earlier chapter I commented on an aspect of Edwards's personal writing which has become something of a critical commonplace—his description of an almost entirely interior landscape. That chapter contrasted Samson Occom's relentlessly material world to Edwards's metaphysical one. Lee's narrative (much like Occom's) presents a contrast as well. In Edwards' interior landscape, psychic distress is presumed to be an obvious manifestation either of the devil or of sinful human nature, whereas in Lee's work, this spiritual landscape shifts to an exterior, social one where the causes of distress include the church. For Lee, the suffering caused by a tradition of female silence supplants her initially spiritual or supernatural torment. So, for instance, following her vision of Satan as an enormous dog, she details the corollary theological and spiritual unease she experiences: "I was the most ignorant creature in the world. . . . Every circumstance, however, was so directed as still to continue and increase the sorrows of my heart, which I now know to have been a godly sorrow which wrought repentance, which is not to be repented of. Even the falling of the dead leaves from the forests, and the dried spires of the mown grass, showed me that I too must die, in like manner" (32).

The psychological troubles she presents here as originating from Satan as well as from "godly sorrow" for sin are eventually construed within a human social context. As the narrative progresses, the conflicts concern external, material realities; Lee locates her opposition more and more clearly within particular persons (who prohibit her from realizing her call) and institutions (which prohibit her authority). So her "enemy," initially experienced as grief, psychic distress, and inclinations toward suicide originating with Satan (who urges her toward self-destruction, for instance, in passages where she struggles with inclinations to drown herself), eventually becomes specifically identified as the institutional church that forbids her to preach. In these encounters of conflict, Lee denounces not the straightforward Satan of the earliest sections of her narrative but the hierarchies of race and gender—which she typifies as resulting from resistance to the spirit of God—that would falsely justify both Christian slaveholders and Methodist bishops who refused to authorize female preachers.

When Lee describes her first encounter with Richard Allen over the issue of women preachers, she says that after he issues his prohibition, she feels immediately relieved—by which she seems to underscore the absence of personal ambition in her calling (thus reasserting her spiritual credentials): "But as to women preaching, he said that our Discipline knew nothing at all about it—that he did not call for women preachers. This I was glad to hear, because it removed the fear of the cross—but no sooner did this feeling cross my mind, than I found that a love of souls had in a measure departed from me; that holy energy which burned within me, as a fire, began to be smothered. This I soon perceived" (36). More important in the passage than her presentation of herself as a reluctant preacher (and hence in line with a biblical tradition), however, is the way Lee obliquely ascribes to Allen (and by extension the institutional church) responsibility for her diminished divine ardor: her spiritual troubles are caused not by spiritual forces but by the human religious community. And the context, established in her narrative and familiar to readers of the Bible, is human reluctance to realize or enact a divine call. She is, she writes, "glad to hear" Allen's prohibition, as it relieves her of a responsibility to obey her call. But in the context of the familiar biblical narratives of reluctant preachers and prophets called by God, resistance is consistently transformed by divine power, often quite dramatically. Rhetorically, then, Lee's readers would have been ready to interpret the church's resistance in the context of other narratives of human resistance to the divine. Indeed, she emphasizes the point, first by noting the immediate, personal spiritual effects and then by launching a direct, fully articulated argument against a conventional view of women's religious roles. The negative spiritual consequences of the prohibition she argues, "bring[s] into disrepute even the word of life" (36).

Having established the consequences of the church's disallowing her divine call, Lee then sets out a careful theological argument in favor of allowing women to preach, modeling the legitimacy of her call as she does so. She begins with a warning, underscoring the diminished spiritual passion she experienced as a result of Allen's refutation, and then segues into a direct confrontation with the assumptions that informed his (and the tradition's) position: "O how careful ought we to be, lest through our by-laws of church government and discipline, we bring into disrepute even the word of life. For as unseemly as it may appear now-a-days for a woman to preach, it should be remembered that nothing is impossible with God. And why should it be thought impossible, heterodox, or improper for a woman to preach? seeing the Saviour died for the woman as well as the man" (36). She begins by articulating an opposition between tradition and scripture, the central theological distinction and persistent rallying cry of Protestantism. Here tradition is specifically figured as the church—bureaucratic and human-authored—in contrast with (and able to "bring into disrepute") the Bible, "the word of life," a well-worn rhetorical path in arguments distinguishing Protestantism from Roman Catholicism. As in her reference to the novel-reading Catholic woman who takes away her Bible, Lee taps a rich source here by obliquely connecting her critique of the prohibition of women preachers to Protestant rejection of Roman Catholicism.

By using inclusive personal pronouns as she describes these shortcomings of the church, Lee implies that she is participant rather than victim; rhetorically she positions herself as an insider, one who understands or perhaps even sympathizes with the process that leads to mistaken conclusions. The tension in the paragraph resides between, on the one hand, traditions and practices that make the idea of women preaching "unseemly," "impossible," "heterodox," and "improper" at that particular moment ("now-a-days") and, on the other hand, the power of God, to which "nothing is impossible."

The assertion that "nothing is impossible with God" has multiple biblical origins that provide a rich context for her specific argument that what is humanly perceived as impossible *is* possible, even likely or essential, in divine terms.[10] Several instances of this rhetoric occur in gospel passages where the notion of human impossibility is used to portray great faith (e.g., Matt. 17.20, where faith may move mountains) and divine power of salvation for God's followers (e.g., Matt. 19.23–26). In each of these instances impossibility is overturned by divine power in surprising ways. At the same time, in both biblical passages there is human agency. In the first, the believer will accomplish the extraordinary (overcome the impossible) by true faith in God: Jesus tells the disciples, "For verily I say unto you, if ye have faith as a grain of a mustard seed, ye shall say unto this mountain, Remove hence to yonder place; and it shall remove; and nothing shall be impossible unto you." In the second, God will accomplish the impossible act of salvation for humans, even the most unsalvageable of humans—in this case, the wealthy: "Then said Jesus unto his disciples, Verily I say unto you that a rich man will hardly enter into the kingdom of heaven. And again I say unto you, It is easier for a camel to go through the eye of a needle, than for a rich man to enter the kingdom of God. When his disciples heard it, they were exceedingly amazed, saying, Who then can be saved? But Jesus beheld them, and said unto them, With men this is impossible; but with God all things are possible." Both texts seem to inform and enrich Lee's overall theological sensibility in the passage above, which emphasizes the surprising power of faith, perhaps especially in the context of extraordinary and unexpected events (moving mountains, moving entrenched traditions to allow women to preach) and the overturning of human hierarchies (which feature the rich and, perhaps by suggestion, whites and men at the top) and established seats of power.

A third biblical passage provides perhaps the richest source for Lee's thinking as she notes divine and human relationships to the "impossible." The nativity account in the Gospel of Luke beings with narratives of miraculous pregnancies: not only the annunciation to Mary but the story of her cousin Elizabeth, "who was called barren." In arguing that God can overcome impossibility, Lee cites a biblical text with implicit resonance to her explicit argument about the presumptions and traditions concerning where and how divine activity occurs. Even more specifically, in recalling this context she echoes the angel's assertion in what is perhaps the most famous biblical narrative of God's encounter with a woman, a dramatic narrative of divine grace in an impossible place—the life and body of a woman. She calls attention to a biblical legacy not only of the theological message of divine power in the face of apparent human impossibility but also of a specific record of God's working in miraculous ways with and through a woman, just as Lee suggests that God has done both at Pentecost and then in her own call and proclamation.

The problematic implications of this text as an argument for a liberatory Christianity, one that challenges sexual hierarchies and prescribed roles, are myriad. Centuries of male artists, for instance, whose paintings of this encounter between the divine and a human woman, provide some evidence of the inescapably masculinist interpretive traditions of Christianity. Nevertheless, this motif has long inspired feminist readers interested in critiques of patriarchal power within Christianity. Brigitte Kahl, for instance, in a 1993 essay, "Toward a Materialist-Feminist Reading" (of the Bible), argues that the beginning of the Gospel of Luke (perhaps the most gender inclusive and most attentive to issues of social justice of the four gospels) features "Mary's messianic theology . . . articulated in the context of a radically de-patriarchalized social reality," and further that this text is "strategically decisive, . . . function[ing] as a kind of hermeneutical key" to other scriptures (236, 238). Central to Kahl's interpretive work are Lee's key issues: the presence of male silence and female speech in the biblical narrative: Zacharias is struck dumb and rendered powerless (for his unbelief concerning Elizabeth's pregnancy), while "the new language of faith is developed in the community of two pregnant women completely occupying the 'father's house.'" Zacharias regains his speech only when he has publicly acknowledged the "naming power" of Elizabeth (236). Frances Gage's famous story of Sojourner Truth's 1851 speech anticipates the core of these same interpretive moves, when she imaginatively constructs Sojourner Truth challenging her audience: "Whar did your Christ come from? From God and a woman. Man had nothing to do with him."[11] Lee, reading scripture through the lens of her own experience of exclusion decades earlier than Frances Gage and Sojourner Truth, grasps the interpretive potential of Luke's text and appropriates its significance for herself personally as well as for the larger liberatory argument she makes in her life narrative.

Lee proceeds to establish her theological point more explicitly, inviting readers into the heart of her theology with a rhetorical question, this time substantiating her argument by way of a second biblical Mary: If Christ died for all, as Christians contend, then how is it possible to distinguish between the rights afforded to any one class of individuals and another?

> If a man may preach, because the Saviour died for him, why not the woman? seeing he died for her also. Is he not a whole Saviour, instead of a half one? as those who hold it wrong for a woman to preach would seem to make it appear.
>
> Did not Mary *first* preach the risen Saviour, and is not the doctrine of the resurrection the very climax of Christianity—hangs not all our hope on this, as argued by St. Paul? Then did not Mary, a woman, preach the gospel? For she preached the resurrection of the crucified Son of God. (36)

Though she does not further develop it, her theology again anticipates closely that of later feminist theologians (some of whom are still arguing for the rights of women to preach and to receive official recognition or ordination within their respective traditions). Feminist theologian and historian Rosemary Radford Ruether begins her 1998 *Women and Redemption* on a foundation quite similar to Lee's in this passage—that within Christian belief systems the central work of salvation is all encompassing, crossing lines of human distinction and consequently dismantling all exclusionary notions, all hierarchies. Ivone Gebara makes a similar argument regarding resurrection as the foundational issue for feminist revisionist thinking about Christianity.

Lee, turning her attention to the figure of Mary Magdalene, recalls her as the first "preacher" of the resurrected Christ. All four gospels tell the story of Mary Magdalene (and the books of Matthew, Mark, and Luke note the role of "the other Mary," the mother of James, the women with Mary Magdalene in this account) as first at the tomb of Jesus, first to see the resurrected Christ, and first to receive the command to go and tell others what they had witnessed. Women's roles in the gospels' resurrection accounts have been key for many feminist exegetes who, like Lee, emphasize the paradigmatic quality of women's ministry at the cross (where they were last to leave) and at the tomb (where they were first to arrive) and among the male disciples after the resurrection (where they bring the news of the risen Christ), envisioning a less hierarchical moment which is then subsumed in official codes and prohibitions. Lee's refutation of Allen's prohibition—which has an oratorical quality, so that it is at once about women preaching and a record of a woman preacher effectively making her point—works in concert with the rest of the account, specifically with Lee's repeated records of ineffective male preachers failing to make their point, failing to speak, failing to convert, failing to manifest signs of the spirit, failing, in general, in the activities at which Lee triumphs, the activities tradition would have denied to her.[12]

Jarena Lee's critique of religious presumptions concerning gender is implicitly and explicitly embedded in her Protestant sense of biblically authorized resistance to traditional authority. Like the other writers discussed here, she directly articulates and rejects the limits of her own tradition, even as she wholeheartedly embraces that tradition. She presents herself as a reforming minister, called, quite clearly, not only to preach the gospel but also to "convert" those within her own community to a more expansive vision of their own religious ideas: namely, to a realization of women's agency and power. She envisions women's and men's power legitimated in precisely the same way: both women and men will preach and speak when/as/if they are inspired and thus authorized by the Holy Spirit, the only credential that mattered in her construction of things. Those not so authorized will not see the divine effects that follow authentically inspired ministry. Conversely, those (such as herself) who are authentically supernaturally gifted will inspire responses. Church guidelines and prohibitions are thus rendered not powerless (for she herself has experienced their inhibiting power) but irrelevant.

Lee's sense of personal agency compels her to seize power because of her understanding of her own oppression and the church's, *her* church's, complicity in it. Her outsider status, in terms of both race (the analysis of which had already been articulated by male African American ministers and bishops) and gender (which those same men had failed altogether to see), situates her to see and name the failures of her religion and to present, then, a narrative of dissent in a genre whose purpose is to inspire conformity to religious piety and earnest belief.

Just as Lee's sense of herself within her tradition and within the genre of spiritual autobiography is important to the voice she develops, her sense of her audience is crucial as well. Perhaps even more explicitly than the other writers here, she writes to a mixed audience and then claims authority on the basis of her identity as an African American and as a woman, assuming that the injustices of her experiences, based on her identity, would resonate with much of her audience. She writes as a woman, is identified with women, both to women and to men, particularly to African American men within her religious tradition. Because her focus is on the gendered struggle she has faced in her quest to realize her call to preach, she writes with an aggressive sense of herself as a divinely inspired female speaker, interrogating the practices of the male ministry in the name of scripture and experience. At the same time, she speaks within a racist tradition—to and about men of color who had established a place for themselves within that tradition; thus she identifies strongly with those men as well. Masculine religious practice and specifically male ministerial discourse have shaped Lee's oppressive experiences; she both subverts and employs that same set of traditions and discourse in constructing her sense of agency as well as her text.

7

FINDING A WAY IN THE FOREST
The Religious Discourse of Race and Justice in the Autobiographies of William Apess

☦

> ... this cruel and unnatural conduct was the effect of some cause. I attribute it in a great measure to the whites ...
>
> William Apess

MOST OF WHAT is known about the work of William Apess comes from his own published autobiographical writing. A significant voice in the public conversation about Native American–white relations in the 1830s, Apess was an Indian rights activist, a Christian missionary concerned with Indian conversions, and an autobiographer. His texts, which blend Christian didactics with strikingly progressive social analysis, provide a record of Apess's complex thinking about race and religion through the penetrating lens of his own experience. Barry O'Connell, in the introduction to his groundbreaking 1992 edition of Apess's complete works, notes the ways Apess anticipates contemporary thinking about race.[1] His texts complicate the conversation about nineteenth-century racial discourse and enrich our sense of the overall history of cultural contact and conflict in the United States. The way Apess tells his life story reveals the theoretical and critical framework that informs all his other writings and, indeed, the activism that he engaged in on behalf of others: Indians and people of mixed race in and beyond the Mashpee community in New England. O'Connell; Scott Michaelsen; Anne Dannenberg; and other readers (including my undergraduate students, for example) note with interest Apess's progressive, polemical politics and his sense of identification with all people of color. In many ways he seems surprisingly modern in his sense of the overlapping issues for nonwhites, as well as for those marginalized by religion.

Apess's discourse about race and the exploitation of Native and African Americans not only lends itself to analyses in minority and postcolonial criticism—specifically, for example, Abdul JanMohamed and David Lloyd's argument about the complex alignment of issues and authority for writers of color, or Homi Bhabha's concept of resembling and resistant hybridity—but also anticipates the very theorizing of these critics (Donaldson, "Son" 210). Malini Schueller and Edward Watts have recently explored the rich intersections of early American studies and postcolonial theory. In concert with these critics, Apess "interrogates [the] idea of purported cultural hegemony by demonstrating on the local, vernacular level the extent to which American cultural history has always been a contradictory set of narratives depicting an endless entanglement of imperial and colonial experiences and identities" (Schueller and Watts 5). Examining his voice, the way he recounts and interprets his experiences with whites and the Christianity he adopts, allows readers to understand the rich interplay between religion, culture, and the authoritative sense of self he presents. In his autobiographies, Apess calls readers to a challenging ideological journey, one that synthesizes an earnest (and, in some ways, entirely predictable) concern with Christian conversion and a specifically political position in favor of Native American sovereignty.

Like the other writers I discuss, Apess presents his life story through the lens of revival religion, but he takes pains to distinguish that religion—specifically Methodism—from other versions of Christianity. Apess survived an early childhood marked by the relentless trauma of family and cultural violence, alcoholism, abandonment, and poverty. His narrow escape delivered him to another set of struggles: indentured servitude in a series of households, where he encountered various strains of Protestant Christianity, and more violence. He rejected the more respectable Christianity of his household masters (in part, he says, to spite them) and embraced Methodism—via the powerful phenomenon of the camp meeting—instead. Interestingly, this is the specific religious culture and theology that Abigail Bailey (and thousands of similarly disposed white American Christians of the later eighteenth and early nineteenth centuries) disparaged. Whereas Bailey distinguished her own (clearly more respectable, in her estimation) piety from the disorder, noise, and vulgarity associated with Methodism,

Apess, like Jarena Lee, found his first experience of authentic religion there, deriving, in addition, a sense of affiliation by way of the twinned biases against both Native Americans and Methodism.[2]

Born in 1798 Massachusetts, near Colrain, Apess records a few early years of "comparative comfort," when he resided in harmony with both his parents, but then narrates an account of familial disintegration and violence. When he was four years old, his parents separated and left him to the care of his grandparents, at whose hands he and his siblings suffered neglect and physical abuse. He survived the abuse and then spent the rest of his childhood "bound out" in service to various white families near Colrain. He was converted in a camp meeting led by his Aunt Sally George, identified by Barry O'Connell as a key spiritual and political leader of the Pequot (lx).[3] As a teen, he fled his indenture and enlisted in a New York militia during the War of 1812. He wandered for several years after the war, held scattered jobs, and affiliated with Native Americans in eastern Ontario. In late 1816 he returned to New England, sought out his family of origin, reaffirmed his Pequot identity, and confirmed his commitment to Methodism with baptism in 1818. Soon thereafter he met (at a camp meeting) and married Mary Wood, whose spiritual autobiography he would later include in *Five Christian Indians*.

Apess led local Methodist societies and traveled in and around New England, preaching mostly to mixed groups of African and Native Americans. When the Methodist Episcopal church denied his request to become a licensed preacher (just as it had Jarena Lee's), he joined and was ordained by the Protestant Methodists in 1829. It was at this time that he wrote *A Son of the Forest*, the first published English autobiography by a Native American. He continued to preach, both about Christianity and about the injustices done to Indians. In 1833 he became involved in the Mashpee community, playing a significant role in the Mashpee Revolt, a dispute over sovereignty, specifically over control of lands, goods, governance, and religious leadership.[4] For his effective and fairly high-profile leadership in what David Carlson has called "the first successful example of civil disobedience in Native American history," Apess was arrested, sentenced to jail, and fined for disturbing the peace. The Mashpee, however, were subsequently granted the right to elect their own selectmen (Carlson 111). Apess continued to preach, speak publicly, and publish until his death in 1839.

Apess's writings span a narrow time frame coinciding with a decade dominated by the aggressive U.S. national policy of Indian removal spearheaded by President Andrew Jackson.[5] Appearing between 1829 and 1836, Apess's published writings include multiple versions of *A Son of the Forest* and a briefer autobiographical account contained within his collection of conversion narratives, *The Experiences of Five Christian Indians* (which went through two editions), as well as sermons and essays: *An Indian's Looking Glass for the White Man* (attached to *Five Christian Indians*); *The Increase of the Kingdom of Christ* and a companion essay, *The Indians: The Ten Lost Tribes*; a tribute to seventeenth-century Native American leader King Philip (*Eulogy on King Philip*); and an essay advocating Indian sovereignty (*Indian Nullification of the Unconstitutional Laws of Massachusetts*), the last work an argument that emerged from his experience with the Mashpee, which compels us to read both his life-writing and his polemics in light of contemporary critical discussions of sovereignty.[6]

All of Apess's publications might be understood as autobiography (Ruoff, "Three"; G. Sayre). His sense of purpose throughout his writing reflects his varied strategies to survive, to make sense of the forces that shaped his extraordinarily complex cross-cultural experiences, and to argue for Christianity and Indian rights. In grounding even his argumentative texts on readings of his own life, he anticipates the multiple strategies of later life writers interested in questions of power. His negotiation for space—even psychic and spiritual space—within a dominant culture and his articulate presentation of that negotiation easily calls to mind, for instance, W. E. B. Du Bois's classic paradigm of double-consciousness, as well as contemporary critics of race and gender in autobiography such as Françoise Lionnet. Further, as a self-consciously Christian writer, Apess draws on the same alternative sense of authority—experiential theology versus ecclesiastical or official theology—that characterizes many of the narratives discussed here and anticipates the religious arguments that emerge in contemporary autobiographical work by writers of color—in *mujerista* and womanist and liberation theology. Like theirs, his source of authority is consistently twofold: his firsthand experience of racist abuse, and his interpretation of that violence by way of a critically conscious and occasionally subversive Christianity that specifically analyzes issues of justice and power. Autobiography and political protest in his texts are embedded and inextricable. His conversion narratives and spiritual autobiographies include, indeed depend upon, an exposé of the white Christians who have mistreated him. Just as Apess seems fully sincere in his religious expression, so he seems fully aware of the strategic power of Christian rhetoric: evangelical Christianity wholly inflected by his sense of Pequot tradition and Pequot political struggles, his experience of racism, and his certainty that his religion could and did speak powerfully to those issues.

Apess's Christianity insists on race-consciousness. Interestingly, that insistence occurs in the context, first, of nineteenth-century racial assumptions—specifically fixed notions of Native American identity and culture, including the unassimilability of Indians—and, second, of evangelical Christian missionary activity founded on the premises of theological redemption and cultural erasure. Apess asserts the significance of race in the context of his encounter with nineteenth-century evangelical Christians who made limited assertions about egalitarian ideas—consistently spiritualized into a theoretical, theological reality, limited to the nonmaterial, noncivic world: Indians could come to "salvation," for instance, just like everyone else. The characteristic evangelical commitment to a need for personal regeneration, predicated on an assumption of human depravity, allowed white Christians to identify in intriguing, thoroughly racialized metaphoric moves with the alienated "savage" by way of the "stranger" and "heathen" of the Bible (particularly of the Old Testament), whom they encountered in real material terms as they continued to encroach on and supplant Native American communities.

Apess's argument concerning race consciousness consisted of a call to awareness of the way his audience's assumptions about racial identity had so thoroughly shaped their social practice. In making this call he seems to affirm a number of corollary arguments, including one of the central assertions of the period (certainly, an assertion that formed the foundation for the unashamed violence of Jackson's Indian removal): that Indians were unassimilable. But his agreement on this issue comes with an important difference: the assertion of Indian sovereignty, morally substantiated, in part, by the violence of European Christians. Apess presumes what Vine Deloria asserted in 1970 was at the heart of the concept of Native American sovereignty: "Inherent in [the] peculiar experience on this continent is hidden the basic recognition of power and sovereignty" (115). In commenting on Deloria's definition, Robert Warrior elaborates that "the U.S. government, through discrimination and through its historical legislation—its treaties, amendments, or statutes—recognizes the presence of discrete racial, cultural, and religious groups within its borders"; consequently, and in contrast to other foundations for political identity, sovereignty requires action rather than demands or arguments for independence (Warrior *Tribal* 90–91). Apess's autobiography provides a fully substantiated assertion of sovereignty; autobiography functions here in part as a case study—a life story as exemplum—a practice that harks back to a rich tradition of spiritual autobiography, not only among the writers already discussed but also within the first generation of American Puritan life writers.[7]

The voice of social protest that develops in *A Son of the Forest*, the Apess text I am most concerned with here, depends upon the author's presentation of his racial identity and his cultural and religious education concerning ethnicity. To a certain extent, Apess's sense of self and authority is complex in ways typical of autobiographical writing. Readers may readily note, for instance, the disjunction (similar to that found in Olaudah Equiano's autobiography) between the naive voice of Apess's autobiographical subject and the more mature voice of the autobiographer as he comments on, interprets, and distinguishes himself from that subject. As Louis Renza describes this familiar dynamic, the autobiographer "knows as well as writes about his past from the limiting perspective of his present self-image . . . and thus adopts, wanting to express the 'truth' about this past, specific verbal strategies to transcend the limitation" ("Veto" 2). But a closer look both bears out and further complicates Renza's sense of the interplay of original and textual self. In Apess's work, the familiar autobiographical negotiation between speaker, subject, and their shared yet distinct identities is marked by the author's profound concern with articulating the complexities of his shifting race consciousness: his commitment to invite readers to connect to his journey from hatred of Indians and employment of vicious Indian stereotypes to reidentification as a Pequot and, finally, to a specific and apparently unavoidable political position—a commitment to Native American rights to land and self-determination.

This ideological journey that he requires readers to share would have presented an enormous challenge, because the end point—a political and certainly minority position—would have been, to say the least, quite distant for nearly all his white Christian readers. But Apess presents his challenge in a particularly inviting mode, accomplishing the autobiographical negotiation in large part by the authority of his own Christian conversion account—and the traditional religious rhetoric accompanying that conversion—as well as by the authority of his own experience as a person of color who participates in European racism, witnesses it, and is himself personally subject to it. That is, he experiences a Christian message—specifically the antihierarchical gospel of the Methodist camp meeting—as transformative, in the midst of other experiences exposing Christian practices that fail to reflect the ideal, the more egalitarian theology, in which he believes.[8]

Like Equiano, Apess surfaces a Christian concern for justice and compassion, providing exposés of hypocritical Christians who overlook the call to neighborly love in the Golden Rule; in "An Indian's Looking Glass for the White Man," he directly appeals to Christian readers to live up to their own best religious ideals in their interactions with Indians. But also like Equiano, who presents biblical voices and narratives that parallel his own, Apess provides an analysis of his own experience—including his own racial self-hatred—thereby crafting a compelling social critique that ultimately suggests the culpability of his sympathetic readers for the violent racism of the United States. That is, he requires his sympathetic Christian readers to make a spiritual—and, consequently, ideological and political—journey similar to his own, to move from hostile racial stereotypes—even, as *Son of the Forest* acknowledges, in the face of compelling substantiation—to a more complex interrogation of the relations between Native Americans and European Americans, including, for example, an analysis of the origins of those racial stereotypes. His presentation of his own naive and unavoidable integration into white, Indian-hating culture—including his absorption of white caricatures of Native Americans—confronts readers with a complex treatment of race. He seems to speak directly to readers who wrestle with the perceived shortcomings of texts such as Equiano's for the twenty-first century, those texts where contemporary readers note and are profoundly discomfited by the degree to which the autobiographer—as he endures contact with European culture—adopts the ways, voice, religion, and assumptions of European Christianity.

Apess speaks of and to the white culture that attempted to deny him his original culture and, at the same time, gave him a means to articulate back to whites a critique of that experience, providing what he calls elsewhere a "An Indian's Looking Glass for the White Man."[9] His acknowledgment of his own race hatred—coupled with his insistence on showing that despite his initially uncritical adoption of white cultural practices, he is still subject to the racialized viciousness of "kind"

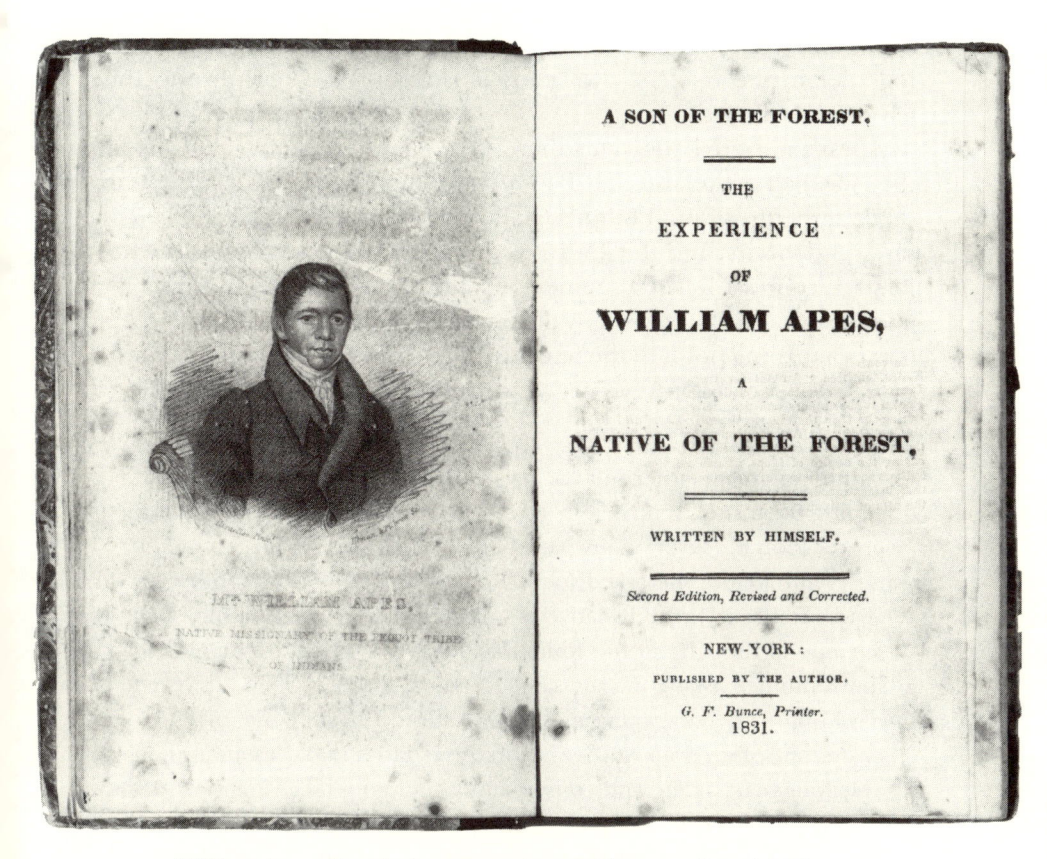

William Apess, frontispiece portrait and title page, *Son of the Forest*.
Courtesy Rosenbach Museum and Library, Philadelphia.

patrons who aim to care for abused Native Americans—provides an exposé for his readers. The call to transformation, requisite in the spiritual autobiographies of this period and generally in the Protestant religious tradition, addresses the reader's race consciousness in more profound ways than it does his or her spiritual condition. Like the other writers discussed here, Apess was familiar with the autobiographical tradition within Christianity in general and in early America in particular, its varied forms of conversion narratives, Indian captivities, personal memoirs, and slave narratives.[10] He had read many of these texts, including not only Mary Rowlandson's narrative but quite likely Equiano's as well (O'Connell xiii). Questions of race consciousness and racial identity are bound together with questions of spiritual transformation in Apess's story, just as, he suggests, they are bound together in the readers' own consciousness of and response to this Christian Indian.

Apess's narrative indicates that his mother was Pequot and his father was half white and half Pequot, although he claims a lineage to the Wampanoag King Philip.[11] He frankly describes the alcoholism of his grandparents and the kindness of white Christian neighbors who, in stark contrast to the cruelties of some of his own kin, insured his and the other children's survival. A critical incident of abuse, which becomes a turning point in the narrative and a pivotal moment in Apess's concept of racial identity—the main subject he explores throughout the narrative—occurs when his grandmother nearly kills him:

> Shortly after my father left us, my grandmother, who had been out among the whites, returned in a state of intoxication and, without any provocation whatever on my part, began to belabor me most unmercifully with a club; she asked me if I hated her, and I very innocently answered her in the affirmative as I did not then know what the word meant and thought all the while that I was answering aright; and so she continued asking me the same question, and I as often answered her in the same way, whereupon she continued beating me, by which means one of my arms was broken in three different places. I was then only four years of age and consequently could not take care of or defend myself—and I was equally unable to seek safety in flight. But my uncle who lived in another part of the house, being alarmed for my safety came down to take me away, when my grandfather made toward him with a firebrand, but very fortunately he succeeded in rescuing me and thus saved my life, for had he not come at the time he did, I would most certainly have been killed. My grandparents who acted in this unfeeling and cruel manner were by my mother's side—those by my father's side were Christians, lived and died happy in the love of God; and if I continue faithful in improving that measure of grace with which God hath blessed me, I expect to meet them in a world of unmingled and ceaseless joys. (6)

He subsequently describes his further rescue by the selectmen of the town, who place him under the care of the Furman family, white Christians who have previously helped Apess and his siblings. Apess carefully specifies the brutality of his own non-Christian kin, the compassionate intervention of the Christian Indian side of his family, and the kindness of white Christian neighbors and civil authorities, noting that since he was "entirely disabled in consequence of the wounds I had received, I was supported at the expense of the town for about twelve months." He describes Mrs. Furman as "kind, benevolent, and tenderhearted," repeatedly attributing his survival to her care.

Apess the mature autobiographer seems to reinforce assumptions likely held by his white Christian readers as he presents them with simple categories: cruel, violent (unconverted) Indians; kind, pacific (converted) Indians; and virtuous white Christian protectors. His experience with his alcoholic grandmother, along with his parents' abandonment of the family, would have powerfully reinforced the vicious Indian stereotypes shared by many of his readers, eager for an account by a converted Indian of his transformation from savage ways. Apess's description of his wrenching experiences seems, at first, to fill that need, his grandmother's vices substantiating—with compelling evidence—racist images of drunk, savage Indians. Moreover, the distance between the respectable, articulate Christian autobiographer, and his terrifying, violent grandmother serves to reassure readers further; the narrative proves both the need for and the efficacy of Christian efforts to convert or obliterate savage Indians.

He goes on in the narrative to describe the extent to which he grew to hate and fear Indians, documenting the psychic and cultural consequences of his survival of the abuse. He is then indentured to white families, however, whose care for him is marked by their cultural distance from and hostility toward Pequots. Deprived of both kin and culture, harboring powerful memories of family violence that nearly killed him, he initially absorbs the values and assumptions of his new community. He recounts, for instance, his abject terror of "Indians," recalling how as a youth he once ran terrified from those he believed to be Native Americans as he encountered them in the forest. By revealing his own race hatred, which, surely, he knew would coincide with readers' fears and hostility, Apess provides whites with a way into his story, a powerful way of connecting to him despite racial difference. White readers could reasonably appreciate his terror, given the images and assumptions about Native Americans that they would have brought to the text, which would have worked in concert with Apess's own apparently substantiating account of his nearly fatal childhood.

Both accounts—that of the abuse of his grandmother and that of his flight in the forest from those he believed to be savages—depict Apess's immediate, dramatic difference from "Indians," who are typified as dangerous, cruel, and violent. Apess's presentation of his own identity would have reassured readers that he was not, as it were, any ordinary Indian; he invites them to identify with the autobiographical subject's fear of and distance from the racial other whom he simultaneously embodies and rejects. He seems, then, at first glance, to engage in exceptionalism, distinguishing himself from the racial mass. The grandmother's speech further emphasizes his difference and distance, even from her; his beating is provoked by her repeated questioning—*does* he hate her? But his confused response invites analysis; it may well have been both the obvious failure of vocabulary to which Apess refers ("I did not then know what the word meant and thought all the while that I was answering aright" [6]) and actual linguistic confusion between a grandmother and a child who speak with varied proficiency two or more different languages—a suggestion that further complicates the presentation of Apess's relationship to his racial and cultural identity (Sayre 16). The boy's repeated answer aggravates her wrath and, ironically, seals his response to her. Indeed, he does (come to) hate her, and to identify with the white townspeople he says she has been "out among."

Apess the autobiographer, however, in contrast to the youthful subject of the narrative, requires readers to come to terms with more complex meanings of his frank account of his Pequot family's mistreatment of him, just as the experiences he goes on to recount required him to reassess his racial identity and the meanings of the race relations he has observed. In case, for instance, readers might miss the implications of his grandmother's having been "out among" the whites—a veiled reference to the troubled state of affairs among the Pequot, who at this time were compelled increasingly to labor for whites as a result of settlers' land thefts—Apess goes on to contextualize her violence and alcohol abuse by reminding readers of white Christians' hand in shaping the particular cultural influences that victimized both him and his grandmother.[12] He invites his audience to read into his grandmother's poignant question her own self-hatred, resulting from the trauma of dispossession. Further, he invites readers into a critique, first, of the exceptionalism that the narrative seemed to endorse and, then, of selective Christian compassion that would spur concern for *one* Indian victim of *one* Indian villain, implicitly questioning white Christians who would position themselves as rescuers of an individual without interrogating the larger causes of and their part in the violence that afflicted countless others.

Here, in effect, is the alternative, critical perspective concerning the identity he refers to earlier in his glowing references to his father's Christian Indian kin. He confronts the presumed response of his reader, appropriating the reader's voice, which he presents in quotation marks, articulating the Christian compassion that works in concert with racist assumptions by failing to engage in larger questions concerning the meanings of his grandmother's violence. The result is a striking account of the violent practices and consequent effects of Christian dispossession of Indians from their lands, history, and culture:

> In view of this treatment I presume that the reader will exclaim, "What savages your grandparents were to treat unoffending, helpless children in this cruel manner." But this cruel and unnatural conduct was the effect of some cause. I attribute it in a great measure to the whites, inasmuch as they introduced among my countrymen that bane of comfort and happiness, ardent spirits—seduced them into a love of it and, when under its happy influence, wronged them out of their lawful possessions—that land, where reposed the ashes of their sires; and not only so, but they committed violence of the most revolting kind upon the persons of the female portion of the tribe, who, previous to the introduction among them of the arts, and vices, and debaucheries of the whites, were as unoffending and happy as they roamed over their goodly possessions as any people on whom the sun of heaven ever shone. The consequence was that they were scattered abroad. Now many of them were seen reeling about intoxicated with liquor, neglecting to provide for themselves and families, who before were assiduously engaged in supplying the necessities of those depending upon them for support. I do not make this statement in order to justify those who had treated me so unkindly, but simply to show that inasmuch as I was thus treated only when they were under the influence of spiritous liquor, that the whites were justly chargeable with at least some portion of my sufferings. (6–7)

The meaning of his abuse, he says, is the meaning of all the troubles of Native Americans since European invasion. His grandmother and her people have acquired alcoholism and consequent violence from whites. Her personal horrific abuse of her grandchild parallels earlier widespread incidents of cultural violence, including the sexual violence that accompanied settlement, and, further, provides a metaphor for the first violence of land theft.

Apess's analysis of the nature and meaning of the cultural conflict is underscored by his initial account of it, in which he describes first contact as occurring between friendly, peaceable Indians and dishonest, violent white men who "claim," in twin impulses of conquest and exploitation, Indian land and Indian women. At the outset of the autobiography as he describes his heritage, he tells readers that his powerful ancestor King Philip was "overcome by treachery," by the "violation of [Indians'] inherent rights by those to whom they had extended the hand of friendship," and that further, this initial injustice of land theft was followed by a "more intense and heart-corroding affliction, that of having their daughters claimed by the conquerors, and however much subsequent efforts were made to soothe their sorrows, in this particular, they considered the glory of their nation as having departed" (4). Apess frames his own life story and the story of his nation not, initially, in terms of his personal conversion to Christianity but in terms of violent cultural displacement, quite specifically including sexual violence. Harking back to Equiano's social criticism, he notes the alignment of violent forces of conquest as well as the complex of psychological and social deteriorations that result.

These are the events that lead, ironically, to Apess's existence as well as to his religious conversion. His "fair and beautiful" grandmother, he claims, is King Philip's granddaughter, and his grandfather is a white man. Their son, Apess's father, "on attaining a sufficient age to act for himself... joined the Pequot tribe, to which he was maternally connected. He was well-received, and in a short time afterward married a female of the tribe, in whose veins a single drop of the white man's blood never flowed" (4). Apess underscores the self-conscious agency of his father's choices: to refuse the white side of his heritage, to affiliate with the Pequots, to marry a racially pure—here construed as emphatically nonwhite—woman. Inverting assumptions about cultural preferences and superiority, he has his father rejecting the white culture of his paternal side and reidentifying with the maternal, Indian side of his lineage, a move that Apess's own story will echo. Further inverting assumptions and arguments of white readers, he constructs racial purity specifically from the exclusion of white blood (conjured by the image of a "single drop," which would become important rhetoric in discussions of racial identity and separation later in the century). Further, the strategic arrangement of Apess's narrative of his childhood beating speaks to this analysis: his chronology of events suggests that his grandmother beats him after and because she has been "out among the whites." The structure of the narrative suggests a further glossing of her question of whether he "hates" her: she recognizes the cultural confusion and hostility she herself represents in her service to whites, the confusion he experiences and will eventually, inevitably, feel in the midst of the familial and cultural disruption that the narrative highlights and ultimately attributes to the larger narrative occurring here.

The later incident—when young Apess mistakes dark-skinned whites for Indians and runs away terrified—reveals his sense of his readers' needs as well as his insistence on complicating those same readers' presuppositions with the complexities of his identity and experience. First, his commentary on the strange incident rattles what might otherwise have been merely an amusing anecdote about childish misapprehension:

> It may be proper for me here to remark that the great fear I entertained of my brethren was occasioned by the many stories I had heard of their cruelty toward the whites—how they were in the habit of killing and scalping men, women, and children. But the whites did not tell me that they were in a great majority of instances the aggressors—that they had imbrued their hands in the lifeblood of my brethren, driven them from their once peaceful and happy homes—that they had introduced among them the fatal and exterminating diseases of civilized life. If the whites had told me how cruel they had been to the "poor Indian," I should have apprehended as much harm from them. (11)

The misapprehension, then, is multiple: first enacted by Apess as a reasonable response to the European culture with which he then identified, then repeated by readers. Further, like the white families he lives among, like his readers, young Apess cannot recognize a true Indian. Rather, he runs from whites whom he judges to be dangerous because they have dark skin. But just as his childish mistake points out his own confused identity, so too it points out the arbitrariness and unreliability of the system of judgment he has uncritically internalized. His following commentary reveals the foolishness of the stories he has absorbed from whites. Historically, in fact, the whites are the savages, their crimes documented. So his flight in the forest, although based on a mistake, turns out to reveal perhaps more accurate locations of savage and civilized behavior. And the detail of the setting in which he encounters these whites, the "forest," underscores larger questions concerning identity: the forest—land relatively untouched by "settlement" culture—recalls the days before the Europeans' arrival, the days Apess thoroughly sentimentally idealizes throughout the narrative.[13]

For white readers the forest was the location both for imaginary, mythic representations of Indians—"sons of the forest," the racially inflected appellation that Apess both affirms and interrogates in his autobiography's title—and for disrupted Indian communities. Ultimately, Apess's life story challenges the identity and location of his white readers. What are these whites doing in the forest, the narrative seems to ask? How had the forest—and perhaps by extension the entire world, "new" to Europeans—come to be their habitation? He answers the implied questions by delineating the profoundly destructive effects of white interactions with the "sons of the forest."

Apess presents his racial experiences in terms of skin color, emphasizing the physiognomic marker that has shaped his existence from the start. Scott Michaelsen notes this terminology, the rhetorically strategic references to color that call attention to the markings of race, the physical appearances of Indians, Africans, and Europeans, and to morally charged metaphorical uses of color as well, examining both the complexity and contradictory quality of Apess's arguments. For Michaelsen (and many other contemporary readers), Apess thoroughly compromises his own argument and position by advocating, unequivocally, a call for Indians to become Christians. Like a number of other Indian activists of the period, he envisions Christianization as both inescapable reality and appropriate goal. Although he insists that the terms of encounter must change, must become nonviolent and culturally accommodating, his Christianity—much like John Marrant's—includes a vision of a multicolored and nonhierarchical spiritual community identified by European religion. Ultimately, Michaelsen determines that Apess's apparently militant critique, his dismantling of racial hierarchies and his indictment of the race crimes of Europeans, is merely a momentary victory, undercut by a final argument that he thinks thoroughly capitulates to white Christianity (69).

Such a judgment, however, may say more about our own prevailing ideologies of race than about Apess's remarkably complex (given his own historical and ideological contexts) assertions about identity.[14] It also fails to acknowledge the ways he subverts and reinvents the Christianity he inherits from the likes of the Furmans as well as from the socially progressive (but perhaps politically naive) Methodists at the camp meetings. I think, for example, of Arnold Krupat's early assessment of Apess's work, which he determined was insufficiently authentic because it was written and in English and "derive[ed] entirely from Christian culture"; further, Apess served as an example that when "the Native lost his land, he lost his voice as well" (*Voice* 145, 147). Similar to Krupat's original judgment is Gary Ashwill's uncomplicated distinction between "acculturated" and "unacculturated" Native Americans, where Apess is easily categorized as the former. Questions of authenticity and identity have since continued to be problematized, of course. But Krupat, one of the most important voices in the recovery and analysis of early Native American literatures, revised his judgments, particularly in his discussion of "An Indian's Looking Glass," which he subsequently called a "brilliant and violent attack on racism" characterized by a "new strength and stylistic assurance" (*Ethnocriticism* 225).[15]

The increasingly rich critical conversation about Apess seems to document the difficulty of categorizing Apess's perspective as well as its generative quality. Both Todd Vogel and David Carlson each acknowledge the complexity of Apess's presentation of his own cultural and political identity, in the contexts of rhetoric and law, respectively. Carolyn Haynes recognizes not only the complex and galvanizing role of Methodism in his self-construction but also the dialectic quality of his "mutually sustaining, interactive" understanding of religion, race, nation, class, and gender; she identifies Apess's perspective as "bifocal" (29, 42). Laura Donaldson, who is similarly sensitive to the complex and empowering function of Methodism for Apess, rejects bifocality along with syncretism and postcolonial hybridity as inadequate paradigms for Apess's "entangled interculturalism," arguing instead for the concept—drawn from the work of the Cherokee historian Rayna Green—of "retraditionalization," which allows, in Donaldson's reading, for recognition of Christianity's complex role, working not only in concert with but also in contrast to oppressive colonialist structures ("Making" 38, 41). Gordon Sayre provides another postcolonial reading. Apess disturbs existing postcolonial (and other) paradigms, even as he anticipates the continued critique offered by postcolonial criticism.[16]

The crucial context here, as in the discussion of Samson Occom's narrative, is recent work on Native American sovereignty, which Occom seemed to anticipate and which Apess made explicit when he argued the case for political sovereignty for the Mashpee in the context of land rights disputes. His commitment to intellectual sovereignty, which he, like the contemporary Cherokee Religious Studies scholar and activist Jace Weaver, articulates in theological or hermeneutical terms, is clearly argued in the autobiographical texts that constitute his overarching polemical work.[17] Apess repeatedly teases apart threads of Christianity from the imperial fabric in which it arrived. He presents a construct I imagine his white readers would have found unthinkable—the Christian Pequot or, perhaps—in a phrase that might more accurately conjure up practices, positions, even creeds that might be indistinguishable from culture—Christian Pequot*ism*. Ultimately, he presents not (emphatically not) an Indian Christian, but a more distinct identity altogether, one that insistently reaffirms Pequot identity and self-determination, rather than assimilation (and corollary cultural losses) into a monolithic belief system authored by and indistinguishable from European culture.

Further, the unthinkable quality of his alternative presentation seems to resonate in critical writing about Apess, which initially seemed to overlook, erode, or apologize for his vigorous commitment to Christianity, precisely because of the ways that it is assumed to be in profound contradiction with his vigorous commitment to his own Pequot identity and to solidarity with the Mashpee. Of course, it is easy now to see the limits of Apess's nineteenth-century analysis: he idealizes precontact Native Americans in ways that ultimately reinscribe European cultural judgments; he adopts the religion and culture of violent colonizers; he becomes a missionary to Native Americans. But for all his apparent religious compliance, and despite his earnest piety, Apess presents conventional Christianity—at least the white version of Christianity—as an enormous failure. His final comment on the incident discussed above, for example, that if he had known of white cruelty to Indians, he "should have apprehended as much harm from them," is both an abstraction reflecting the autobiographer's more complex sense of self, including his critical view of European settlement, and a specific indication of the actual treatment by whites that follows.

The rest of the narrative goes on to recount the ways that his Indian identity, despite his distance from the cultural practices, language, and communities of his original kin, lead the Christian whites with whom he is in contact to mistreat him. His account recalls the subtle and penetrating critique offered by Occom in his concluding story of the Indian boy who is beaten repeatedly because of his race; the Furmans and each of his subsequent masters mistreat him because of his culturally remote but physically apparent Indian identity. Appess's own presentation to readers strategically suggests that it is precisely that abuse which relentlessly underscores his Pequot identity, further exposing the white Christians who initially "saved" him. The family dramas that ensue, at and after the Furmans, condemn the Christian missionizing activities of whites with Indians. For what, Apess's own narrative asks, are Indians "saved"? The terms of cultural contact are denounced here, as are the prescribed cultural hierarchies of his readers.

Ultimately Apess is persuaded to reidentify with Native American communities and causes, not because of the Christian gospel he comes to believe in and preach to other Indians but, rather, because of Indian-hating white Christians, whose beliefs and actions he knows intimately. All of his education and experience, including, certainly, his early abandonment and abuse, might well have led him to become an uncomplicated example of a thoroughly Christianized and acculturated Indian. But, as with Samson Occom, such development cannot occur, precisely because of the pervasive racism of Christian traditions and practices. In the moments, for example, when Apess may begin to think he has replaced his original family and has begun, perhaps, to compensate for the early and life-shaping losses he survived, the family he lives with sells his indenture or physically abuses him. Thus he is reminded of his true status—determined by race—within the dominant culture: he is an outsider and will be, always, despite his seemingly thorough adoption of European ways. Moreover, he is powerless; Christians believe he cannot—and the narrative seems finally to assert emphatically that he will not—alter his identity, despite compelling and dramatic theological abstractions of conversion and transformation. The only family toward which he can feel true allegiance is that of his original kin, which, somewhat ironically, is the identity his white Christian brethren insist on seeing. Whites' savage treatment of him, then, compels him to recover his original identity and to interrogate the larger meanings of those original losses, echoed in the abuse he survives at the hands of the apparently kind whites who rescue him from his apparently cruel grandmother.

The need for Apess's reassertion of his Pequot identity is established throughout the narrative by the constant state of impermanence that characterizes his childhood as he moves among whites: relationships are fragile, frequently hostile and violent; all adults are unreliable. The

Furmans—the family that for a year nursed him back to health after his childhood injuries—reiterate the violence, abandonment, and confusion that he endured with his grandparents. When he is bound out to the Furmans initially, he believes he is treated as part of their family. Apess describes the family as poor (Furman was a cooper) but says that they had become so attached to him during his convalescence that they chose to keep him in service until he was of age. He goes to school, learns to read and write, and receives instruction in Christianity from Mrs. Furman. Initially, he finds Mr. Furman's parental guidance and discipline (for example, concerning decorum in church after he had misbehaved) "wholesome and timely," and he describes Mrs. Furman herself as "upright and exemplary" (9). The mature autobiographer "blesses God" for the literacy and Christian education he gains at the hands of the Furmans, calling readers' attention to his own religious assent and suggesting, further, his religious credentials: his authority and insight, and his ability to distinguish good Christianity from bad, the discrimination on which the rest of his analysis of his experiences with whites depends.

Apess goes on, however, to relate in some detail how he was harmed by the Furmans (and by subsequent white families), recording incidents of physical and psychological abuse, all of which, he notes, were racially inflected. Thus he delineates the severe limits and vicious effects of the Christian charity he has initially counted as blessings. The welcomes extended to him by family and church are all contingent upon the racism and violence that grounded those institutions. When, for instance, Apess is unjustly accused of threatening a housegirl with a knife, Furman immediately believes the false accusations and again whips Apess "for a long while," calling him an "Indian dog" as he beats him (12). Although Apess's own comment in this paragraph specifically contextualizes the account of the beating within a larger, more predictable religious story in which the autobiographer faults himself for an earlier misdeed and untruth, which he believes eroded his childish credibility with his foster family, the structure of the autobiography and the particular placement of this incident contextualizes the story within the larger repeated occurrences of racial violence and abuse. Apess's innocence and Furman's specifically racially identified violence underscore Apess's true offense, which is neither the threatened violence for which he is unjustly punished nor his earlier infractions that eroded trust;

rather, the offense is that despite conversion and family attachment, he remains, for Furman, an "Indian dog."

Further, the narrative juxtaposes Apess's supposed crime of threatening violence with the relentless actual violence of his Christian overseers, which recalls and recapitulates the original abuse at the hands of his own kin. Although that early incident is unequivocally presented for readers' condemnation, the later violence is presented in increasingly complex ways, which invite readers to make connections to that early abuse and to Apess's incisive analyses of its causes and meanings. Apess says, for example, that Furman "regretted" his haste in making an incorrect judgment, once the truth of the boy's innocence was confirmed. But Furman nonetheless persists in his violence: he later responds to Apess's severe illness by giving him "a dreadful whipping," because, as Apess says, "he really thought, I believe, that the devil was in me and supposed that the birch was the best mode of ejecting him" (13).

While Mrs. Furman encourages Apess in his moves toward Christianity, Mr. Furman discourages him, specifically prohibiting him from attending Methodist camp meetings. Apess's record of his childhood distress over Furman's prohibitions against Methodism emphasizes his extreme emotional state and, further, presents that distress in terms of other losses, all occurring within the Furman family—the place where, under different circumstances, Apess might have been afforded a more reliable place of belonging. The juxtaposition of events presented by the adult autobiographer underscores emotional intensity, loss, and isolation:

> He supposed that I only went for the purpose of seeing the boys and playing with them. This thing caused me a great deal of grief; I went for many days with my head and heart bowed down. No one had any idea of the mental agony I suffered, and perhaps the mind of no untutored child of my age was ever more seriously exercised. Sometimes I was tried and tempted—then I would be overcome by the fear of death. By day and night I was in a continual ferment. To add to my fears about this time, death entered the family of Mr. Furman and removed his mother-in-law. I was much affected, as the old lady was the first corpse I had ever seen. She had always been so kind to me that I missed her quite as much as her children, and I had been allowed to call her mother. (13).

Apess dramatically emphasizes the actual terms of his relations with the Furman family. His articulation of grief over his loss of one specific and apparently somewhat loving relationship, as well as the obvious limits of that relationship (with a woman he was "allowed" to call mother), emphasizes the ways in which his original losses are recapitulated, always, in racially charged terms.

Each subsequent selling of his indenture deepens the sense of abandonment conveyed by the narrative and anticipates subsequent betrayals. Peers who might have provided a place of solace or belonging prove to be no better than the families: one boy betrays him to Furman as the two plan to run away together, and the hired girl sets him up to be a victim of Furman's violence. Further, his family of origin, which might have become a place of refuge, continues to disappoint him. The father whose abandonment he records in the first lines of the autobiography hovers over Apess's narrative consciousness, even though he never quite materializes as a significant presence in the action or the events that take place. Several times Apess longs for or plans a visit to his father but fails to carry out his intention. And when he does go, his cryptic and halting account of the visit is poignantly anticlimactic; his silence on an encounter long and energetically sought for speaks his disappointment, reiterating the abandonment and isolation he has so often experienced.

Even the Christians at the camp meetings fail to accept him. When he has what he believes are genuine spiritual experiences, the other believers condemn them as inauthentic, concluding in this case that Apess's problem is not his race but his age: "They did not ascribe [my changed "deportment"] to the influence of divine grace, inasmuch as they all considered me *too young* to be impressed with a sense of divine things. They were filled with unbelief. I need not describe the peculiar feelings of my soul" (13). This proclamation of his refusal to describe his own emotional state reveals, first of all, unspeakable rage and sadness as a consequence of others' failure to accept him, and second, an important corollary, his kinship with the reader. His "I need not describe" assumes that the reader understands and will participate in his sense of loss, even without his description. The reader's experience of the text bears out the authenticity of Apess's spiritual identity. And the implicit claims of community are rhetorically strategic, potentially unsettling the sympathies and sense of identity of Apess's readers, as they are asked to make sounder judgments than those of the individuals Apess describes in his narrative.

As is typical of a religious autobiography, readers are asked to examine their behavior and the state of their souls in light of the autobiographer's spiritual reflections. But Apess's texts require his readers to reflect on *others'* behavior, on the consequences of their treatment of the autobiographical subject. Not only is Furman's overt violence relevant here but less lethal hostilities as well. A discussion of "nicknames" (that is, racial epithets), for instance, and the context for that discussion as well, are particularly revealing and worth quoting at length:

> After a while I became very fond of attending on the Word of God—then again I would meet the enemy of my soul, who would strive to lead me away, and in many instances he was but too successful, and to this day I remember that nothing scarcely grieved me so much, when my mind had thus been petted, than to be called by a nickname. If I was spoke to in the spirit of kindness, I would be instantly disarmed of my stubbornness and ready to perform anything required of me. I know of nothing so trying to a child as to be repeatedly called by an improper name. I thought it disgraceful to be called an Indian; it was considered as a slur upon an oppressed and scattered nation, and I have often been led to inquire where the whites received this word, which they so often threw as an opprobrious epithet at the sons of the forest. I could not find it in the Bible and therefore concluded that it was a word imported for the special purpose of degrading us. At other times I thought it was derived from *in-gen-uity*. But the proper term which ought to be applied to our nation, to distinguish it from the rest of the human family, is that of "Native"—and I humbly conceive that the natives of this country are the only people under heaven who have a just title to the name, inasmuch as we are the only people who retain the original complexion of our father Adam. Notwithstanding my thoughts on this matter, so completely was I weaned from the interests and affections of my brethren that a mere threat of being sent away among the Indians into the dreary woods had a much better effect in making me obedient to the commands of my superiors than any corporal punishment that they ever inflicted. I had received a lesson in the unnatural treatment of my own relations which could not be effaced, and I thought that, if those who should have loved and protected me treated me with such unkindness,

surely I had not reason to expect mercy or favor at the hands of those who knew me in no other relation than that of a cast-off member of the tribe. A threat, of the kind alluded to, invariably produced obedience on my part, so far as I understood the nature of the command. (10)

Apess documents the race hatred and confusion that characterized his childhood, even as he provides a nascent analytical argument for his Christian readers about the effects (spiritual and otherwise) of the Christian racism embedded in evangelism and missionizing efforts. He so feared being returned to his own kin—the "Indians" in the "dreary woods" who had treated him so unnaturally—that the threat of reunification with his family caused him to be on his best—that is, most religiously and culturally compliant—behavior. But the voice of the mature autobiographer provides commentary here, explicitly calling into question the origins of that racial hostility and implicitly questioning the virtue of religious and cultural compliance. The whole paragraph provides a criticism of the very term he uses to name his own people. So his account of his fear of those he calls "Indians" occurs in the context of his critique of the European origins and derogatory intentions of this term. He calls attention both to the power relations (of those named and those doing the naming) and the race hostility that characterize the cultural conflict in which he is so thoroughly enmeshed.

His earlier description of his childhood terror of his own people is presented within his very different but substantially and specifically documented fear of whites. If the introductory narrative of his terrible, life-changing beating by his grandmother records horrific evidence for his fear and hatred of Native Americans, the subsequent narrative of his terrible, mind-changing abuse by whites records horrific evidence for his fear and hatred of European Americans. Thus the autobiography serves as an invitation to understand and appreciate Apess's religious and racial identity; he requires readers to scramble their own ideas and assumptions about Native and European Americans.

Further, the paragraph establishes Indian-hating, name-calling Christians as a primary source of *spiritual* difficulty for the Christian autobiographer. In a rhetorical move reminiscent of Jarena Lee's account of the spiritual effects of institutionalized religion's gender prohibitions, Apess confronts evangelical Christian readers on their core concerns: conversion and personal piety: rather than aligning with the Holy Spirit's sanctifying powers, Christians are affiliated with opposing, evil forces. The autobiographical subject here wishes to be obedient to God but finds himself led astray by, as he says, the "enemy of [his] soul." His standard Christian rhetoric is neither surprising nor extraordinary but just what a reader might expect in a spiritual autobiography by an American evangelical Christian. Yet as the sentence continues, Apess reveals that, in fact, the agent for Satan, his soul's "enemy," is the (name-calling European) Christian. Further complicating matters for his white Christian readers, Apess goes on to clarify that the derogatory name that grieves him and leads him astray is "Indian," the standard term used by Europeans to refer to Apess and other Native people in the United States.

There would have been at least two potential implications for white readers. First, they are invited into the very confusion regarding identities that characterizes much of Apess's experience. Second, they are presented with issues of racial identity and race hatred framed as specifically *spiritual* issues. The autobiographical account makes an insistent demand: if readers are to empathize with the vulnerable, earnestly religious young persona featured in this memoir, they must come to know that what may have been understood as the "Indian Problem" is, instead, quite emphatically a "Christian Problem." Social critique and spiritual autobiography merge in ways that suggest Apess's purposely shifting his focal point for didactic purposes. Nowhere does he present an uncomplicated story of an exemplary Christian conversion, the straightforward goal of missionizing efforts, the characteristic feature of many, many published Christian autobiographies of the period, and the presumed goal of his text. So although Apess sincerely supports and works toward further Christianization of Natives, in the end his religious text presents a profoundly conflicted model of religious transformation: cultural encounter and conversion lead the marginalized Christian into a fairly complex social and political critique of conventional Christianity. Indeed, in Apess's conception of things, that sense of informed critique and incisive analysis seems to be the object, the final purpose, even, of "true" Christianity, which in his presentation is profoundly aligned not only with personal piety but with personal compassion and social justice. Religious autobiography seems to aim toward the reader's spiritual self-evaluation and rebirth in decidedly political terms.

The conventional reversals of Christian autobiography—from dark to light, death to rebirth, sin to salvation, distance from to intimacy with God—are replaced here with another reversal. It is one still rooted in concepts of identity crucial to the personal theological realities at the heart of traditional stories of sin and salvation, but in Apess's case the reversal is not only personal and theological but also importantly cultural, ideological, and political. In his experience, Christianity itself exposes the racism that leads him to vigorous reidentification with the Pequots, Methodism, and a powerful sense of Indian identity and sovereignty, which are of a piece with his own authority to occupy the pulpit, to publish, and to be involved in social activism. By his own description of this transformative journey—as important to the autobiography as the Christian conversion at its center—he invites readers to undergo a similar transformation, to recognize and interrogate their assumptions about racial identity, and to move toward a more complex and compassionate application of their Christian principles. This complex journey, is, finally, the one he calls his readers to participate in.

As in the other life narratives discussed here, Apess's Christian story is subordinated to the material realities he must survive. The spiritual story—of his eventual (and repeated) conversions and sanctification, of internal and heavenly conflicts and powers (Apess's rebellions and illnesses, which might have been presented in entirely spiritual terms)—can be understood only within the fundamental concerns of physical survival, and the causes of that struggle: the betrayal and violence of every adult in his life. Readers may have purchased Apess's *Son of the Forest* at a camp meeting expecting to find a message of redemption and sanctification dramatically told by a converted savage, a "son of the forest." But instead, Apess delivers a scathing critique of mainstream Christianity and converts the spiritual life-story genre into an examination of the causes and effects of Christian racism. The narrative ultimately becomes an account of the shortcomings of the church and of individual Christians, and a theological argument for an alternative.

8

RELIGIOUS IMPERATIVES, DEMOCRATIC VOICES, AND AUTOBIOGRAPHICAL PREOCCUPATIONS

☦

> Improve your privileges while they stay.
> Phillis Wheatley

ARGUABLY THE most prominent eighteenth-century writer of color in early America, certainly the most conventionally "literary," the poet Phillis Wheatley did not leave behind a prose narrative of her own life story. She documented her self-construction, nonetheless, in the many, presumably more formal and less personal, texts she did leave behind—a significant body of published poetry that earned her notoriety in the form of both suspicion and praise. What we know of her biography suggests multiple connections to the writers discussed in this book: like theirs, Wheatley's voice, her rhetorical authority throughout her poetry, depends upon an earnest commitment to Christianity; like them, she writes from a simultaneously didactic and autobiographical foundation; and like them, she subtly (and occasionally not so subtly) records her recognition of the limits, failures, and profound hypocrisies of the religious tradition she earnestly and piously embraced. Wheatley's work and its critical reception suggest the persistence, relevance, and possible wider scope of the issues explored in this book. The threads and commonalities of the autobiographical writers echo and surface in her work, reiterating the central assertions of my discussion.

Phyllis Wheatley allows another glimpse at the crucial religious dynamic in play, as well as readerly resistance and denial concerning religion as a textual feature worth serious analysis. Her poems, even her authority to write them, are inscribed upon a foundation of fairly conventional Christian piety, derived (like the autobiographers') from eighteenth-century revival religion. Indeed, her earnest Christianity has frequently been understood as (in part) accounting for self or race hatred in her poetic texts. Like many African and Native American writers in the early period, she has frequently disappointed and dismayed twenty-first-century readers looking for a racial and cultural self more authentic than what is thought possible amid the didactic Christianity she offers to readers.[1]

Although many of her eighteenth-century interrogators questioned her authorship in the context of the obvious feature of her identity (how could an African slave girl write pious heroic couplets?), her later detractors questioned her identity in the context of the obvious feature of her authorship (how could an African slave girl write pious heroic couplets?). Henry Louis Gates examined eighteenth-century responses to Wheatley, noting the irony of her consistently vexed critical reception over two centuries (*Trials*). Crucial then and now is an understanding of Wheatley's expression of piety, which has proved to be as troubling as her representation of her racial self; they are intertwined. Objections to her piety have quite frequently been corollary to objections to her presentation of herself as African American.

First, there is the now famous authorial inquisition she faced in Boston, where seventeen men—all of them elite, educated, public figures and most of them prominent churchmen—examined Wheatley to determine whether she was, in fact, the author of her poems. Enslaved as a very young girl in Africa, she endured the Middle Passage and was purchased by the Wheatleys of Boston. The Wheatleys noted and encouraged her remarkable intellect, teaching her to read and write and instructing her in Latin, classical mythology, theology, rhetoric, and the tradition of British letters. Within a few years she was writing poems, which the Wheatleys had published in New England newspapers. Her early success resulted from her popularity in circles of influence within revivalist Christianity. She first earned international notoriety with an elegy for none other than evangelist George Whitefield, which she sent to the wealthy and influential patroness of Methodism, Selina Hastings, the same Countess of Huntingdon who was so important to the career of John Marrant.[2] That poem's London publication in 1771 made Wheatley both a literary celebrity and a political flashpoint, given

Phillis Wheatley, frontispiece portrait, *Poems on Various Subjects, Religious and Moral.* Courtesy Schomburg Center, New York Public Library.

that she was a slave—now an extraordinarily accomplished slave—at a moment of increasingly intense political and religious discussions of abolition on both sides of the Atlantic. Wheatley's Whitefield poem became enormously popular, sustaining multiple printings in England and America.

As the poet's notoriety grew, however, so did doubts about her authorship. Hence the inquisition, initiated by her owner, John Wheatley, who called upon New England patriarchs (most of them representing civil and religious influence) to establish beyond doubt Phillis Wheatley's authority and authenticity. She passed the examination, and the testimony of her judges became part of the publication of her subsequent volume of poetry:

> WE whose Names are underwritten, do assure the World, that the POEMS specified in the following Page, were (as we verily believe) written by Phillis, a young Negro Girl, who was but a few Years since, brought an uncultivated Barbarian from Africa, and has ever since been, and now is, under the Disadvantage of serving as a Slave in a Family in this Town. She has been examined by some of the best Judges, and is thought qualified to write them. (8)[3]

As Henry Louis Gates notes in his imaginative discussion of this scene of interrogation, the testimonial of the Boston men was designed to counter racist assertions made by intellectuals and philosophers—including Hume, Kant, and Descartes—which suggested that it was impossible for an African to have written these works (*Trials*).

While some took issue with her race, however, others, anticipating the critical reception her work would later provoke, took issue with her religion. Thomas Jefferson, for example, in a frequently quoted argument, asserted that Wheatley's verse proved not the humanity of black slaves (as his abolitionist contemporaries argued was the unavoidable conclusion to be reached from reading her work) but, rather, the limits of their imagination. An African might exercise the lower "senses" but could not access the higher "imagination." Wheatley's poetry, then, simply proved the divide between piety and real aesthetic expression: "Misery is often the parent of the most affecting touches in poetry. Among the blacks is misery enough, God knows, but not poetry. Love is the peculiar oestrum of the poet. Their love is ardent, but it kindles the senses only, not the imagination. Religion, indeed, has produced a Phillis Whatley [*sic*] but it could not produce a poet. The compositions composed under her name are below the dignity of criticism" (267). Jefferson's argument parallels the less strident one articulated by his contemporary Mary Wollstonecraft concerning Olaudah Equiano (discussed in chapter 4); both assert, as an obvious and inarguable fact, that piety negates aesthetics. Indeed, to Jefferson, Wheatley's earnest religion suggested a failure of true imagination and hence of humanity. Pious poetry does not, cannot, result from an invocation of authentic "love," the exclusive province of true poetry; pious poetry results, rather, from "misery."

It seems the height of irony that nearly two hundred years later she would be criticized for the same feature—her piety—but toward a different end by writers in the Black Arts Movement. Amiri Baraka deemed her poems imitative, "ludicrous departures from the huge black voices that splintered southern nights with their *hollers, chant, arwhoolies,* and *ballits*"; Seymour L. Gross described her as a pious Uncle Tom (both qtd in Gates *Trials* 76). In the case of the later critics, then, piety negates racial authenticity and, presumably, critical self-consciousness along with it. Failures to appreciate Wheatley often occur, at least in part, around her religious sensibility and the way that sensibility informs, liberates, and restricts the rhetorical power of her texts. Obviously pious, she was consequently presumed not to be self-aware, not capable of political or social critique or of any sort of complexity, let alone irony. Alice Walker offered a somewhat more nuanced and sympathetic version of the critiques of the 1960s and '70s: in the widely reprinted 1983 essay *In Search of Our Mothers' Gardens,* she presented Wheatley as the example of a DuBoisian double-consciousness, a raced version of Virginia Woolf's "contrary instincts" (235–37).

Wheatley's "instincts" however, appear profoundly *more* contrary if one widens the scope of the critical lens to look beyond, for example, her personification in "Liberty and Peace" of freedom as a golden-haired goddess (which preoccupied Walker and other critics as well). Readers of Wheatley's letters know the telling moment when, in correspondence with Samson Occom about a year after her volume of poetry was published, she articulated the limits and ironies of their conversion to Christianity, their shared experiences of spiritual liberation and immediate, this-worldly exploitation and abuse. The letter, now typically included in anthologies of American literature, does much to complicate what appears at first to students as straightforward and undeniable self and race hatred in "On Being Brought from Africa," her most anthologized poem. To Occom she wrote:

> In every human Breast, God has implanted a Principle, which we call Love of Freedom; it is impatient of Oppression, and pants for Deliverance; and by the Leave of our Modern Egyptians I will assert, that the same Principle lives in us. God grant Deliverance in his own way and Time, and get him honor upon all those whose Avarice impels them to countenance and help forward the Calamities of their Fellow Creatures. This I desire not for their Hurt, but to convince them of the strange Absurdity of their Conduct whose Words and Actions are so diametrically opposite. How well the Cry for Liberty and the reverse Disposition for the Exercise of Oppressive Power over others agree,—I humbly think it does not require the Penetration of a Philosopher to determine. (153)

The letter evidences Wheatley's profound sense of connection not only to the political and literary elites of New England and their privileged counterparts across the Atlantic but to other American writers of color. The presumptions in the letter are manifold: that the Native American Occom will share her sense of the obvious injustice and irony of their experiences of structural, legally sanctioned, racial oppression in the context of revolutionary rhetoric about liberty and independence, and that he will appreciate the biblical reference to Exodus 1, with which she contextualizes and critiques that experience when she recasts American patriots not as heroes of freedom but as "Modern Egyptian" enslavers and exploiters, building empires on the violently enforced toil of others.

Even absent the illuminating letter to Occom, however, reading her poems as autobiography, which both the problematic critical legacy and the letter invite one to do, turns up much of the same ambivalent blend of dissent and piety as is evidenced in the prose works already discussed. Though the major part of her work consisted of poetry written either "on" or "to" various individuals both notable and obscure, the matter of the poet's *self*-construction in these works is a sizable and complex topic.[4] Examining the corollary issue of just how a teenage slave girl acquired the remarkable rhetorical authority evident in the poems and thinking of her in the context of the writers already examined reveal important connections.

Wheatley frequently exhorts and encourages readers (real and imagined) from a platform that sounds very much like a pulpit. Using ministerial tones that seem, at least, surprising she directs one sermonic text, for example, to the "young men" of Harvard ("To the University of Cambridge, in New England"). She begins by recognizing her own identity as an African but, in contrast to "On Being Brought," she imagines herself here not as passive victim but, curiously, as agent, as if she has willed her own slavery—indeed, as if she were a traveler or adventurer rather than a kidnapped slave: "I *left* my native shore" (ll, my emphasis). Then, in apparent contrast, she notes that to the white men at university "'tis giv'n to scan the heights / Above, to traverse the ethereal space, / And mark the systems of revolving worlds." But "still more," she says, these students have received the "blissful news" of Christianity (11–12). After recounting for them her Christian message of salvation, she ends her poem with a commanding warning:

> Improve your privileges while they stay,
> Ye pupils, and each hour redeem, that bears
> Or good or bad report of you to heav'n.
> Let sin, that baneful evil to the soul,
> By you be shunn'd, nor once remit your guard;
> Suppress the deadly serpent in its egg.
> Ye blooming plants of human race divine,
> An *Ethiop* tells you 'tis your greatest foe;
> Its transient sweetness turns to endless pain,
> And in immense perdition sinks the soul. (12)

Wheatley addresses her readers as the autobiographers do—as a minister. Employing an authoritative tone, she seems to speak to these particular readers, her most privileged white male contemporaries, as if she understands her own authority precisely by way of her difference from her audience, those "sons of science" who are afforded opportunities unavailable to her but clearly not unimagined. That distance and difference is emphasized further in her subtly ironic identification of the students as "blooming plants of *human race divine*" (my emphasis) and hersels as an "*Ethiop*." In that context, then, her message serves to remind them of what she argues is the central meaning of Christianity: humility. Calling them to mind Christ's "hands out-strecht" in "compassion," in "mercy," his refusal to resent his "revilers" (12), she articulates a compassionate Christianity which then provides the foundation for the warning she issues in the stanza quoted above. Explicitly recognizing and naming the "privileges" of her hearers, she urges them to "improve" upon them in a poem seeming to argue that true Christianity consists of humility and compassion, which constitute, if not precisely the opposites of privilege, at least its moral checks. She seizes authority as she invites them to curb (or at least take note of) their own. The same presumption of moral authority occurs repeatedly in Wheatley's rhetorical encounters with the most privileged of readers imaginable—in her decisions to pen a eulogy for Whitefield, write encomiums for both George Washington and George III, solicit a meeting with Ben Franklin, correspond with philanthropists, and denounce the slave trade to the Earl of Dartmouth.

The rhetorical parallels between Wheatley and the autobiographers discussed here, the strategies and conflicts, the complex self-construction informed by theological imperatives of self-examination, personal narrative, and outsider authority, widen the scope of possibility of meaning and enhance the relevance of the convergence of issues among these writers. In one of several anthologies that continues to move discussion of early writing by African and Native American writers into classrooms and critical journals, Vincent Carretta observes that "for most of the Black writers, Protestant Christianity with its emphasis on direct knowledge of the Bible was the primary motive for literacy. Virtually all the Afro-British publications in prose took the form of spiritual autobiographies that trace the transition from pagan beliefs to the Christianity shared with the authors' British readers" (*Unchained* 9).[5] The shared Christianity of these texts functioned in complex, profoundly important ways for writers of color in the early period. The Protestant Christianity in evidence in the autobiographical writings of Samson Occom, John Marrant, Abigail Bailey, Olaudah Equiano, Jarena Lee, and William Apess is fundamentally shaped by the authors' experiences on the margin rather than at the center of institutional, official religious power. Protestant Christianity remains crucially and complexly constant, frequently evident in an insistence on the spiritual and ideological meaning of social injustice as a reality caused not by the elsewhere emphatically sovereign God present in American Protestant theology but by human greed, cultural arrogance, and institutional obliviousness; evident, further, in religious rhetoric, in the dynamic and contradictory pressures of constraint and liberation, in biblical intertextuality, and in interrogations of established hierarchies. Like these autobiographers, then, the poet Phillis Wheatley grounds her expressions of piety in experiences both of personal and spiritual liberation and of racial exclusion and prohibition in the context of

Protestant Christianity. Like them, she seems to gain a voice and a political stance via Christianity, notwithstanding the fact that her piety has frequently provoked resistance among her most sophisticated and politically engaged readers, particularly those who have looked for a certain kind of authenticity.[6]

The dynamics in play in American revivalist religion—of culture, power, and political and social critique of entrenched religious institutions—allowed marginalized writers (including and perhaps especially writers marginalized specifically by those religious traditions) to seize the rhetorical platform of autobiographical writing in order to speak of the ironies and failures of their religious, social, material, and political experiences. Traditionally, personal narratives allowed religious writers to speak their faith in order to testify to the workings of God. In the context of revival religion, the genre became a vigorous extension of democratic theological inclinations, a particularly hospitable site for the complex and challenging messages the writers conveyed to their contemporaries. Protestantism's emphasis on *language*—the text of the Bible, preachers' sermons, the commentaries on and conversation about and memorization of the scriptures—helped shape a context in which the words about one's own life had a powerful significance, potentially, at least, as a spirit-inspired gloss on the authorized sacred narratives that served as the center of meaning for revivalist believers. As Rodger Payne has argued in a study of white early American autobiographers: "If conversion was theologically egalitarian—at least in theory—because it presented to and demanded of all the choice of grace or damnation, spiritual autobiography and conversion narratives were similarly the first 'democratic' forms of literature because they legitimated the narrative self they produced on the basis of their use of the discourse of conversion" (47).

Personal narratives about religion, especially about conversion, are in some ways formulaic, predictably adhering to identifiable conventions, both discursive and experiential. Critical attention often focuses on the complex acts of self-construction in these works. But there is more at stake here. According to Payne, "Far from being merely imitative texts, evangelical spiritual autobiographies were part of a new vernacular and modernist literature that reflected the language of popular democracy, but they were not without the tension that accompanies any new discursive formation" (48). Furthermore, although Payne and others have fruitfully examined the crises and strains evident in notions of the self and theological orthodoxy for white writers, the discursive tension identifiable in texts by women and writers of color occurs around the scope, purpose, and meaning of the story of the religious self. Careful readings of writers from outside the mainstream, those prohibited from traditional sites of power and privilege because of race and sex, reveal that the construction of the self—including the expected story of conversion—often occurred in the context of their awareness of a deeply flawed external social world (which included their families and churches). The writers' religious argument, then, concerned not only personal conversion but institutional and societal change as well.

The theological moorings and social practices at the foundation of American spiritual autobiography in the late eighteenth and early nineteenth centuries, emerging from revival Christianity, led to other religious and social effects: for example, the significance of the pulpit—actually, rhetorically, and metaphorically—for the writers in this study. Individuals unlikely on the one hand, to take on authoritative roles, such as Phillis Wheatley or Harriet Beecher Stowe (both of them famous examples of writers criticized for self-deprecation, cultural betrayal, and sentimentality), would, on the other hand, take up the position, tone, and rhetorical strategies of the minister. Samson Occom, John Marrant, Olaudah Equiano, Jarena Lee, and William Apess turn their preacherly rhetoric back on the religious communities to which they remained loyal. Each of those writers experienced rhetorical enfranchisement, including access to public roles as preachers, which were both officially sanctioned and severely limited (by unofficial, itinerating, or missionary status that authorized them for ministry only with marginalized, mostly nonwhite communities). Such roles positioned them, after all, to preach. Revivalist religion, which was specifically "populist and anti-intellectual, [including] the Freewill Baptists, Christians, Methodists and African Methodists, created a religious culture in which even the most humble convert—the poor, the unlearned, the slave, or the female—felt qualified to preach the gospel" (Brekus 145). Great Awakening religion's emphasis on experience, on immediate and unpredictable revelation, involved not only a rejection of all things Roman Catholic—including, quite specifically, priestly hierarchies—but also an endorsement of a "priesthood of all believers," one of the rallying cries of the Protestant Reformation, which persisted into revivalist Christianity in specific ways, such as, for example, a widened scope of how, when, where, and by whom the gospel would be preached. Universal priesthood meant expanded rhetorical opportunities for those "priestly" believers of all sorts.

The experience of authority itself was transformative for writers located outside the traditional mainstream of the power and privilege of Anglo-American cultures. This is especially apparent, as I argue, in the autobiographical writing of Abigail Bailey, who, though least clearly fitted to the group discussed here, becomes consequently instructive. Even (or, perhaps, especially) for this least socially critical or socially aware writer, the pulpit, in however limited a sense, seems to have moved her toward a deeper sense of agency, power, and autonomy, features of the autobiographical speaker that make her final self-presentation markedly different from that of the subject of the *Memoirs* proper. All these writers saw and understood the rhetorical power and significance of such a role, particularly as an opportunity for issuing judgments on faithful brethren poised to listen because of the particular contexts: revival religion's emphasis on individual authority and on the unpredictability of the movement of the spirit; and the spiritual traditions of life-writing, which emphasized narration, reflection, and self-improvement.

The autobiographical speaker understood his or her life as a biblical narrative, as a revelatory exemplum, part of the sermonic discourse of the tradition. An outsider's sensibility, once informed by the crucial, typically defining, inside experience of injustice, morphed the message from the personal, spiritually understood benefits of salvation to a call for this-worldly justice, even when (as was so often the case in the writers examined here) such a call meant identifying the hypocrisy of the authoritative community that had led the speaker to the conversion experience to begin with. They may be, in Patricia Collins's terms, definitive "outsiders within," who see up close and personal the power dynamics at work in the dominant cultural group, into which they have been invited to participate in limited terms. Like the subjects of Collins's study, they have had a lifetime of experience of "self-affirmation [from] seeing white power demystified." The close contact with locations of power afforded by their embrace of revival religion allowed these writers "a distinct view of the contradictions between the dominant group's actions and ideologies." According to Collins, the "outsider-within stance functions to create a new angle of vision on the process of suppression" (11–12).

The inclusion—theological, institutional, experiential—offered by revival religion to writers who were otherwise marginalized in eighteenth- and early nineteenth-century America instilled a sense of power and agency; at the same time, specific exclusions—the limits, boundaries, and prohibitions experienced by each—provoked the social critique embedded in these texts. Apess could not initially obtain a license to preach, nor could he get official authorization for publication of his life narrative on his own terms. Jarena Lee's experience of exclusion becomes the subject of her autobiography: she is prohibited from preaching; then she is prohibited, like Apess, from publishing her version of her autobiography. Further, the difficulties experienced by these speakers goes far beyond exclusion. Acts of violence recur in many of these texts: Occom speaks metaphorically, describing an imaginary Indian boy repeatedly beaten because of his race. In a horrible example of the historical uncanny, Apess becomes that poor Indian boy, literally beaten, first by his family of origin and then repeatedly by the white foster father/master who raises him. Like Apess, Marrant describes scenes of brutal violence, first within his family of origin and then later at the plantation with slaves. Equiano both suffers and witnesses the violence he comes to see as inextricable from the system of slavery, which he experiences as both victim and participant. Bailey's lifetime of family violence is transformative, not, as she first expects, of her brutal husband but of her family, which is entirely disrupted, and also of herself, of her sense of power and agency. When Abigail identifies with Phoebe as a victim of her husband, she comes to see a way to resist the violence. Her emergent sense of Phoebe as a separate person experiencing harm compels her to identify and resist her husband's violence, recasting it from potentially meaningful metaphor to moral reprehensibility. Violence as both spiritual analogue and experiential reality becomes a key vehicle for meaning here.

Suffering and violence, along with consequent interpretive dilemmas, emerge as recurring features of these texts. Although this set of writers shares no specific theology of suffering, they do importantly all reject a theology of divine authorship of suffering. (Indeed, Bailey's memoir can be read as a journey toward such a rejection.) Equiano's uneducated friend who philosophizes that he and his fellow Christian slaves will find justice not on earth but only when they "look up to God Mighty in the top" (110) articulates compellingly the precise theological position that these writers refuse, a position they argue against (implicitly or explicitly) in their life narratives. These autobiographers require their Christian readers to identify biblically and personally with the victims of injustice and, consequently, to evaluate the social practices that perpetuate injustice.

Apess and Marrant, for their parts, must convey and then correct what they assume will be their readers' interpretive assumptions concerning racial violence. In multiple instances in *Son of the Forest,* Apess addresses the "problem" of violence as he knows his white readers would understand it: as initiated by the savage behavior of Native Americans. Insistently contextualizing his own injuries at the hands of his brethren, he argues that they are "the effect of some cause" which must be "attribute[d] in a great measure to the whites," and he proceeds to chronicle the effects of cultural contact with Europeans (7). Similarly, he later argues by colonial inversion, again acknowledging and confronting his readers' assumptions about frontier violence: "But let the thing be changed. Suppose an overwhelming army should march into the United States for the purpose of subduing it and enslaving the citizens; how quick would they fly to arms, gather in multitudes around the tree of liberty, and contend for their rights with the last drop of their blood. And should the enemy succeed, would they not eventually rise and endeavor to regain liberty? And who would blame them for it?" (31). Similarly, Marrant writes an apologetic for Indian hostility: "When they recollect that the white people drove them from the American shores, they are full of resentment," leading them to unite and murder as many white men, women, and children as "they could lay hold of" (88). Marrant later tells a violent slaveholder that "the blood he had spilt... would be required by God at his hands" (92).

For Equiano, the violence of slavery is the easy identifier of hypocritical religion: "O Ye nominal Christians," he says, "might not an African ask you 'learned you this from your God, who says unto you, do unto all men as you would men should do unto you?'" (61). Each writer seems, to varying degrees, to make sense of violence by a fundamental expression or experience of compassion. Each one identifies with the experience and perspective of the sufferer. Each one's critique depends upon the perspective realized by the one suffering the effects of institutionally designed, approved, or ignored violence. In the highly metaphorized, spiritual worlds of these autobiographers, violence, like nearly all material circumstances, becomes a vehicle for religious meaning. Interestingly, however, these writers (with the important exception of Abigail Bailey at the outset of her narrative) do not interpret violence as a means of sanctification; they do not adopt a submissive posture of suffering in silence, see the violence as grace-filled, or long for heavenly rather than earthly reprieve. Rather, they oppose it, refusing to conceive of themselves as recipients of a divinely designed violence. In the end, the truth they learn from the suffering or the sufferer, and the consequent recognition of meaning they demand from readers, reflects institutional or social concerns rather than exclusively personal and spiritual matters.

Their perspectives anticipate the emergence of Critical Race Theory, which, among other things, asserts that the perspective of the sufferer, the experience of victimization, defines and justifies a socially critical moral stance, a particular one that speaks of and to the social injustice at the foundation of the experience of violence. The legal scholar Mari J. Matsuda, an early proponent, explains some of the premises of the theory (sounding as if she is in direct dialogue with Equiano's philosophizing friend who looks to "God mighty in the top"): "Those who have experienced discrimination speak with a special voice to which we should listen. Looking to the bottom—adopting the perspective of those who have seen and felt the falsity of the liberal promise—can assist critical scholars in the task of fathoming the phenomenology of law and defining the elements of justice" (1). Critical Race Theory goes beyond identifying with the position of the sufferer: presuming that theory must be informed by concrete experiences of oppression, it asserts that "when notions of right and wrong, justice and injustice, are examined not from an abstract position, but from the position of groups who have suffered through history, moral relativism recedes and identifiable normative priorities emerge" (2). What Matsuda calls a "new epistemological source" becomes, for Critical Race Theory scholars, a foundation for legal arguments.

Autobiography may be understood as a set of rhetorical conventions for just such a source. The autobiographers here locate a foundation of experiential knowing as an authoritative hermeneutical lens, through which they view both their lives and the practices of their religious traditions. By presenting their own experience, their own exclusion, oppression, and suffering, as a failure of the theological and social ideals of their traditions, and by seizing their right to rhetorical authority within those traditions, these writers speak of and enact the change they envision, the unrealized ideals they endorse.

The historian Catherine Albanese describes religion in the United States in the context of cultural exchange: messy, asymmetrical, askew, a story of "meeting and change ... in which the encounter with the other becomes the invited or (mostly) uninvited gift that transforms the contacting parties." Early Americans, she argues, professed religions that "bore the signs of contact with those who were other and different. American religions were *changed* religions, even if they evoked the stuff of tradition and the trappings of former cultures and times" (202–3). Generalizations made about Christianity in the early period, however, particularly those made in the context of literary studies, have too frequently assumed a Protestantism which, if not precisely monolithic, is defined institutionally or historically by representatives at the center of official Protestant traditions: seminary-trained, officially empowered, often well-published and widely recognized religious spokesmen. So we recall, for example, William Bradford, Jonathan Edwards, and Cotton Mather as speaking for and representing early American Protestantism. All of them white, all of them male, educated, elite, they have come to define what literary scholars mean when they speak of early American Christianity. But these writers espouse a set of beliefs and experiences markedly different in important ways from the religious perspectives expressed in the more thoroughly "changed" religion evidenced in the life-writing of Occom, Marrant, Equiano, Bailey, Lee, and Apess—that messy, contradictory, deeply experiential and frequently subversive religion in abundant evidence in works by early American women and writers of color.

Protestant Christianity appears nearly everywhere in the English autobiographical texts of early American women and writers of color. Religious experience, an emphasis on its authority, and a rhetoric of personal transformation and inversions of hierarchies provided the experiential and theoretical platform on which many white women and writers of color constructed prophetic selves that could preach to the most authoritative representatives of the tradition. The complex constellation of issues in the changed religion of the Protestantism of U.S. writers from the margins of those traditions includes the way biblical narrative, imagery, and rhetoric informed their presentations of themselves and their experiences as individuals who had both a story to tell and a lesson to teach. The appeal of religion for these writers, the nuances of this blend of personal piety and political, institutional, or cultural dissent within a diverse array of texts, presents a history of

American religious autobiography in contrast to the one represented by the white writers whose texts have been too long presumed to tell the whole story of early American experience. Further, autobiographies by women and writers of color constitute not only "changed" religion but a changed genre as well. The rules and presumptions concerning life-writing shift here, forecasting a literature of piety and dissent that will then inform major religious and social reform movements of subsequent centuries.

NOTES

1. Margins and Centers

1. In a recent work of traditional intellectual history (ignoring all but the most canonical writers), James Block argues that Protestant ideas were both foundational to an American concept of agency and, ultimately, ineffectual. Block's focus and methodology are quite different from mine here, but our discussions share a recognition of the historical significance, complexity, and contradictory effects of American Protestantism.

2. For a more detailed account of the period and corollary scholarly debates among historians, see Susan Juster (*Disorderly*) and Jeffrey Richards's informative review essay.

3. For detailed studies of the religious and cultural history of the Great Awakening and its contexts which pay particular attention to the question of the loosening of authority and social hierarchies, see Richard Bushman (*Great Awakening*); Michael Crawford; Mary Maples Dunn; Clarke Garrett; David Hall; Amy Schrager Lang; Harry Stout; and Donald Weber.

4. The dynamic interplay between writers of color and communities of color is particularly addressed by Joanna Brooks.

5. Jon Butler's argument, in the main, concerns an objection to historians' practice of generalizing the effects, practices, and beliefs characteristic of regional movements into a general notion of the Great Awakening.

6. Malini Johar Schueller and Edward Watts have explored the usefulness of postcolonial approaches specifically for early American texts.

7. Shea's original work drew on earlier discussions of spiritual autobiography in Puritan and Quaker traditions (see his bibliographical essay, 271–77, in the 1988 publication) and his thoroughgoing revisitation of the field of study in the "Bibliographical Supplement" (279–86). For a historical sense of the critical discussion of the genre of spiritual autobiography specifically within the English Protestant tradition, see Margaret Botrall, John Morris, and Dean Ebner. Within the burgeoning field of autobiography studies, recent critical discussions include examinations of spiritual life-writing within the Protestant tradition. Forms that may be read as spiritual autobiographies include conversion narratives, Quaker journals, Indian captivity narratives, travel writing, and slave narratives. See, for example, Carol Edkins's essay on American Quaker and Puritan women's writing. On conversion narratives

(as precursor to later autobiographical forms); see Patricia Caldwell; Mary Cochran Grimes; John O. King; and Jerald Brauer.

8. I am thinking here both of Bassard's 1992 essay ("Gender and Genre") in which she shows how scholars have been unable to engage in serious critical inquiry concerning religious issues in nineteenth-century works by African American women, as well as of the larger discussion in her 1999 *Spiritual Interrogations*, which I draw on in the discussions that follow. More recently, Joanna Brooks's *American Lazarus* looks quite specifically at the religious and historical contexts for a set of texts by Native and African American writers, addressing overall concerns that I share (including an acknowledgment of the challenge these texts present to readers who are not biblically literate). For the most part, Brooks sets aside autobiographical narratives in order to examine other textual forms, a concern she contextualizes both in the history of canon formation and what she rejects as a preoccupation with subjectivity (12–13). Brooks's work establishes groundbreaking readings of, in some cases, heretofore wholly neglected texts (Samson Occom's hymnal, for instance). The genre of religious autobiography, and particularly the way that genre was practiced by early writers of color, is far from an exhausted topic, however, particularly as those works are understood in light of the recent boom in autobiography studies, most of which attend exclusively or primarily to recent or contemporary texts or to a history of autobiography mainly imagined via European writers. Helen Thomas situates slave narratives in the context of British romanticism, paying particular attention to the effects of Methodism and revivalist Christianity.

2. Samson Occom

1. Occom is referred to as a "first" by others as well: Murray calls him the first Indian writer of significance (44); Peyer says Native American literature in English begins with Occom (208); Michael Elliott notes that he is the first Native American ordained as a Christian minister (233). The sermon for Moses Paul went through nineteen editions and was translated into Welsh in 1827 (Ruoff, *American Indian Literatures* 62). The execution sermon, an important early American genre, was usually delivered before the execution of a convicted criminal. The purpose, generally, of these sermons was to impress hearers with the seriousness of the crimes of the condemned, and to provoke them, in the face of one criminal's guilt and certain death, to reflect on their own morality and mortality and to repent (see Bosco; Minnick). Murray discusses the particular power of Occom's sermon's orchestration—a virtuous Indian preaching a warning about a wicked Indian—calling it a "moral tableau." Noting that Occum speaks to several separate audiences within the sermon, he suggests that the writer's overall intent, as he allows

each component to "overhear" the other audiences' parts, is marginally subversive (45–47).

2. Wheelock ran a private school and was the pastor of the Second Congregational Church of Lebanon, Connecticut. Occom entered the school in December 1743 and remained under Wheelock's instruction for four years, until his poor eyesight and ill health caused him to abandon his studies. He was an excellent student whose performance prompted Wheelock to concentrate his educational efforts on Native Americans by founding the famous Indian Charity School (Peyer 209–10).

3. See Axtell on Wheelock's founding of Dartmouth.

4. Michael Elliott notes that accusations of drunkenness followed Occom throughout his career and were repeated by writers such as Timothy Dwight, even though he believed they were unfounded. Elliott also distinguishes between early American notions of "drunkard" and "being overtaken with strong drink" as he discusses the pervasive stereotype of the drunken Indian in early New England and now (251, 239).

5. Occom's narrative remained unpublished until 1982, when Bernd Peyer included it in his anthology. I use Peyer's transcription here (*Elders*). The typescript is located in the Dartmouth College Library Special Collections.

6. Since the original version of this essay was published in John Hawley's *Christian Encounters with the Other* in 1998, new discussions of Samson Occom have appeared, including David Carlson's *Sovereign Selves*, which examines Occom's historical and biographical contexts and presents him as a precursor to William Apess. Hilary Wyss's *Writing Indians* and Keely McCarthy's "Conversion, Identity, and the Indian Missionary" examine a number of the concerns addressed here, in particular the complex presentation of the self in the context of conversion and missionary activity in Occom's writing. Wyss and McCarthy discuss letters and diary entries not included in my discussion.

7. See Von Lonkhuyzen on the role of goods and technology, including literacy, in the conversions of Native Americans in New England in the early period. Occom's letters indicate a special concern for literacy and for improving his own and other Indians' material circumstances via Christianity. Weinstein attributes Occom's interest in religion, and his loyalty to Christianity, entirely to this concern.

8. See Richardson; Blodgett; Weinstein; and Carlson for fuller discussions of the Mason Controversy and Occom's biography.

9. Occom's dates are 1723 to 1792; Edwards's are 1703 to 1758. Edwards's "Personal Narrative" was written in 1739, then published posthumously in 1765, three years before Occom began his "Short Narrative."

10. Edwards's first discussion of religious awakening occurs in his 1737 *Faithful Narrative of the Surprising Work of God*, an account of his experiences with his own congregation at Northampton in 1734–35. His 1746

Treatise concerning Religious Affections, provides a fuller analysis of the Great Awakening.

11. Notable discussions of Edwards's style include those of William J. Scheick (*Writings*); Sandra Gustafson; Daniel B. Shea ("Art"); Stuart Piggin and Dianne Cook; and Dennis Barbour.

12. Keely McCarthy has also recently noted the Pauline source for these lines. Others, including David Murray, Dana Nelson, and Bernd Peyer, have remarked on their strong tone but have not heard the Pauline resonance.

13. Michael Elliott, using Victor Turner's anthropological work as a starting point, describes Occom's authoritative position and voice as "liminal" but permanently rather than temporarily so. Drawing on the correspondence between Occom and Wheelock, Elliott provides a rich analysis of the possible layers of meanings in Occom's words about himself and his colleagues. Both Nelson and McCarthy also attend to the complexities of Occom's self-presentation, including a discussion of the suggestiveness of this passage.

14. Brooks examines Occom's hymnal, *A Choice Collection of Hymns and Spiritual Songs,* an important work to the Brotherton community, as the "most extensive and influential project of [Occom's] literary career" (55). Her discussion establishes the significance of Occom's work in particular as a part of the democratization of American Protestant culture at this moment and indicates the significance of hymnody for early African American and American Indian communities and literatures.

3. John Marrant

1. The two other most widely read captivity narratives were Mary Rowlandson's 1682 *The Soveraignty and Goodness of God* and John Williams's 1707 *The Redeemed Captive, Returning unto Zion.* Nellie McKay calls the Indian captivity narrative "America's first unique autobiographical account" (31). For discussions of the significance of captivity narratives and the metaphor of captivity in U.S. literature and culture, see Burnham; Kolodny (*Land*); Breitwieser, Derounian-Stodola; and Slotkin. Anthologies of captivity narratives, such as those edited by Vaughan and Clark and by VanDerBeets, provide overviews of the genre, as does John Sekora in his discussion of the captivity genre as a context for understanding the emergence of the narrative of Briton Hammon, whose 1760 *Narrative of the Uncommon Sufferings and Surprizing Deliverance* may be the earliest published slave narrative.

2. Potkay's and Burr's introduction to Marrant's *Narrative* includes a full record of his life. A second autobiographical text, Marrant's *Journal,* which recorded his life experiences after the *Narrative,* was published in June or July of 1790. The other Marrant publication that has generated some scholarly

attention is his 1789 *Sermon* delivered to Freemasons and possibly edited by Prince Hall.

3. See Joanna Brooks's recent study for a fuller discussion of the Countess's "Connexion," and its context and significance for early American evangelicals. On Selina Hastings, see John R. Tyson's recent studies; Boyd Stanley Schlenther; and Edwin Welch.

4. Cedric May discusses in greater detail the particulars of Marrant's relationship to theological disputes within Methodism.

5. Vincent Carretta selected the same edition of the *Narrative* for inclusion in his 1996 collection, *Unchained Voices*.

6. Several recent studies provide analyses of cross-cultural contact initiated by European Christians, paying particular attention to conversion. See, for example, John Hawley; Nicholas Griffiths and Fernando Cervantes; Malini Schueller and Edward Watts; and Gauri Viswanathan.

7. See Ryken et al. for a fuller discussion of the suffering servant motif in general and the suffering servant passages in particular.

8. Slotkin's discussion of the racial violence of the frontier in establishing a U.S. national identity (*Regeneration*) provides one possible meaningful context for Marrant's text. Rene Girard's *Violence and the Sacred* (taken up in subsequent chapters) provides another.

4. Olaudah Equiano

1. See Valerie Smith; Chinosole; Wilfred Samuels; and Robin Sabino and Jennifer Hall as examples of readings that attempt either to dismiss or ignore Equiano's religious perspective altogether or to present religion as a kind of rhetorical disguise, useful for audience appeal but either somewhat or wholly inauthentic. Ferguson, on the other hand, sees the significance of Equiano's religion and argues that it informs a racial self-hatred consistent with the Christian racism exemplified in many other texts.

2. Carretta quotes Wollstonecraft's review (from *The Analytical Review*, May 1789) at length (*Equiano* 331–32).

3. Despite Equiano's address to members of Parliament at the outset of the *Narrative*, and his public offers to give testimony, he was not invited to give evidence at Parliamentary hearings. He did witness the popular response to his *Narrative*, but he did not live to see either the abolition of the African slave trade (in 1807) or the abolition of slavery in British colonies (in 1838). See Carretta (*Equiano* and *Unchained*) for a fuller history not only of abolition and Equiano's conversion to it (which Carretta argues is as significant as his religious conversion) but also of the transition from widespread practices of slavery across cultures to a race-based slave system, which becomes the legacy that Equiano (and the abolitionists who came after him)

had to address. Equiano died in 1797. For the details of his life not fully expounded in his *Narrative*, I am indebted to Vincent Carretta's work, first in the Penguin edition (which is the source referenced in quotations from the *Narrative* in this chapter) and second in the groundbreaking 2005 biography of Equiano, which provides richer and more specific historical contexts than were previously available. For example, Carretta posits that Equiano not only relied on Anthony Benezet (whom he cites) as a source for his recollections and descriptions of Africa in the early part of the *Narrative*, but may have fabricated his own African birth altogether; new evidence (baptismal and naval records) unearthed by Carretta indicates that Equiano was born in America—specifically, in South Carolina.

4. Concerning Christianity as a shaping force for Equiano's interpretive and narrative authority, Adam Potkay (in opposition to readers who emphasize his lack of control and loss of his original cultural self) argues that Equiano "wills, guides, shapes, and controls" the transformation he describes by way of religion, even more specifically by reenacting the biblical narrative's move between Old and New Testament ("Olaudah" 680). Tanya Caldwell sees Christianity as one among several sources that give Equiano his profoundly British (rather than African) voice. Katalin Orban argues that Equiano commands authority specifically on the grounds of Christianity (659). And Susan Marren examines how Christianity and, more specifically, scripture allow Equiano to "circumvent the white person's language and its closed categories of meaning" (102).

5. Angelo Costanzo notes the significance of biblical references and quotations, of biblical types in line with a tradition of Puritan typology, throughout early slave narratives.

6. Forrest Wood discusses the centrality of this particular biblical appeal in eighteenth-century antislavery literature (62), including Equiano's confrontation with readers at the end of chapter 2 in the *Narrative*.

7. Equiano's "Ebo" have been identified with the Ibo in Nigeria (Achebe; Edwards and Shaw) and his "Issaka" with the Ika (Wood 165) and Isseke in Nigeria (Achebe; Acholonu).

8. In "Appendix B: A Note on the Illustrations" in the Penguin edition of Equiano (315) Carretta observes the way the author's portrait evolves somewhat from earlier to later editions of the *Narrative*; in the biography, Carretta contextualizes the author's portrait with other eighteenth-century visual representations (280–92). Lynn Casmier-Paz examines the rhetorical function of portraits in slave narratives and discusses Equiano's in specific, emphasizing, as I do, the significance and particularity of the biblical text.

9. Following Equiano's own practice, I use the King James Version (1611) of all biblical texts cited.

10. Carretta notes that Equiano has to have been mistaken concerning the time he heard George Whitefield: given the chronology of travel for both men, it would have been impossible for Equiano to have heard Whitefield in Philadelphia in 1766 or '67, as he says he did; he probably heard the evangelist in Savannah, Georgia, in February 1765 (*Equiano* 378 n. 3).

11. Tanya Caldwell highlights Equiano's British cultural moorings and readerly appeal, as she connects him to Defoe, Burke, Adam Smith, and the Bible; however, her presentation of the *Interesting Narrative* as a text that, consequently, "would not rock the boat," and of Equiano as nostalgically inclined toward conformity to the system of eighteenth-century English government and empire (267, 272), ignores the complexity of Equiano's religion as well as the specifics of his political and publication history. Similarly, Adam Potkay, in a discussion of teaching Equiano ("History"), argues for a recognition of Christianity as the primary lens for this text, faulting those who see strong evidence of African cultures informing the narrative; however, Potkay seems to underestimate the subversive power and complexity of Equiano's religion.

12. The verse Equiano quotes is not in Psalm 126. He may be thinking of another passage or conflating several passages. Biblical texts that use similar (though not precisely the same) language include several other passages from Psalms:13.5, 28.7, 33.21, 86.12. A number of these texts fit the tone and thematic concerns of Equiano's discussion of his manumission, as they describe oppression and liberation. Equiano may also have been recalling the words of a Bible commentary, such as Matthew Henry's, which he owned. See Carretta's note 70 in Equiano's *Narrative* (246).

13. Equiano recalls the story of the prophet Elijah from 2 Kings 2.1–18. His quoted words do not match the biblical text precisely but nonetheless call to mind the chariot and horses of fire described in the Bible, which transport Elijah into heaven.

14. Carretta's footnote (*Narrative*) suggests that Equiano refers here to the story of the plagues in Exodus 7, yet he seems to be thinking rather more specifically of the incident in Exodus 2 that he discusses here.

15. In his 1967 edition of Equiano's *Narrative*, Paul Edwards notes that early black writers Ottobah Cugoano and James Gronniosaw also made use of the "talking book" (188 n.40). Gates asserts that the motif is first named by Zora Neale Hurston and referred to by Ishmael Reed (*Signifying* xxv).

16. The date of Gronniosaw's *Narrative*, sometimes listed as 1770, was determined to be 1772 by Carretta (*Unchained* 53–54).

17. In addition to my discussion of this instance in the earlier version of this chapter in *African American Review*, Carretta examines it in "Property of the Author" and in *Equiano*, where it leads him into a rich discussion of the frontispiece portrait as a visual element of the trope of the Talking Book (287–90).

18. In addition to the critics already discussed in this chapter, Marion Rust; Samantha Early; Douglas Anderson; Ide Corley; and Clement Okafor emphasize the complexity of Equiano's self-presentation.

19. Early in the *Narrative*, Equiano writes of having been a "predestinarian" from his earliest days (119). See also Carretta's note on predestinarianism (*Narrative* 275).

5. Abigail Abbot Bailey

1. Taves's introduction, one of the few published discussions of Bailey's *Memoirs*, establishes the religious, social, and historical contexts examined in this chapter. Students and scholars of early America are indebted to Taves for her recovery of this work and her informed introduction and rich set of footnotes in the republication. My discussion of Bailey's biography and the religious and cultural contexts draws upon Taves's work.

2. Important recent discussions of intimate violence in early America include the collection of essays edited by Daniels and Kennedy, and Elizabeth Pleck's historical discussion of family violence and social policy in early America. Susan Lentz examines the legal history of domestic abuse (and she notes Bailey's narrative as an example of the high evidentiary standards for prosecuting domestic violence). *The Hanging of Ephraim Wheeler* (Irene Quenzler Brown and Richard D. Brown) provides another early account of domestic violence and incest (though not by way of a published autobiographical account).

3. For sociological and psychological analyses of perpetrators of domestic abuse, specifically in the context of Christianity, see Brown and Bohn; Arriaga and Oskamp; and Renzetti, Edleson, and Bergen. See also Roy; Dobash and Dobash; and Breines and Gordon.

4. Abigail Bailey successfully divorced and gained a property settlement from Asa, but she did not pursue prosecution on any of the grounds that she might have, including cruelty, adultery, incest, rape. While prosecution in similar cases was unusual, it was not unprecedented. Marriage in early New England was viewed in the context of covenantal theology as a contract, an agreement between unequal parties. The submission of the lesser partner (the wife in a marriage covenant) in any such agreement depended upon the responsible, faithful carrying-out of the covenant by the superior partner. For a fuller discussion, see Taves, (Introduction) as well as Susan Lentz's study of domestic violence, and the account of Ephraim Wheeler's trial and execution (Brown and Brown), mentioned above.

5. Taves notes that Phineas Bailey, one of Abigail and Asa's sons, produced his own memoir, which corroborates his mother's account concerning Asa's abuse.

6. For discussions of gender, and specifically women's social and domestic roles in early American Protestantism, see, for example, Dunn; Karlsen; Keller; Malmsheimer; Moran; Morgan; Ulrich; and Porterfield.

7. See the collection of essays edited by Joanne Carlson Brown and Carole R. Bohn, *Christianity, Patriarchy, and Abuse: A Feminist Critique*. The Promise Keepers movement (founded in 1990) provides one rather striking twenty-first-century example of traditional patriarchal religion (and covenantal theology) in action, as evangelical men vow to strengthen their God-given authority within the family and their wives, in response, retrench into what they see as biblically prescribed and straightforwardly subordinate roles. In 2007, Promise Keepers offered regular conventions across the United States, sold Podcasts and merchandise, and greeted visitors to their website by announcing "men, you know we're in a war."

8. Charles Chauncy (1705–1787) was Jonathan Edwards's famous opponent concerning the role of emotion in religious life. Theologically more liberal than Edwards and others who defended religious revivalism, Chauncy argued against awakening experiences in *Seasonable Thoughts*.

9. See, for example, Girard, *Violence and the Sacred* and *Things Hidden since the Foundation of the World* (the latter a discussion mainly of biblical texts) and *The Scapegoat*. James Williams, among others, provides an overview of Girardian thought.

10. The tone and meaning of this aspect of Bailey's narrative are reminiscent of a number of early Puritan autobiographies, perhaps most notably Anne Bradstreet's record of her struggle to "wean" her affections, which has generated a rich critical discussion of Puritan belief and practice in general and Bradstreet's spirituality and poetics in particular.

11. Abigail's original editor, drawing on information from Phineas Bailey, one of the Bailey children, informs readers of Asa's fate. After fighting a divorce and property settlement for several years, he was eventually arrested and held in jail until he agreed to a property settlement. Once divorced, he briefly lived with his oldest sons, with whom he was "peevish and unreasonable." He then "married a vile widow,—a turbulent being, who in some degree repaid his cruelties." The Bailey sons returned to their mother, while Asa reportedly became a Methodist preacher—and subsequently lived in "poverty, disgrace, and misery" (179). As for Abigail Bailey herself, she was reunited with her younger children for four years, then "put out" all but the two youngest, some to the homes of their older siblings. Thereafter, she lived for ten years with the family of her church deacon in Piermont, New Hampshire, and then with various grown children until her death in 1815.

12. In a discussion of the captivity narrative genre, Kathryn Zabelle Derounian-Stodola notes how recent scholarship has emphasized the way writers gain agency by way of experience and publication (246).

6. Jarena Lee

1. Carol V. R. George's *Segregated Sabbaths: Richard Allen and the Rise of Independent Black Churches, 1760–1840* provides a fuller discussion of the emergence of the African Methodist Episcopal denomination. Interestingly, George acknowledges only Allen's final decision to approve Lee's requests to preach, omitting his previous prohibitions (detailed by Lee and further substantiated by other historians). George contextualizes Allen's views on women's ordination in the context of Methodist doctrine and practice. She discusses Allen's refusal to grant an earlier request from another woman, Dorothy Ripley, to preach at Bethel Church, suggesting, as does William Andrews, that his resistance to women preachers may have resulted from his relationship with official Methodist hierarchy; the earlier request came prior to the AME's complete severing of official ties to the Methodist church in 1816 (Introduction 128).

2. I am drawing biographical details from Lee's own narratives, from William L. Andrews's introduction to her work, and from George's historical sketch. For more on the history of early nineteenth-century religious camp meetings, see Ann Taves (*Fits*); and Dickson Bruce.

3. For more on the circumstances of Lee's publication history, see Frances Smith Foster (*Written*); and Elizabeth Grammer.

4. Nell Painter (drawing in part on Elizabeth Massey's work) includes a discussion of Sojourner Truth's shifting portrait images, which I found instructive in thinking about the implications of Lee's appearance in this image.

5. All citations of Lee's narrative refer to the text of Andrews's edition in *Sisters of the Spirit*.

6. See the first chapter of Equiano's narrative, and Apess's now widely anthologized "An Indian's Looking Glass for the White Man" (*On Our Own Ground*).

7. Lee's implicit reenactment is suggestive of the Protestant (and particularly Puritan) notion of typology, where believers regularly imagine themselves reliving biblical events in contemporary contexts. Biblical typology, a rich use of biblical allusion, has been an especially common characteristic of African American literature from the early period on into the twentieth century, including, for instance, the work of James Baldwin, Amiri Baraka, and Claude Brown (Foster, "Biblical Tradition").

8. See, for example, Carroll Smith-Rosenberg's "Domesticating Virtue"; and Cathy Davidson's *Revolution and the Word*.

9. Samuel Morse, son of an influential Congregational preacher, would later invent the telegraph. His arguments against Catholicism's influence in the United States were first published in his brother's weekly periodical, *The*

New York Observer, in 1834. A year later they were collected and published as *Foreign Conspiracy Against the Liberties of the United States.*

10. The most likely biblical sources—not all of which are explored in my discussion—include Matthew 17.20, 19.26; Mark 10.27; Luke 1.37, 18.27.

11. I emphasize Gage rather than Sojourner Truth as the source of the imagery here because Nell Irvin Painter has persuasively demonstrated that Gage's account (in an unlikely dialect and including this reference) is less reliable than Marius Robinson's contemporary report on the same speech. Painter's *Sojourner Truth: A Life, a Symbol* examines the mythmaking surrounding Sojourner Truth, in particular the way she functioned for nineteenth- and twentieth-century white feminists.

12. By the time of the publication of Lee's manuscript, Allen and the African Methodist Episcopal church had revised their position to allow "itinerating" women preachers. Throughout the nineteenth and early twentieth centuries, women in various Methodist traditions became licensed and unlicensed itinerating preachers; AME readers would have witnessed that shift. And congregational experience soon produced published testimony and discussion of the same issue (still a topic of controversy in many Christian traditions). Nancy Hardesty examines defenses of female preaching urged by two white women in the Methodist tradition—Phoebe Palmer in her 1859 *Promise of the Father* and, a generation later, Frances Willard in her 1888 *Woman in the Pulpit*. The first woman ordained as a regular (nonitinerating) minister in the United States was Antoinette Blackwell, in a Congregational church in 1853. The AME church approved full ordination for women in 1948.

7. William Apess

1. I draw on O'Connell's work, and on Maureen Konkle's important recent study of Apess in the context of Native American intellectual resistance. Both works inform the overview of Apess's career and publication history presented here. O'Connell's edition of Apess's work (as well as the earlier inclusion of Apess's writing in the landmark first edition of the *Heath Anthology of American Literature*) has generated an increasingly significant critical conversation among literary critics and historians (see Gordon Sayre, who, in addition to citing some errors of fact, faults O'Connell for too heavy an editorial presence in *On Our Own Ground*, and for "assimilating" Apess into a community of minority writers). Apess is discussed in several recent treatments of early American history (Waldstreicher; Lepore; Richter), and, in contrast to many earlier discussions of his work, much recent scholarship has examined Christianity, specifically Methodism, as an empowering force for Apess's political critique.

2. Karim Tiro and Carolyn Haynes explore further the impact of the converged prejudices against both Native Americans and Methodism.

3. Carolyn Haynes, drawing on the ethnohistorical work of Jack Campisi, further points out that Aunt Sally George was part of a robust tradition of Pequot women leaders in this period, and that the presence of female leadership is one of several overlaps between Methodist and Pequot cultures.

4. Donald Nielson; Scott Stevens; and David Carlson discuss in detail the Mashpee Revolt and Apess's important role in it.

5. Kim McQuaid, in the first serious critical study of Apess, provided an overview of his career specifically in the context of Jackson's presidency. McQuaid's essay contains some factual errors concerning his biography, which Barry O'Connell corrects in *On Our Own Ground*. Konkle subsequently corrects some speculation and assumptions and fills in gaps in O'Connell's account, providing important information about Apess's later life and death (including multiple newspaper accounts of his death) not available elsewhere.

6. Theresa Gaul provides a suggestive and historically contextualizing reading of Apess's critically neglected *Indian Nullification*.

7. Scott Manning Stevens discusses Apess's work in the context of Puritan autobiography.

8. Haynes discusses Apess in the context of Methodism in greater detail. See Taves (*Fits*), and the earlier study by Dickson Bruce for further discussion of Methodist practice, the role of emotion, and religious democratization in the context of camp meetings.

9. Michaelsen provides a close reading of how the "looking glass" functions in this text, which is now frequently taught in university classrooms. Konkle notes other uses of the looking glass in argumentative rhetoric in the eighteenth and nineteenth centuries (117).

10. Apess himself writes within even more localized traditions; all of his writing was published by the Methodists and sold at camp meetings and other religious gatherings (Tiro; Haynes).

11. O'Connell notes here that Apess is either confused or has deliberately elided the histories of Indian nations. Both Maureen Konkle and Roumiana Velikova discuss Apess's "error" at length, contextualizing it, first, in the history of the Wampanoag and Pequot and, second, in Apess's immediate historical and political moments. Further, O'Connell suggests that Apess's mother may have been part African American, a suggestion Konkle refutes (115).

12. Krupat, among others, notes that by Apess's era, "Pequot cultural integrity was at a low point. That is to say that aboriginal lands had been usurped or heavily encroached upon by whites so that traditional ecological and cultural practices were severely disrupted, where they were not entirely destroyed" (*Ethnocriticism* 221–22). See also Warrior (*People*); Stevens;

Tiro; and Campisi for more on Pequot history in Apess's era. Pequot history provides a particularly compressed example of the violence and destruction caused by European contact with Indians (including the historical fact that the Pequot nation has frequently—and for several centuries—been inaccurately described by scholarly and creative writers as eradicated).

13. Laura Mielke analyzes Apess's subversive use of sentimental rhetoric within the autobiographical mode.

14. Michaelsen's argument about Apess is part of a larger critique of the fundamentally anthropological vision that informed nineteenth-century cross-racial interactions and that continues, in his compelling analysis, to shape contemporary notions, including "multiculturalism."

15. Scott Michaelsen further examines critical reactions to Apess by Krupat, Murray, and Ashwill in this regard (201 n. 11).

16. Haynes; Donaldson; and Tiro attend to the function of religion. Haynes argues that the social derision (identified, importantly, as a "shame" component) provoked by Methodism among more privileged Christians was key to Apess's experience and to the bifocal understanding he presents to and demands from readers. Donaldson focuses not on the psychological and social element of shame in her analysis of Apess's Methodism but on sound, noise, aurality. Tiro notes the significance not merely of Methodism but of Methodism at the particular historical moment of Apess's writing, when the denomination changed from a dissenting and racially diverse sect to one of the largest (more respectable and much less diverse) Protestant denominations (654). In an earlier study, David Murray examines the presence of social critique in the published sermons of Occom (where it is veiled) and Apess (where it is direct) (63).

17. Carlson examines Apess and Occom in this context.

8. Religious Imperatives

1. Frances Smith Foster's study of African American women's writing (*Written by Herself*) offers a contextualized study of Wheatley, examining the complex autobiographical strain as well as the problematics of "authenticity" in her work.

2. Samuel Rogal has examined Wheatley's Methodist connection.

3. All quotations from Wheatley's texts, including this testimonial from her 1773 *Poems*, are from Wheatley's *Complete Writings*, edited by Vincent Carretta.

4. Recent critical study of Wheatley has attended to her self-construction, to the slippery relationship between self, speaker, and reader in these poems. See, for example, Daniel Black for a discussion of masking and subterfuge; Mary McAleer Balkun on performative rhetoric; Daniel Ennis on identity

construction in the context of the American Revolution, and Carla Willard on irony.

5. Carretta notes further that Venture Smith's 1798 text is "the only example of a work written or dictated by a Black during the period [of the eighteenth century] that is entitled a 'narrative' but is not a story of conversion, and his reference to the 'christian land' in which he lives is clearly ironic" (*Unchained* 9).

6. Todd Vogel engages these concerns in his study of the rhetoric of nineteenth-century writers, which includes a study of William Apess.

WORKS CITED

Achebe, Chinua. *Morning Yet on Creation Day: Essays.* London: Heinemann, 1975.

Acholonu, Catherine Obianju. "The Home of Olaudah Equiano—A Linguistic and Anthropological Search." *Journal of Commonwealth Literature* 22 (1987): 5–16.

Albanese, Catherine. "Exchanging Selves, Exchanging Souls: Contact, Combination, and American Religious History." *Retelling U.S. Religious History.* Ed. Thomas A. Tweed. Berkeley: U of California P, 1997. 200–226.

———. Foreword. *Religion and Domestic Violence in Early New England: The Memoirs of Abigail Abbot Bailey.* Ed. Ann Taves. Bloomington: Indiana UP, 1989. vii–viii.

Aldridge, William. "Preface." Marrant. *Narrative.* 75–76.

Anderson, Douglas. "Division below the Surface: Olaudah Equiano's *Interesting Narrative.*" *Studies in Romanticism* 43 (2004): 439–60.

Andrews, William L. "African American Autobiography Criticism: Retrospect and Prospect." *American Autobiography: Retrospect and Prospect.* Ed. Paul John Eakin. Madison: U of Wisconsin P, 1991. 195–215.

———. Introduction. *Sisters of the Spirit: Three Black Women's Autobiographies of the Nineteenth Century.* Ed. William L. Andrews. Bloomington: Indiana UP, 1986. 1–21.

———. *To Tell a Free Story: The First Century of Afro-American Autobiography.* Bloomington: Illinois UP, 1986.

Anzaldúa, Gloria. *Borderlands/La Frontera: The New Mestiza.* San Francisco: Aunt Lute, 1987.

Apess, William. *On Our Own Ground: The Complete Writings of William Apess, a Pequot.* Ed. Barry O'Connell. Amherst: U of Massachusetts P, 1992.

Aquino, María Pilar. "Including Women's Experience: A Latina Feminist Perspective." *In the Embrace of God: Feminist Approaches to Theological Anthropology.* Ed. Ann O'Hara Graff. Maryknoll, NY: Orbis, 1995. 51–70.

Arriaga, Ximena B., and Stuart Oskamp. *Violence in Intimate Relationships.* Thousand Oaks, CA: Sage, 1999.

Ashwill, Gary. "Savagism and Its Discontents: James Fenimore Cooper and His Native American Contemporaries." *American Transcendental Quarterly* 8 (1994): 211–27.

Axtell, James. *The European and the Indian: Essays in the Ethnohistory of Colonial North America.* New York: Oxford UP, 1981.

Bailey, Abigail Abbot. *Memoirs of Mrs. Abigail Bailey.* 1815. *Religion and Domestic Violence in Early New England: The Memoirs of Abigail Abbot Bailey.* Ed. Ann Taves. Bloomington: Indiana UP, 1989.

Bakhtin, M.M. *Speech Genres and Other Late Essays.* Austin: U of Texas Press, 1986.

Balkun, Mary McAleer. "Phillis Wheatley's Construction of Otherness and the Rhetoric of Performed Ideology." *African American Review* 36 (2002): 121–35.

Barbour, Dennis H. "The Metaphor of Sexuality in Jonathan Edwards' 'Personal Narrative.'" *Christianity and Literature* 47 (1998): 285–94.

Bassard, Katherine Clay. "Gender and Genre: Black Women's Autobiography and the Ideology of Literacy." *African American Review* 26 (1992): 119–29.

———. *Spiritual Interrogations: Culture, Gender, and Community in Early African American Women's Writing.* Princeton: Princeton UP, 1999.

Bednarowski, Mary. *The Religious Imagination of American Women.* Bloomington: Indiana UP, 1999.

Bhabha, Homi. *The Location of Culture.* London: Routledge, 1994.

Black, Daniel P. "Literary Subterfuge: Early African American Writing and the Trope of the Mask." *CLA Journal* 48 (2005): 387–403.

Block, James E. *A Nation of Agents: The American Path to a Modern Self and Society.* Cambridge: Harvard UP, 2002.

Blodgett, Harold. *Samson Occom.* Dartmouth Coll, Manuscript Ser. 3. Hanover, NH: Dartmouth College, 1935.

Bosco, Ronald A. "Lectures at the Pillory: The Early American Execution Sermon." *American Quarterly* 30 (1978): 156–76.

Bottrall, Margaret. *Every Man a Phoenix.* London: Murray, 1958.

Boyd, Richard. "Violence and Sacrificial Displacement." *Arizona Quarterly: A Journal of American Literature, Culture, and Theory* 50 (1994): 51–69.

Bradstreet, Anne. "My Dear Children." *The Works of Anne Bradstreet.* Ed. Jeanine Hensley. Cambridge: Belknap P of Harvard UP, 1967.

Braude, Ann. "Women's History *Is* American Religious History." *Retelling U.S. Religious History.* Ed. Thomas A. Tweed. Berkeley: U of California P, 1997. 87–107.

Brauer, Jerald. "Conversion: From Puritanism to Revivalism." *Journal of Religion* 58 (1978): 227–43.

Breines, Wini, and Linda Gordon. "The New Scholarship on Family Violence." *Signs: Journal of Women in Culture* 8 (1983): 490–531.

Breitwieser, Mitchell Robert. *American Puritanism and the Defense of Mourning: Religion, Grief, and Ethnology in Mary White Rowlandson's Captivity Narrative.* Madison: U of Wisconsin P, 1990.

Brekus, Catherine A. *Strangers and Pilgrims: Female Preaching in America, 1740–1845.* Chapel Hill: U of North Carolina P, 1998.
Brooks, Joanna. *American Lazarus: Religion and the Rise of African and Native American Literatures.* New York: Oxford UP, 2003.
Brown, Irene Q. and Richard D. Brown. *The Hanging of Ephraim Wheeler: A Story of Rape, Incest, and Justice in Early America.* Cambridge: Belknap P of Harvard UP, 2003.
Brown, Joanne Carlson, and Carole R. Bohn, eds. *Christianity, Patriarchy, and Abuse: A Feminist Critique.* New York: Pilgrim, 1990.
Bruce, Dickson. *And They All Sang Hallelujah: Plain-Folk Camp-Meeting Religion, 1800–1845.* Knoxville: U of Tennessee P, 1974.
Burnham, Michelle. *Captivity and Sentiment: Cultural Exchange in American Literature, 1682–1861.* Hanover, NH: UP of New England, 1997.
Bushman, Richard L. *The Great Awakening: Documents on the Revival of Religion, 1740–1745.* 1969. Chapel Hill: U of North Carolina P, 1989.
———. *From Puritan to Yankee: Character and the Social Order in Connecticut, 1690–1795.* Cambridge: Harvard UP, 1967.
———. Butler, Jon. *Awash in a Sea of Faith: Christianizing the American People.* Cambridge: Harvard UP, 1990.
Caldwell, Patricia. *The Puritan Conversion Narrative: The Beginnings of American Expression.* Cambridge: Cambridge UP, 1983.
Caldwell, Tanya. "'Talking Too Much English': Languages of Economy and Politics in Equiano's *The Interesting Narrative.*" *Early American Literature* 34 (1999): 263–82.
Campisi, Jack. "Emergence of the Mashantucket Pequot Tribe." *The Pequots in Southern New England.* Ed. Laurence Hauptman and James Wherry. Norman: U of Oklahoma P, 1993. 117–40.
Cannon, Katie Geneva. "Christian Ethics and Theology in Womanist Perspective." *Journal of Feminist Studies in Religion* 5 (1989): 92–94.
———. *Katie's Canon: Womanism and the Soul of the Black Community.* New York: Continuum, 1995.
Carlson, David J. *Sovereign Selves: American Indian Autobiography and the Law.* Urbana: U of Illinois P, 2006.
Carretta, Vincent. *Equiano, the African: Biography of a Self-Made Man.* Athens: U of Georgia P, 2005.
———. Introduction. *The Interesting Narrative.* By Olaudah Equiano. New York: Penguin, 1995. ix–xxiv.
———. "Property of Author." *Genius in Bondage: Literature of the Black Atlantic.* Ed. Vincent Carretta and Philip Gould. Lexington: U of Kentucky P, 2001.
———, ed. *Unchained Voices: An Anthology of Black Authors in the English-Speaking World of the 18th Century.* Lexington: U of Kentucky P, 1996.

Works Cited

Casmier-Paz, Lynn A. "Slave Narratives and the Rhetoric of Author Portraiture." *New Literary History* 34 (2003): 91–116.

Chauncy, Charles. *Seasonable Thoughts on the State of Religion in New England.* Boston: Rogers and Fowle, 1743.

Chinosole. "Tryin' to Get Over: Narrative Posture in Equiano's Autobiography." *The Art of the Slave Narrative.* Ed. John Sekora and Darwin T. Turner. Macomb: Western Illinois U, 1982. 45–54.

Collins, Patricia Hill. *Black Feminist Thought: Knowledge, Consciousness, and the Politics of Empowerment.* New York: Routledge, 1991.

Conforti, Joseph A. *Jonathan Edwards, Religious Tradition, and American Culture.* Chapel Hill: U of North Carolina P, 1995.

Corley, Ide. "The Subject of Abolitoinist Rhetoric: Freedom and Trauma in *The Life of Olaudah Equiano.*" *Modern Language Studies* 32.2 (2002): 129–156.

Costanzo, Angelo. *Surprising Narrative: Olaudah Equiano and the Beginnings of Black Autobiography.* New York: Greenwood, 1987.

Crawford, Michael J. *Seasons of Grace: Colonial New England's Revival Tradition in Its British Context.* New York: Oxford UP, 1991.

Cugoano, Ottobah. *Thoughts and Sentiments on the Evils of Slavery.* 1787.

Daly, Robert. "Powers of Humility and the Presence of Readers in Anne Bradstreet and Phillis Wheatley." *Studies in Puritan American Spirituality* 4 (1993):1–24.

Daniels, Christine, and Michael V. Kennedy, eds. *Over the Threshold: Intimate Violence in Early America.* New York: Routledge, 1998.

Dannenberg, Anne Marie. "'Where, Then, Shall We Place the Hero of the Wilderness': William Apess's *Eulogy on King Phillip* and Doctrines of Racial Destiny." *Early Native American Writing: New Critical Essays.* Ed. Helen Jaskowski. Cambridge: Cambridge UP, 1996. 66–82.

Davidson, Cathy. *Revolution and the Word: The Rise of the Novel in America.* New York: Oxford UP, 1986.

Deloria, Vine. *We Talk, You Listen: New Tribes, New Turf.* New York: Macmillan, 1970.

Derounian, Kathryn Zabelle. "The Publication, Promotion, and Distribution of Mary Rowlandson's Captivity Narrative in the Seventeenth Century." *Early American Literature* 23 (1988): 239–61.

Derounian-Stodola, Kathryn Zabelle and James Arthur Levernier. *The Indian Captivity Narrative, 1550–1900.* New York: Twayne, 1993.

Derounian-Stodola, Kathryn Zabelle. "Captivity Narratives." *Teaching the Literatures of Early America.* Ed. Carla Mulford. New York: MLA, 1999. 243–55.

Dobash, R. Emerson, and Russell Dobash. *Violence against Wives.* New York: Free Press, 1979.

Donaldson, Laura. "Making a Joyful Noise: William Apess and the Search for Postcolonial Method(ism)." Schueller and Watts 29–44.

———. "Son of the Forest, Child of God: William Apess and the Scene of Postcolonial Nativity." *Postcolonial America.* Ed. C. Richard King. Urbana: U of Illinois P, 2000. 201–22.

Du Bois, W. E. B. *Souls of Black Folk.* Chicago: A. C. McClurg & Co., 1903.

Dunn, Mary Maples. "Congregational and Quaker Women in the Early Colonial Period." *Women in American Religion.* Ed. Janet Wilson James. Philadelphia: U of Pennsylvania P, 1980. 27–45.

Early, Samantha Manchester. "Writing from the Center or the Margins? Olaudah Equiano's Writing Reassessed." *African Studies Review* 46.3 (2003): 1–16.

Ebner, Dean. *Autobiography in Seventeenth-Century England: Theology and the Self.* The Hague: Mouton, 1971.

Edkins, Carol. "Quest for Community: Spiritual Autobiographies of Eighteenth-Century Quaker and Puritan Women in America." *Women's Autobiography: Essays in Criticism.* Ed. Estelle C. Jelinek. Bloomington: Indiana UP, 1980.

Edwards, Jonathan. *A Jonathan Edwards Reader.* Ed. John E. Smith et al. New Haven: Yale UP, 1995.

———. *A Faithful Narrative of the Surprising Work of God.* 1737. J. Edwards 57–87.

———. "Personal Narrative." C. 1739. J. Edwards 281–96.

———. *A Treatise concerning Religious Affections.* 1746. J. Edwards 137–71.

Edwards, Paul. "Equiano's Lost Family: 'Master' and 'Father' in *The Interesting Narrative.*" *Slavery and Abolition* 11 (1990): 216–26.

—. *Equiano's Travels: His Autobiography.* Oxford: Heinemann, 1967.

Edwards, Paul, and Rosalind Shaw. "The Invisible *Chi* in Equiano's *Interesting Narrative.*" *Journal of Religion in Africa* 19.2 (1989): 146–56.

Elliott, Emory. *The Cambridge Introduction to Early American Literature.* New York: Cambridge UP, 2002.

Elliott, Michael. "'This Indian Bait': Samson Occom and the Voice of Liminality." *Early American Literature* 29 (1994): 233–251.

Emerson, Ralph Waldo. *Nature. Essays and Lectures.* New York: Library of America, 1982.

Ennis, Daniel J. "Poetry and American Revolutionary Identity: The Case of Phillis Wheatley and John Paul Jones." *Studies in Eighteenth-Century Culture* 31 (2002): 85–98.

Equiano, Olaudah. *The Interesting Narrative of the Life of Olaudah Equiano.* 1789. New York: Penguin, 1995.

Fanon, Frantz. *Black Skin, White Masks.* Trans. Charles Lam Markmann. New York: Grove, 1967.

———. *The Wretched of the Earth.* 1963. Trans. Constance Farrington. New York: Grove, 1968.

Ferguson, Sally Ann. "Christian Violence and the Slave Narrative." *American Literature* 68 (1996): 297–320.

Foster, Frances Smith. "Biblical Tradition." *African American Literature*. Ed. William L. Andrews et al. New York: Oxford UP, 1997.

———. *Written by Herself: Literary Production by African American Women, 1746–1892*. Bloomington: Indiana UP, 1993.

Foster, Hannah Smith. *The Coquette*. 1797. Oxford: Oxford UP, 1987.

Franchot, Jenny. "Invisible Domain: Religion and American Literary Studies." *American Literature* 67 (1995): 833–42.

Gage, Frances. "Reminiscences of Sojourner Truth." *History of Women Suffrage*. Ed. Elizabeth Cady Stanton, Susan B. Anthony, and Matilda J. Gage. Rochester, NY: 1881. 114–17.

Garrett, Clarke. *Spirit Possession and Popular Religion: From the Camisards to the Shakers*. Baltimore: Johns Hopkins UP, 1987.

Gates, Henry Louis, Jr. *Figures in Black: Words, Signs, and the Racial Self*. New York: Oxford UP, 1987.

———. *The Signifying Monkey: A Theory of African-American Literary Criticism*. New York: Oxford UP, 1988.

———. *The Trials of Phillis Wheatley: America's First Black Poet and Encounters with the Founding Fathers*. New York: Civitas, 2003.

Gaul, Theresa Strouth. "Dialogue and Public Discourse in William Apess's *Indian Nullification*." *American Transcendental Quarterly* ns 15 (2001): 275–92.

Gebara, Ivone. "The Face of Transcendence as a Challenge to the Reading of the Bible in Latin America." *Searching the Scriptures*. Ed. Elisabeth Schüssler Fiorenza. New York: Crossroad, 1997. 172–86.

George, Carol V. R. *Segregated Sabbaths: Richard Allen and the Emergence of Independent Black Churches, 1760–1840*. New York: Oxford UP, 1973.

Gilmore, Leigh. *Autobiographics: A Feminist Theory of Women's Self-Representation*. Ithaca: Cornell UP, 1994.

———. *The Limits of Autobiography: Trauma and Testimony*. Ithaca: Cornell UP, 2001.

Girard, Rene. *The Scapegoat*. Trans. Yvonne Freccero. Stanford: Stanford UP, 1986.

———. *Things Hidden since the Foundation of the World*. Trans. Stephen Bann and Michael Metteer. Stanford: Stanford UP, 1987.

———. *Violence and the Sacred*. Trans. Patrick Gregory. Baltimore: Johns Hopkins UP, 1978.

Gordon, Judith S. *Helping Survivors of Domestic Violence: The Effectiveness of Medical, Mental Health, and Community Services*. New York: Garland, 1998.

Grammer, Elizabeth Elkin. *Some Wild Visions: Autobiographies by Female Itinerant Evangelists in Nineteenth-Century America*. New York: Oxford UP, 2003.

Green, Rayna. *Native American Women: A Contextual Bibliography.* Bloomington: Indiana UP, 1983.
Griffiths, Nicholas, and Fernando Cervantes, eds. *Spiritual Encounters: Interactions between Christianity and Native Religions in Colonial America.* Lincoln: U of Nebraska P, 1999.
Grimes, Mary Cochran. "Saving Grace among Puritans and Quakers: A Study of 17th and 18th Century Conversion Experiences." *Quaker History* 72 (1983): 3–26.
Gronniosaw, James Albert Ukawsaw. *A Narrative of the Most Remarkable Particulars in the Life of James Albert Ukawsaw Gronniosaw, an African prince, written by himself.* Newport, RI: 1774.
Gura, Philip. *A Glimpse of Sion's Glory: Puritan Radicalism in New England, 1620–1660.* Middletown, CT: Wesleyan UP, 1984.
———. *Jonathan Edwards: America's Evangelical.* New York: Hill and Wang, 2005.
Gustafson, Sandra. "Jonathan Edwards and the Reconstruction of 'Feminine' Speech." *American Literary History* 6 (1994): 185–212.
Gutiérrez, Gustavo. *A Theology of Liberation: History, Politics, and Salvation.* Maryknoll, NY: Orbis, 1973.
Hall, David D. *Worlds of Wonder, Days of Judgment: Popular Religious Belief in Early New England.* New York: Knopf, 1989.
Hammon, Jupiter. *America's First Negro Poet: The Complete Works of Jupiter Hammon of Long Island.* Ed. and intro. Stanley Austin Ransom Jr. Port Washington, NY: Kennikat, 1970.
Hardesty, Nancy. "Minister as Prophet? Or as Mother?" *Women in New Worlds: Historical Perspectives on the Wesleyan Tradition.* Ed. Hilah F. Thomas and Rosemary Skinner Keller. Nashville: Abingdon, 1981. 88–101.
Harper, Frances Ellen Watkins. *Iola Leroy, or Shadows Uplifted.* 1893. Ed. Frances Smith Foster. Schomburg Library Edition of Nineteenth-Century Black Women Writers. New York: Oxford UP, 1988.
Harris, Sharon M. "Introduction: 'And Their Words Do Follow Them'—The Writings of Early American Women." *American Women Writers to 1800.* New York: Oxford UP, 1996. 3–30.
Hatch, Nathan O. *The Democratization of American Christianity.* New Haven: Yale UP, 1989.
Hawley, John C. ed. *Christian Encounters with the Other.* New York: New York UP, 1998.
Haynes, Carolyn. *Divine Destiny: Gender and Race in Nineteenth-Century Protestantism.* Jackson: UP of Mississippi, 1998.
Hedges, Elaine. "The Nineteenth Century Diarist and Her Quilts." *Feminist Studies* 8.2 (1982): 293–99.

Henderson, Mae. "Speaking in Tongues: Dialogics, Dialectics, and the Black Woman Writer's Literary Tradition." *Changing Our Own Words: Essays on Criticism, Theory, and Writing by Black Women*. New Brunswick, NJ: Rutgers UP, 1989. 16–37.

Irigaray, Luce. *This Sex Which Is Not One*. Trans. Catherine Porter. Ithaca: Cornell UP, 1985.

Isaac, Rhys. *The Transformation of Virginia, 1740–1790*. Chapel Hill: U North Carolina P, 1999.

Isasi-Díaz, Ada María. *Mujerista Theology: A Theology for the Twenty-first Century*. Maryknoll, NY: Orbis, 1996.

JanMohamed, Abdul, and David Lloyd. *The Nature and Context of Minority Discourse*. New York: Oxford UP, 1990.

Jefferson, Thomas. *Writings*. New York: Library of America. 1984.

Johnson, David E., and Scott Michaelsen. "Border Secrets: An Introduction." *Border Theory: The Limits of Cultural Politics*. Ed. David E. Johnson and Scott Michaelsen. Minneapolis: U of Minnesota P, 1997.

Joyner, Charles. "'Believer, I Know': The Emergence of African American Christianity." *African American Christianity: Essays in History*. Ed. Paul E. Johnson. Berkeley: U of California P, 1994. 18–46.

Juster, Susan. *Disorderly Women: Sexual Politics and Evangelicalism in Revolutionary New England*. Ithaca: Cornell UP, 1994.

———. "To Slay the Beast: Visionary Women in the Early Republic." Juster and MacFarlane 19–37.

Juster, Susan, and Lisa MacFarlane. "Introduction: 'A Sperit in de Body.'" *A Mighty Baptism: Race, Gender, and the Creation of American Protestantism*. Ed. Susan Juster and Lisa MacFarlane. Ithaca: Cornell UP, 1996. 1–18.

Kahl, Brigitte. "Toward a Materialist-Feminist Reading." *Searching the Scriptures: A Feminist Introduction*. Ed. Elisabeth Schussler Fiorenza. New York: Crossroad, 1993. 225–40.

Karlsen, Carol F. *The Devil in the Shape of a Woman: Witchcraft in Colonial New England*. New York: Norton, 1987.

Keller, Rosemary Skinner. "New England Women: Ideology and Experience in First Generation Puritanism, 1630–1650." *Women and Religion in America*, Ed. Rosemary Radford Ruether and Rosemary Skinner Keller. Vol. 2. San Francisco: Harper, 1983. 132–44. 3 vols.

King, John O., III. *The Iron of Melancholy: Structures of Spiritual Conversion in America from the Puritan Conscience to Victorian Neurosis*. Middletown, CT: Wesleyan UP, 1983.

Kolodny, Annette. "Among the Indians: The Uses of Captivity." *New York Times Book Review*, 31 Jan. 1993, I 26–29.

———. *The Land Before Her: Fantasy and Experience of the American Frontiers, 1630–1860*. Chapel Hill: U of North Carolina P, 1984.

Konkle, Maureen. *Writing Indian Nations: Native Intellectuals and the Politics of Historiography.* Chapel Hill: U of North Carolina P, 2004.

Krupat, Arnold. *Ethnocriticism: Ethnography, History, Literature.* Berkeley: U of California P, 1992.

———. Introduction. *Native American Autobiography: An Anthology.* Ed. Arnold Krupat. Madison: U of Wisconsin P, 1994. 3–19.

———. "Native American Autobiography and the Synecdochic Self." *American Autobiography: Retrospect and Prospect.* Ed. Paul John Eakin. Madison: U of Wisconsin P, 1991. 171–94.

———. *The Voice in the Margin: Native American Literature and the Canon.* Berkeley: U of California P, 1989.

Lang, Amy Schrager. *Prophetic Women: Anne Hutchinson and the Problem of Dissent in the Literature of New England.* Berkeley: U of California P, 1987.

Lauter, Paul, et al. *Heath Anthology of American Literature.* Lexington: Heath, 1989.

Lee, Jarena. *The Life and Religious Experience of Jarena Lee. Sisters of the Spirit: Three Black Women's Autobiographies of the Nineteenth Century.* Ed. and intro. William L. Andrews. Bloomington: Indiana UP, 1986. 25–48.

Lepore, Jill. *The Name of War: King Philip's War and the Origins of American Identity.* New York: Knopf, 1998.

Leverenz, David. *The Language of Puritan Feeling: An Exploration in Literature, Psychology, and Social History.* New Brunswick, NJ: Rutgers UP, 1980.

Lionnet, Françoise. *Autobiographical Voices: Race, Gender, Self-Portraiture.* Ithaca: Cornell UP, 1989.

Lovejoy, David S. *Religious Enthusiasm in the New World: Heresy to Revolution.* Cambridge: Harvard UP, 1985.

Lyerly, Cynthia Lynn. "Passion, Desire, and Ecstasy: The Experiential Religion of Southern Methodist Women, 1770–1810." *The Devil's Lane: Sex and Race in the Early South.* Ed. Catherine Clinton and Michele Gillespie. New York: Oxford UP, 1997.

Malmsheimer, Lonna M. "Daughters of Zion: New England Roots of American Feminism." *New England Quarterly* 50 (1977): 484–504.

Marrant, John. *A Narrative of the Lord's Wonderful Dealings with John Marrant, a Black, (Now Going to Preach the Gospel in Nova Scotia) Born in New-York, in North America.* 1785. *Black Atlantic Writers of the 18th Century.* Ed. Adam Potkay and Sandra Burr. New York: St. Martin's, 1995. 75–105.

———. *A Journal of the Rev. John Marrant, From August the 18th, 1785, to the 16th of March, 1790. To which are added Two Sermons: One Preached on Ragged Island on Sabbath Day, the 27th Day of October 1787; the Other at Boston in New England, On Thursday, the 24th of June, 1789.* London: 1790.

———. *A Sermon Preached on the 24th Day of June 1789, Being the Festival of Saint John the Baptists, at the Request of the Right Worshipful the Grand Master*

Prince Hall, and the Rest of the Brethren of the African Lodge of the Honorable Society of Free and Accepted Masons in Boston. Boston: 1789.

Marren, Susan M. "Between Slavery and Freedom: The Transgressive Self in Olaudah Equiano's Autobiography." *PMLA* 108 (1993): 94–105.

Massey, Mary E. *Bonnet Brigades.* New York: Knopf, 1966.

Mather, Cotton. *The Negro Christianized.* Boston, 1706.

———. *Rules for the Society of Negroes.* Boston, 1693.

Matsuda, Mari J. "Looking to the Bottom: Critical Legal Studies and Reparations" 22 Harv. C.R.-C.L.L. Rev. 323 (1987).

May, Cedric. "John Marrant and the Narrative Construction of an Early Black Methodist Episcopal." *African American Review* 38 (2004): 553–70.

McCarthy, Keely. "Conversion, Identity, and the Indian Missionary." *Early American Literature* 36 (2001): 353–69.

McKay, Michelle, and William J. Scheick. "The Other Song in Phillis Wheatley's 'On Imagination.'" *Studies in the Literary Imagination* 27 (1994): 71–84.

McKay, Nellie. "Autobiography and the Early Novel." *The Columbia History of the American Novel.* Ed. Emory Elliott. New York: Columbia UP, 1991. 26–45.

McQuaid, Kim. "William Apes, A Pequot: An Indian Reformer in the Jackson Era." *New England Quarterly* 50 (1977): 605–25.

Michaelsen, Scott. *The Limits of Multiculturalism: Interrogating the Origins of American Anthropology.* Minneapolis: U of Minnesota P, 1999.

Mielke, Laura L. "'Native to the Question': William Apess, Black Hawk, and the Sentimental Context of Early Native American Autobiography." *American Indian Quarterly* 26 (2002): 246–70.

Minnick, Wayne C. "The New England Execution Sermon, 1639–1800." *Speech Monographs* 35 (1968): 77–89.

Montgomery, Benilde. "Recapturing John Marrant." *A Mixed Race: Ethnicity in Early America.* Ed. Frank Shuffleton. New York: Oxford UP, 1993.

Moran, Gerald F. "Sisters in Christ: Women and the Church in Seventeenth-Century New England." *Women in American Religion.* Ed. Janet Wilson James. Philadelphia: U of Pennsylvania P, 1980. 45–46.

Morgan, Edmund S. *The Puritan Family: Religion and Domestic Relations in Seventeenth-Century New England.* 1944. New York: Harper, 1966.

Morris, John. *Versions of the Self: Studies in English Autobiography from John Bunyan to John Stuart Mill.* New York: Basic, 1966.

Morse, Samuel. *Foreign Conspiracy Against the Liberties of the United States.* New York: Leavitt, Lord, 1835.

Murphy, Geraldine. "Olaudah Equiano, Accidental Tourist." *Eighteenth-Century Studies* 27 (1994): 551–68.

Murray, David. *Forked Tongues: Speech, Writing and Representation in North American Indian Texts.* Bloomington: Indiana UP, 1991.

Nelson, Dana. "'(I Speak like a Fool but I am Constrained)': Samson Occom's Short Narrative and Economies of the Racial Self." *Early Native American Writing: New Critical Essays*. Ed. Helen Jaskoski. Cambridge: Cambridge UP, 1996. 42–65.

———. "Reading the Written Selves of Colonial America: Franklin, Occom, Equiano, and Palou/Serra." *Resources for American Literary Study* 19 (1993): 246–59.

The New World. Dir. Terrence Malick. Perf. Colin Farrell, Q'Orianka Kilcher, Christopher Plummer, and Christian Bale. New Line Cinema, 2005.

Nielson, Donald. "The Mashpee Revolt of 1833." *New England Quarterly* 58 (1985): 400–20.

Occom, Samson. *A Choice Collection of Hymns and Spiritual Songs*. New London, CT: Press of Thomas and Samuel Green, 1774.

———. *A Sermon Preached at the Execution of Moses Paul, an Indian*. Bennington, VT: William Watson, 1772.

———. "A Short Narrative of My Life." Peyer, *Elders* 12–18.

O'Connell, Barry. Introduction. Apess xii–lxxvii.

Okafor, Clement A. "*The Interesting Narrative of the Life of Oladuah Equiano*: A Triple-Tiered, Trans-Atlantic Testimony." *Literary Griot* 14 (2002): 160–83.

Olsen, Tillie. *Silences*. New York: Delacorte, 1978.

Orban, Katalin. "Dominant and Submerged Discourses in *The Life of Olaudah Equiano*." *African American Review* 27 (1993): 655–65.

Painter, Nell Irvin. *Sojourner Truth: A Life, a Symbol*. New York: Norton, 1996.

Palmer, Phoebe. *The Promise of the Father*. Boston: H.V. Degen, 1859.

Payne, Rodger M. *The Self and the Sacred: Conversion and Autobiography in Early American Protestantism*. Knoxville: U of Tennessee P, 1998.

Peyer, Bernd, ed. *The Elders Wrote: An Anthology of Early Prose by North American Indians, 1768–1931*. Berlin: Reimer, 1982.

———. "Samson Occom: Mohegan Missionary and Writer of the 18th Century." *American Indian Quarterly* 6 (1982): 208–17.

Piggin, Stuart, and Dianne Cook. "Keeping Alive in the Heart and the Head: The Significance of 'Eternal Language' in the Aesthetics of Jonathan Edwards and S. T. Coleridge." *Literature and Theology* 18 (2004): 383–414.

Pleck, Elizabeth. *Domestic Tyranny: The Making of American Social Policy against Family Violence from Colonial Times to the Present*. New York: Oxford UP, 1987.

Porterfield, Amanda. *Female Piety in Puritan New England*. New York: Oxford UP, 1992.

Potkay, Adam. "History, Oratory, and God in Equiano's *Interesting Narrative*." *Eighteenth-Century Studies* 34 (2001): 601–24.

———. Introduction. *Black Atlantic Writers of the 18th Century*. Ed. Adam Potkay and Sandra Burr. New York: St. Martin's, 1995. 1–20.

———. "Olaudah Equiano and the Art of Spiritual Autobiography." *Eighteenth Century Studies* 27 (1994): 677–92.

Potkay, Adam, and Sandra Burr. "About John Marrant." *Black Atlantic Writers of the 18th Century*. Ed. Potkay and Burr. New York: St. Martin's, 1995. 67–74.

Pratt, Mary Louise. *Imperial Eyes: Travel Writing and Transculturation*. London: Routledge, 1992.

Promise Keepers. http://www.promisekeepers.org/ambassadors. 24 April 2007.

Raboteau, Albert J. "African Americans, Exodus, and the American Israel." *African American Christianity: Essays in History*. Ed. Paul E. Johnson. Berkeley: U of California P, 1994. 1–17.

Renza, Louis. "The Veto of the Imagination: A Theory of Autobiography." *Autobiography: Essays Theoretical and Critical*. Ed. James Olney. Princeton: Princeton UP, 1980. 268–95.

———. *"A White Heron" and the Question of Minor Literature*. Madison: U of Wisconsin P, 1984.

Renzetti, Claire M., Jeffrey L. Edleson, and Raquel Kennedy Bergen. *The Sourcebook on Violence against Women*. Thousand Oaks, CA: Sage, 2001.

Richards, Jeffrey H. "Religion, Race, Literature, and Eighteenth-Century America." *American Literary History* 5 (1993): 578–87.

Richardson, Leon Burr. *An Indian Preacher in England*. Dartmouth Coll. Manuscript Ser. 2. Hanover, NH: Dartmouth Coll., 1933.

Richter, Daniel K. *Facing East from Indian Country: A Native History of Early America*. Cambridge: Harvard UP, 2001.

Rogal, Samuel. "Phillis Wheatley's Methodist Connection." *Black American Literature Forum* 21 (1987): 85–95.

Rowlandson, Mary. *The Soveraignty and the Goodness of God, Together With the Faithfulness of His Promises Displayed; Being a Narrative of the Captivity and Restauration of Mrs. Rowlandson*. Boston, 1682.

Rowson, Susanna. *Charlotte Temple*. 1794. Oxford: Oxford UP, 1987.

Roy, Maria, ed. *The Abusive Partner: An Analysis of Domestic Battering*. New York: Van Nostrand, 1982.

Ruether, Rosemary Radford. *Women and Redemption: A Theological History*. Minneapolis, MN: Fortress, 1998.

Ruoff, A. LaVonne Brown. *American Indian Literatures: An Introduction, Bibliographic Review, and Selected Bibliography*. New York: MLA, 1990.

———. "Three Nineteenth-Century American Indian Autobiographers." *Redefining American Literary History*. Ed. A. LaVonne Brown Ruoff and Jerry Ward Jr. New York: MLA, 1990. 251–69.

Rust, Marion. "The Subaltern as Imperialist: Speaking of Olaudah Equiano." *Passing and the Fictions of Identity*. Ed. Elaine K. Ginsberg. Durham, NC: Duke UP, 1996.

Ryken, Leland, et al. *Dictionary of Biblical Imagery*. Downers Grove, IL: InterVarsity, 1998.

Sabino, Robin, and Jennifer Hall. "The Path Not Taken: Cultural Identity in the *Interesting Life* of Olaudah Equiano." *MELUS* 24 (1999): 5–19.

Sáenz, Benjamin Alire. "In the Borderlands of Chicano Identity, There Are Only Fragments." *Border Theory: The Limits of Cultural Politics*. Ed. Scott Michaelsen and David E. Johnson. Minneapolis: U of Minnesota P, 1997. 68–96.

Saffin, John. *A Brief and Candid Answer to a Late Printed Sheet, Entitled, The Selling of Joseph*. Boston, 1701.

Saillant, John. "'Remarkably Emancipated from Bondage, Slavery, and Death': An African American Retelling of the Puritan Captivity Narrative, 1820." *Early American Literature* 29 (1994): 122–40.

Samuels, Wilfred D. "The Disguised Voice in *The Interesting Narrative of Olaudah Equiano*." *Black American Literature Forum* 19 (1985): 64–69.

Sandiford, Keith. *Measuring the Moment: Strategies of Protest in Eighteenth Century Afro-English Writing*. London: Associated UP, 1988.

Sayre, Gordon. "Defying Assimilation, Confounding Authenticity: The Case of William Apess." *Auto/Biography Studies* 11 (1996): 1–18.

Sayre, Robert. "Autobiography and the Making of America." *Autobiography: Essays Theoretical and Critical*. Ed. James Olney. Princeton: Princeton UP, 1980. 146–68.

Scheick, William J. "Logonomic Conflict in Anne Bradstreet's 'A Letter to Her Husband.'" *Essays in Literature* 21 (1994): 166–84.

———. *The Writings of Jonathan Edwards: Theme, Motif, and Style*. College Station: Texas A&M UP, 1975.

Schlenther, Boyd Stanley. *Queen of the Methodists: The Countess of Huntingdon and the Eighteenth-Century Crisis of Faith and Society*. Bishop Auckland, UK: Durham Academic P, 1997.

Schueller, Malini Johar, and Edward Watts, eds. *Messy Beginnings: Postcoloniality and Early American Studies*. New Brunswick, NJ: Rutgers UP, 2003.

Sekora, John. "Red, White, and Black: Indian Captivities, Colonial Printers, and the Early African-American Narrative." *A Mixed Race: Ethnicity in Early America*. Ed. Frank Shuffleton. New York: Oxford UP, 1993.

Sewall, Samuel. *The Selling of Joseph*. Boston, 1700.

Shea, Daniel B., Jr. "The Art and Instruction of Jonathan Edwards' *Personal Narrative*." *The American Puritan Imagination*. Ed. Sacvan Bercovitch. New York: Cambridge UP, 1974. 159–172.

———. "The Prehistory of American Autobiography." *American Autobiography: Retrospect and Prospect*. Ed. Paul John Eakin. Madison: U of Wisconsin P, 1991. 25–46.

———. *Spiritual Autobiography in Early America*. 1968. Madison: U of Wisconsin P, 1988.

Showalter, Elaine. *Sister's Choice*. Oxford: Clarendon, 1991.
Slotkin, Richard. *Regeneration through Violence: The Mythology of the American Frontier, 1600–1800*. Middleton, CT: Weslyan UP, 1973.
Slotkin, Richard, and James K. Folsom. *So Dreadful a Judgment: Puritan Responses to King Philip's War, 1676–1677*. Middleton, CT: Weslyan UP, 1978.
Smith, John. *The General History of Virginia*. 1624.
Smith, Sidonie, and Julia Watson, eds. *Women, Autobiography, Theory: A Reader*. Madison: U of Wisconsin Press, 1998.
Smith, Theophus H. *Conjuring Culture: Biblical Formations of Black America*. New York: Oxford UP, 1994.
Smith, Valerie. *Self-Discovery and Authority in Afro-American Narrative: Original Essays in Criticism and Theory*. Cambridge: Harvard UP, 1987.
Smith-Rosenberg, Carroll. "Domesticating 'Virtue': Coquettes and Revolutionaries in Young America." *Literature and the Body: Essays on Populations and Persons*. Ed. Elaine Scarry. Baltimore: Johns Hopkins UP, 1988. 160–83.
Stevens, Scott Manning. "William Apess's Historical Self." *Northwest Review* 35 (1997): 67–84.
Stout, Harry S. *The New England Soul: Preaching and Religious Culture in Colonial New England*. New York: Oxford UP, 1986.
Stowe, Harriet Beecher. *The Minister's Wooing*. Hartford, CT: Stowe-Day Foundation, 1978.
———. *Oldtown Folks*. Ed. Dorothy Berkson. New Brunswick, NJ: Rutgers UP, 1987.
Taves, Ann. *Fits, Trances, and Visions: Experiencing Religion and Explaining Experience from Wesley to James*. Princeton: Princeton UP, 1999.
———. Introduction. *Religion and Domestic Violence in Early New England: The Memoirs of Abigail Abbot Bailey*. Ed. Taves. Bloomington: Indiana UP, 1989. 1–49.
Tenney, Tabitha Gilman. *Female Quixotism*. 1801. Oxford: Oxford UP, 1992.
Thomas, Helen. *Romanticism and Slave Narratives: Transatlantic Testimonies*. Cambridge: Cambridge UP, 2000.
Tiro, Karim M. "Denominated 'SAVAGE': Methodism, Writing, and Identity in the Works of William Apess, a Pequot." *American Quarterly* 48 (1996): 653–79.
Tyson, John R. "Lady Huntingdon's Reformation." *Church History* 64 (1995): 580–93.
———. "'A Poor, Vile Sinner': Lady Huntingdon's Vocabulary of Weakness and Deference." *Methodist History* 37 (1999): 107–18.
Ulrich, Laurel Thatcher. *Good Wives: Image and Reality in the Lives of Puritan Women in Northern New England, 1650–1750*. New York: Oxford UP, 1980.

VanDerBeets, Richard, ed. *Held Captive by Indians: Selected Narratives, 1642–1836*. Knoxville: U of Tennessee P, 1994.

Van Lonkhuyzen, Harold W. "A Reappraisal of the Praying Indians: Acculturation, Conversion, and Identity at Natick, Massachusetts, 1646–1730." *New England Quarterly* 63 (1990): 396–428.

Vaughan, Alden T., and Edward W. Clark, eds. *Puritans among the Indians: Accounts of Captivity and Redemption, 1676–1724*. Cambridge: Harvard UP, 1981.

Velikova, Roumiana. "'Philip, King of the Pequots': The History of an Error." *Early American Literature* 37 (2002): 311–36.

Viswanathan, Gauri. *Outside the Fold: Conversion, Modernity, and Belief*. Princeton: Princeton UP, 1998.

Vogel, Todd. *Rewriting White: Race, Class, and Cultural Capital in Nineteenth-Century America*. New Brunswick, NJ: Rutgers UP, 2004.

Waldstreicher, David. *In the Midst of Perpetual Fetes: The Making of American Nationalism, 1776–1820*. Chapel Hill: U of North Carolina P, 1997.

Walker, Alice. *In Search of Our Mothers' Gardens*. New York: Harcourt, 1983.

Warrior, Robert Allen. *The People and the Word: Reading Native Non-Fiction*. Minneapolis: U of Minnesota P, 2005.

———. *Tribal Secrets: Recovering American Indian Intellecual Traditions*. Minneapolis: U of Minnesota P, 1995.

Watson, John Fanning. *Methodist Error; or, Friendly Christian Advice to those Methodists who indulge in extravagant emotions and bodily exercises*. Trenton, NJ, 1819.

Weaver, Jace. "From I-Hermeneutics to We-Hermeneutics: Native Americans and the Post-Colonial." *Native American Religious Identity: Unforgotten Gods*. Ed. Jace Weaver. Maryknoll, NY: Orbis, 1998. 1–25.

Weber, Donald. *Rhetoric and History in Revolutionary New England*. New York: Oxford UP, 1988.

Weinstein, Laurie. "Samson Occom: A Charismatic Eighteenth-Century Mohegan Leader." *Enduring Traditions: The Native Peoples of New England*. Ed. Laurie Weinstein. Westport, CT: Bergin, 1994. 91–102.

Welch, Edwin. *Spiritual Pilgrim: A Reassessment of the Life of the Countess of Huntingdon*. Cardiff: U of Wales P, 1995.

Wheatley, Phillis. *Complete Writings*. Ed. Vincent Carretta. New York: Penguin, 2001.

Willard, Carla. "Wheatley's Turns of Praise: Heroic Entrapment and the Paradox of Revolution." *American Litrature* 67 (1995): 233–56.

Willard, Frances. *Woman in the Pulpit*. Boston: Linthrop, 1888.

Williams, Delores S. *Sisters in the Wilderness: The Challenge of Womanist God-Talk*. Maryknoll, NY: Orbis, 1993.

Williams, James G. "The Innocent Victim: Rene Girard on Violence, Sacrifice, and the Sacred." *Religious Studies Review* 14 (1988): 320–26.

Wood, Forrest G. *The Arrogance of Faith: Christianity and Race in America from the Colonial Era to the Twentieth Century.* New York: Knopf, 1990.

Woolman, John. *The Journal and Major Essays of John Woolman.* Ed. Phillips P. Moulton. New York: Oxford UP, 1971.

Wyss, Hilary E. *Writing Indians: Literacy, Christianity, and Native Community in Early America.* Amherst: U of Massachusetts P, 2000.

Zafar, Rafia. *We Wear the Mask: African Americans Write American Literature, 1760–1870.* New York: Columbia UP, 1997.

INDEX

abolition, 6, 191n. 3
acculturation, 13, 61
Acts of Apostles: Equiano's use of, 68, 70–72; Pentecost story in, 124
African American Christianity, 118; characteristics of, 43
African Americans, 5; acculturation process and, 13, 61; biblical typology in literature of, 196n. 7; direct knowledge of Bible as primary motive for literacy among, 178; early life-writing of, 12–13; loyalists, Nova Scotia settlement, 41, 59; Talking Book motif in tradition of, 79–81; Whitefield's influence on black Atlantic writing, 7; womanist theologians within community, 17–18. *See also* Equiano, Olaudah; Lee, Jarena; Marrant, John; slavery
African Methodist Episcopal (AME) church, 118, 196n. 1, 197n. 12; Book Concern rejection of Lee's manuscript, 119–20; as revivalist congregation with focus on experience, 125
agency: American concept of, 187n. 1; Bailey's development of, 88, 89, 101, 102–3, 108–14, 181; human, Moses as example of, 77–78; from inclusion of the marginalized in revivalist religion, 182; Lee's sense of, 134–36, 144–45; power of faith to accomplish the extraordinary, 141
Albanese, Catherine, 93, 98, 185
alcoholism, Indian, 154, 155, 156, 157
Aldridge, William, 38, 41, 42, 45, 59; preface to Marrant's *Narrative*, 43, 44, 49–50
Allen, Richard, 118–19, 120, 130, 133, 134; Lee's refutation of prohibition of, 117, 139–44; views on women's ordination in context of Methodist doctrine and practice, 196n. 1

American Lazarus (Brooks), 188n. 8
American Literature (journal), 17
American Puritan conversion narrative, 12
American Tract Society, 138
Andrews, William L., 12–13, 63, 66, 119, 135, 196n. 1, 196n. 2
Anglo-American experience, assumption of superiority in, 37
anti-Catholic sensibilities, 127–28
Anzaldúa, Gloria, 39, 40
Apess, William, 2, 6, 19, 34, 48, 60, 89, 113, 115, 146–70, 178, 180, 198n. 10; abandonment and isolation felt by, 147, 155, 163, 164, 165–67; acknowledgment of his own race hatred, 152, 155; alternative sense of authority of, 149; authorial control of, 13; brief biography of, 147–48; childhood terror of his own people, 167–68; Christian Pequotism presented by, 162; family of origin, 154–55, 156, 158–59, 163, 166, 168; fear and hatred of European Americans, 168; with Furman family, 154–55, 162, 163, 164–66; integration into white culture, 152, 159, 163–66; Mashpee Revolt and, 148, 161–62, 198n. 4; Methodism of, 147–48, 152, 161, 168, 170, 197n. 1, 199n. 16; Pequot identity and self-determination reaffirmed by, 162, 163–65, 170; primary source of spiritual difficulty for, 168–69; provocation of social critique in, 182; published writings of, 149; on race-consciousness, 150–51; racial identity, pivotal moment in concept of, 154–56. See also *Son of the Forest, A* (Apess)
Aquino, María Pilar, 17, 120
Ashwill, Gary, 161
assimilation, 9, 150, 162, 197n. 1

Augustine, 137
authorial control, issue of, 13
authority: experience of, as transformative, 181; revivalism and challenge to hierarchies of, 4; sense of personal, by way of textual construction, 12. *See also* preaching/preachers, ministers/ministerial authority
autobiographical negotiation between speaker, subject, and their shared yet distinct identities, 151
autobiography studies, burgeoning field of, 187n. 7, 188n. 8
Axtell, James, 29

Bailey, Abigail Abbot, 2, 6, 19, 85–116, 147, 178; agency, development of, 88, 89, 101, 102–3, 108–14, 181; authorial control of, 13; brief biography of, 89–90; differences between more clearly dissident writers and, 114–16; disapproval of emerging unaffiliated or newly affiliated revivalist congregations, 114; discontinuous voice of, 11; divorce and property settlement, 110, 194n. 4; evangelical awakening or rebirth of, 86–87; historical context of religious perspective, 89–90; ideological and personal isolation of, 115–16; inability to comprehend nonspiritual meaning of her experience, 114–15; life after divorce, 111–12, 195n. 11; ministerial self, emerging sense of, 106, 111–14; preoccupation with sovereignty of God, 86, 93–94, 102, 103; private, spiritual experience of oppression, 87–88; progress in making decisions concerning material circumstances, 108–9; provocation of social critique in, 182; religious ecstasy, experiences of and retreat into, 96–98; significance of pulpit to, 181; turning points in transformation of, 100–103, 109–11. See also *Memoirs of Abigail Abbot Bailey* (Bailey)
Bailey, Asa, 90, 91, 103; Abigail's view of, 103–4; abuse of daughter, 90, 95, 96–101; fate of, 195n. 11; response to Abigail's divorce and property settlement actions, 110

Bailey, Phebe, 90; Abigail's realization of effects of Asa's violence on, 100–101; father's sexual abuse/rape of, 90, 95, 96–101
Bailey, Phineas, 194n. 5, 195n. 11
Balkun, Mary McAleer, 199n. 4
baptism, 7, 134–35
Baraka, Amiri, 175
Bassard, Katherine Clay, 17, 61, 188n. 8
Bednarowski, Mary, 18
Benezet, Anthony, 192
Bethel Church (Philadelphia), 118, 119, 125
Bhabha, Homi, 147
biblical narrative, autobiographical speaker's understanding of his or her life as, 181
biblical typology, 196n. 7
Black, Daniel, 199n. 4
Black Arts Movement, 175
Black Skin White Mask (Fanon), 9
Blackwell, Antoinette, 197n. 12
Block, James, 187n. 1
Blodgett, Harold, 23, 24, 25
Bonino, José Míguez, 18
Borderlands/La Frontera (Anzaldúa), 39, 40
border theory, writers identified with, 39–40
boundary space, notion of, 10
Bradford, William, 185
Bradstreet, Anne, 85, 195n. 10
Braude, Anne, 92
Brekus, Catherine, 119
Brooks, Joanna, 16, 17, 34–35, 187n. 4, 188n. 8, 190n. 14, 191n. 3
Brothertown community of Christian Indians, 23, 35
Brown, Irene Quenzler, 194n. 2
Brown, Richard D., 194n. 2
Bruce, Dickson, 198n. 8
Burr, Sandra, 7, 38, 44, 45, 59, 190n. 2
Butler, Jon, 4, 187n. 5
Byrd, William, 36

Caldwell, Patricia, 12
Caldwell, Tanya, 192n. 4, 193
Calvinism, 89; covenantal theology, 110; preoccupation with sovereignty, 36; sense of total human depravity in, 107

Index

Campisi, Jack, 198n. 3
camp-meeting tradition, 125, 147, 148, 152, 166
Cannon, Katie, 17–18, 120
captivity narrative genre, 38–39, 190n. 1, 195n. 12; attempts to make spiritual sense of violence in, 85–86; Indian violence typically portrayed in, 47–48; of Pocahontas and John Smith, 54–55; reevaluations of spirituality as feature of, 109. *See also* Marrant, John
Carlson, David, 148, 161, 189n. 6, 198n. 4
Carretta, Vincent, 7, 63, 64, 65, 178, 191n. 2, 191n. 3, 191n. 5, 192n. 3, 192n. 8, 193n. 10, 193n. 14, 193n. 17, 199n. 3, 200n. 5
Carter, Landon, 36
Casmier-Paz, Lynn, 192n. 8
Catholicism: liberation theologies in Latin American Roman Catholic Church, 18; Protestant American opposition to, 127–28, 140–41, 180, 196n. 9
Charlotte Temple (Rowson), 127
Chauncy, Charles, 98, 195n. 8
Cherokees, Marrant's encounter with, 41, 51–57
Chinosole, 191n. 1
Choice Collection of Hymns and Spiritual Songs, A (Occom), 190n. 14
Christian aggression, social and spiritual effects of, 48. *See also* violence
Christian Encounters with the Other (Hawley), 189n. 6
Christianity: Christian Pequotism of Apess, 162; early American Protestantism, 7, 185–86; evangelical, contradictions of near contemporary expressions of, 8; historical legacy of, featuring those outside of/opposed to established systems of religious and political authority, 71–72; patriarchal nature of, 92–93
Christian Pequotism, 162
"Christian Problem," "Indian Problem" as, 169
Clelland, Robert, 23, 24
Collins, Patricia, 181

colonizer, Equiano's participation as, 80–82
Columbus, Equiano's modeling of self after, 80, 82
commitment to Christian self-effacement, 12
Conforti, Joseph, 137–38
"contact zone," 9
contradictions between dominant group's actions and ideologies, autobiographical speakers' view of, 181
conversion, Christian: African American, facile dismissal as acculturation, 61; of Apess, 151–52; of Lee, 118, 129–31, 135; of Marrant, 41, 43; of Occom, 29; viewed as death and rebirth, 50
"Conversion, Identity, and the Indian Missionary" (McCarthy), 189n. 6
conversion narrative(s), 187n. 7; American Puritan, 12; Equiano's *Interesting Narrative* as, 65; as first 'democratic' forms of literature, 179; self-construction in context of awareness of flawed external social world, 180
Coquette, The (Foster), 127
Corinthians, Paul's second letter to, 30
Costanzo, Angelo, 63, 192n. 5
Countess of Huntingdon's Connexion, 42. *See also* Hastings, Selina (Countess of Huntingdon)
covenantal theology, 93, 194n. 4, 195n. 7
Critical Race Theory, 184
cross-cultural contact. *See* multicultural contact
crucifixion of Jesus, 55–58, 104
Cugoano, Ottobah, 193n. 15
"cultural knots," 40

Daniels, Christine, 194n. 2
Daniel story, Bailey's selective use of, 105
Dannenberg, Anne, 146
Dartmouth College, 21, 23, 24, 30
Davidson, Cathy, 196n. 8
deaths, attempts to make spiritual sense of untimely, 85
Deloria, Vine, 150
democratic theological inclinations, autobiographical writing as extension of, 179

Derounian-Stodola, Kathryn Zabelle, 195
Descartes, René, 174
diary genre, 11
discontinuous voice, 11
discours décousu, 10–11
discursive form of writing, 11
dissent: Protestant tradition of, 7–8; Puritan zero-tolerance policy on, 37
divine power: in face of apparent human impossibility, 141, 142; God's working in miraculous ways with and through woman, 142. *See also* Holy Spirit
domestic violence, 194n. 2; Bailey's *Memoirs* recounting, 85–116. *See also* Bailey, Abigail Abbot
domination, consequence of, in contemporary minority discourse, 9–10
Donaldson, Laura, 147, 161, 199n. 16
drunken Indian stereotype, 189n. 4
dual perspective, acculturation process and, 13
Du Bois, W. E. B., 13, 149
Dunn, Mary Maples, 92
Dwight, Timothy, 189n. 4

early American Protestantism: changed religion of writers from margins, 185–86; contradictory strains of liberation and oppression in, 7; traditional representatives of, 185, 186
Ebo and Hebrew biblical culture, Equiano's parallels between, 67–68, 192n. 7
editions: of Apess's *Son of the Forest*, 149, 197n. 1; of Bailey's *Memoirs*, 91; of Equiano's *Narrative*, 68, 192n. 3, 192n. 8, 193n. 15; of Lee's *Life and Experiences*, 119-20, 135, 196n. 5; of Marrant's *Narrative*, 13, 41, 44-46, 55, 59, 60, 191n. 5
Edkins, Carol, 187n. 7
Edwards, Jonathan, 4, 22, 25–28, 30, 36, 109, 185, 189n. 9, 189n. 10, 195n. 8; interior landscape of, 138–39; Lee's connection to, 137–39; popularity among revivalists of, 137–38
Edwards, Paul, 193n. 15
egalitarian social order: revivalism and loosening of roles, 5; work of Holy Spirit and, 124, 131, 144

Eli and Samuel, story of, 104
Elijah, Equiano's linking of manumission with entrance into heaven of, 73–75, 193n. 13
Elizabeth, miraculous pregnancy of, 142–43
Elliott, Michael, 29, 30, 31, 188n. 1, 189n. 4, 190n. 13
Emerson, Ralph Waldo, 27
empowerment: of "divergent" individuals existing in boundary spaces, 10; from traditions that silence, 8. *See also* agency
Ennis, Daniel, 199n. 4
Equiano, Olaudah, 2, 6, 19, 44, 60, 62–84, 105, 115, 120, 152, 153, 161, 175, 178, 180, 191n. 1, 193n. 11; authorial control of, 13; biography of, 192n. 3; as Christian colonizer, attempt to act as, 80–82; Christianity as central to conception and presentation of himself, 65, 192n. 4; complex sense of his own identity, 79, 80–83; conflicted political stance regarding slavery, 63–64, 71–72, 79; contradictory viewpoints of, 64; conversion to abolition, 191n. 3; internal contradiction of personal piety amidst violence of slave masters, 78–79; manumission, 72–75, 193n. 12; material experiences with Christians shaping Christianity of, 64–65, 83; modeling self after Columbus, 80, 82; provocation of social critique in, 182; as purchaser and overseer of slaves after manumission, 79; reenslavement, resistance to, 78–79, 81–82; rejection of theology of divine authorship of suffering, 182–83; violence of slavery as easy identifier of hypocritical religion for, 183; Whitefield heard by, 70, 193n. 10. *See also Interesting Narrative of Life of Olaudah Equiano* (Equiano), religious authority in
ethical beliefs, as inextricable part of African American Christianity, 43
Eulogy on King Philip (Apess), 149
exclusion, provocation of social critique by, 182

execution sermon, 21, 188n. 1
Exodus: Bailey's focus on submission in reading of, 105; Moses story in, Equiano's use of, 76–78; Wheatley's reference to, in letter to Occom, 176
Experiences of Five Christian Indians, The (Apess), 148, 149
experiential religion/theology, 120, 149; recurring significance of, 6; revivalism and primacy of, 4

Faithful Narrative of Surprising Work of God (Edwards), 189n. 10
Fanon, Frantz, 9
Female Quixotism (Tenney), 127
feminist theologians, Lee's theology anticipating, 143–44
Ferguson, Sally Ann, 191n. 1
forest as location for mythic representations of Indians, 160. See also *Son of the Forest, A* (Apess)
Foster, Frances Smith, 196n. 4, 199n. 1
Foster, Hannah Smith, 127
Franchot, Jenny, 17
freedom, Wheatley on, 175–76

Gage, Frances, 143, 197n. 11
Gates, Henry Louis, 79, 172, 174
Gaul, Theresa, 198n. 6
Gebara, Ivone, 143
gender: experience of Christianity as outsider due to, 2, 3, 6; hierarchies, patriarchal nature of Christianity and, 92–93. See also Bailey, Abigail Abbot; Lee, Jarena; Wheatley, Phillis
George, Aunt Sally, 148, 198n. 3
George, Carol V. R., 196n. 1
Gilmore, Leigh, 13–14
Girard, Rene, 99–100, 191n. 8, 195n. 9
Golden Rule, 65; Apess's exposés of Christians overlooking, 152; Equiano's condemnation of slavery as incompatible with, 65
Gospel of Luke: Equiano's use of, 75–76; nativity account in, Lee's use of, 142–43
Grammer, Elizabeth, 196n. 4
Great Awakening, 3–5, 25, 187n. 3, 187n. 5; disorderliness and multiple dislocations of, 4–5; emphasis on experience, 180; endorsement of "priesthood of all believers," 180–81; New Lights vs. Old Lights, 89–90, 98; religious climate of, 29. See also Edwards, Jonathan; Occom, Samson
Green, Rayna, 161
Gronniosaw, James, 79, 193n. 15–16
Gross, Seymour L., 175
Gura, Philip, 138
Gutiérrez, Gustavo, 18

Hall, Jennifer, 191n. 1
Hall, Prince, 41–42, 191n. 2
Hammon, Briton, 190n. 1
Hammon, Jupiter, 123
Hanging of Ephraim Wheeler, The (Brown and Brown), 194n. 2
Hardesty, Nancy, 197n. 12
hardship. See suffering
Harper, Frances Ellen Watkins, 15
Harris, Sharon, 10–11
Hastings, Selina (Countess of Huntingdon), 6, 41, 42, 46, 172, 191n. 3
Hatch, Nathan O., 7
Hawley, John, 189n. 6
Haynes, Carolyn, 161, 198n. 2, 198n. 3, 198n. 8, 199n. 16
Heath Anthology of American Literature, 197n. 1
Henderson, Mae, 122–23
hermeneutical sovereignty, 34
Holiness movement, 125
Holy Spirit: egalitarian quality of work of, 124, 131, 144; human speech as realm of, 118; manifestations of divine power with arrival of, 124, 125
human agency, Moses as example of, 77–78
Hume, David, 174
Huntingdon, Selina Hastings, Countess of, 6, 41, 42, 46, 172, 191n. 3
Hurston, Zora Neale, 18, 193n. 15
Hutchinson, Anne, 7, 8, 36
hymns, 14, 123, 188n. 8, 190n. 14

identity, religion/religious discourse as source of, 16
impossibility: divine power overcoming, 141, 142; notion of human, 141; power of faith over, 141

incest: as form of adultery rather than child abuse, 98; historical context of, 98–99; Phebe Bailey's sexual abuse/rape by father, 90, 95, 96–101. *See also* rape; sexual violence
Increase of Kingdom of Christ, The (Apess), 149
Indian captivity narratives. *See* captivity narrative genre
Indian Charity School, 189n. 2
Indian Nullification of Unconstitutional Laws of Massachusetts (Apess), 149, 198n. 6
"Indian Problem," as "Christian Problem," 169
Indian removal, U.S. national policy of, 6, 148–49, 150
Indians: The Ten Lost Tribes, The (Apess), 149
"Indian's Looking Glass for White Man, An" (Apess), 149, 152, 161
injustice: acquiescence as Christian virtue in face of, 76; biblical violence in response to, 77; Christian readers required to identify with victims of, 183; racial, Marrant's concern with, 42–43, 45–46; Wheatley's letter to Occom articulating, 175–76
In Search of Our Mothers' Gardens (Walker), 175
intellectual resistance, Native American, 197n. 1
intellectual sovereignty, 34, 162
Interesting Narrative of Life of Olaudah Equiano (Equiano), religious authority in, 62–84: authorial imperative in, 62; biblical literature of social justice used in, 75–76; biblical reference points on frontispiece and title page of, 68–72; challenge to readers' unexamined presumptions about race, 123; conflating spiritual liberation with liberation from slavery, 74; as conversion narrative, 65; descriptions of Africa and Africans, 66–68; Elijah story in, 73–75, 193n. 13; historical legacy of Christianity featuring outsiders highlighted in, 70–72; horrific experience and exploitation chronicled in, 75–76; manumission, biblical references used in account of, 72–75; Moses story in, 76–78; paradoxical imperatives in, 62; political protest woven into biblical parallels throughout, 75; portrait, evolution in early to late editions of, 192n. 8; religious vision in, 84; return to trope of Talking Book in, 79–81; the self presented in, 63, 65; strategic appeals to audience on basis of scriptural text and metaphor, 65–66. *See also* Equiano, Olaudah
intertextuality, 54, 79, 89, 129, 178
Iola Leroy (Harper), 15
Irigaray, Luce, 11
irony of spiritual liberation and racial oppression, Wheatley on, 175–76
Isaac, Rhys, 4
Isaiah, Equiano's use of book of, 68–70, 75–76
Isasi-Díaz, Ada María, 17, 120
Issaka, 192n. 7

Jackson, Andrew, 149, 150
JanMohamed, Abdul, 9–10, 147
Jefferson, Thomas, 6, 174–75
Jenkins, Mr. (plantation owner), 58
Jenkins, Mrs. (plantation owner's wife), 56–58
Jesus, crucifixion of, 55–58, 104
Jewett, David, 23–24
Jews, Equiano's parallels between Ebo culture and culture of, 67–68
Joel, Lee's use of passage from prophet, 123, 124
John of the Cross, 137
Johnson, David E., 40
Jones, Absalom, 118
Journal (Woolman), 14–15
Joyner, Charles, 43
Julian of Norwich, 137
Juster, Susan, 3, 4, 136, 187, 187n. 2
justice: biblical literature of social, 75–76; call for this-worldly, 181; Moses story and, 76–78; theological arguments insisting on, 18

Kahl, Brigitte, 142
Kant, Immanuel, 174
Kennedy, Michael V., 194n. 2

Index

Kibbey, Ann, 136
King, Martin Luther, Jr., 2
Know-Nothings party, 127
Konkle, Maureen, 197n. 1, 198n. 5, 198n. 9, 198n. 11
Krupat, Arnold, 36, 161, 198n. 12

language, Protestantism's emphasis on, 179
Latina community, *mujerista* theologians within, 17, 120
Latin American Roman Catholic Church, liberation theologies in, 18
Lee, Jarena, 2, 6, 48, 86, 87, 89, 114, 115, 116, 117–45, 168, 178, 180; Allen's decision to approve call to preach, 134, 196n. 1; antihierarchical Christianity experienced and preached by, 134; argument for women in public ministry, 132, 140–44; authorial control of, 12–13; brief biography of, 118–20; call to preach, 117, 118–19, 123–25, 131–36; cause of ministerial vocation/compulsion to speak, 130–32; connection to Edwards, 137–39; conversion experience of, 118, 129–31, 135; double outsider status of, 123, 126, 145; effectiveness as preacher, 134; proclamation on behalf of women's rights to public speech, 118; provocation of social critique in, 182; resistance to masculine prohibitions, 117, 139–44; sense of her audience, 145; sense of personal agency, 134–36, 144–45; suicidal thoughts, 137, 138, 139. *See also Life and Religious Experience of Jarena Lee, a Coloured Lady, Giving an Account of Her Call to Preach the Gospel* (Lee)
Lentz, Susan, 194n. 2, 194n. 4
Leverenz, David, 93
liberation, Equiano's account of, 72–75
liberation theologies, 18
liberatory Christianity, nativity account in Gospel of Luke as argument for, 142–43
"Liberty and Peace" (Wheatley), 175
Life and Religious Experience of Jarena Lee, a Coloured Lady, Giving an Account of Her Call to Preach the Gospel (Lee), 119–20: Allen's prohibition of women preaching, 139–40; antibiblical Roman Catholic woman in, 126, 127; baptism, account of, 134–35; call to preach in, 131–36; call to preach in, biblical text providing divine legitimation of, 123–25; church's validation of Lee's preaching, 134; complex, deflected sense of agency in, 134–36; conversion, 129–31, 135; difficulty in realizing call in, 126; dramatic conflicts between good and evil in, 137–40; emphasis on voices, actual sound, audibility, and even volume in, 136; epigraph from Book of Joel, 122–25; male ministerial failure/silence as context and provocation for Lee's ministerial work, 131–32; "My Marriage" section, 128–29; pictorial representation of writer in, 120–22; presenting herself as illustration of Jonah text, 132–34; soul as agent in, 130–31; structure of text, 128; "testimonial/familial" and "competitive/public" means of discourse in, 123; theological argument for allowing women to preach in, 140–44; title page, 122. *See also* Lee, Jarena
Lionnet, Françoise, 10, 117, 149
literacy, conversion to Christianity and, 23, 29, 178, 189n. 7
literary critics, postmodern discomfort with earnest religious expression of, 16–17
Lloyd, David, 10, 147
looking glass in argumentative rhetoric, uses of, 198n. 9. *See also* "Indian's Looking Glass for White Man, An" (Apess)
loudness as characteristic of revivalist religious communities, 136
Lovejoy, David S., 5
Luke, Gospel of, 75–76, 142–43

McCarthy, Keely, 189n. 6, 190n. 12
McKay, Nellie, 190n. 1
McQuaid, Kim, 198n. 5
Magdalene, Mary, 143–44
male authorial privilege, 123
Malik, Terrence, 54

manumission of Equiano, biblical references used in account of, 72–75
Margate, David, 42, 52
Marrant, John, 2, 6, 19, 38–61, 115, 160, 178, 180; apologetic for Indian hostility, 183; authorial control of, 13; boundary-crossing by, 43–45; brief biography, 41–42; conception of God, 52; concern with racial injustice, 42–43, 45–46; conversion experience, 41, 43; encounter with Cherokee, 41, 51–57; familial violence faced by, 44, 46–47, 55; identification with messianic Jesus, 51; on Indian receptivity to Christianity, 47, 48, 59; male authorial privilege, 123; multiple selves and subjectivities experienced by, 39, 40, 44; ordination in England, 41; presented as parallel for David (David and Goliath) by Aldridge, 49–50; provocation of social critique in, 182; publications of, 190n. 2; theology constructed by, 39, 50, 61. See also *Narrative of Lord's Wonderful Dealings with John Marrant, a Black, A* (Marrant)
Marren, Susan, 62, 63, 192n. 4
Mary, annunciation to, 142
Mashpee Revolt, 148, 198n. 4; Apess's argument for political sovereignty and, 161–62
Mason Controversy, 23
Massey, Elizabeth, 196n. 4
material realities, focus on, 6, 16, 179; by Apess, 170; by Bailey, 108; by Equiano, 64, 83; by Lee, 139; by Marrant, 41, 43; by Occom, 22, 28, 36, 138
Mather, Cotton, 7, 185
Matsuda, Mari J., 184
May, Cedric, 191n. 4
Memoirs of Abigail Abbot Bailey (Bailey), 6, 85–116: on Asa's sexual abuse of Phebe, 90, 95, 96–101; biblical texts referenced in, 92, 95–96, 102, 104, 105; conflation of two authority figures of God and Asa in, 93, 94; despiritualization of suffering in, 101; development of agency in, 88, 89, 101, 102–3, 108–14; editorial description of Bailey's later life and death, 111–12; as extended reflection on meaning of suffering, 102–5; focus on radical submission for spiritual growth, 105; intertextuality of, 89; Joseph's "trials" in, reference to, 95–96; letter appended to, showing authoritative self, 112–13; ministerial voices in, 94–96; ministerial voices in, response to, 105–8; personal spiritual sensibility in, 106; prayer diary manuscripts as source of, 90; reevaluations of behavior and spirituality, 109–10; sanctified violence within Christian tradition as context for, 99–100; Smith's criticism of Abigail's inaction, 107–8; Smith's introduction to, 91–92, 106–8; theological revelation about legitimacy of agency and "means," 110–11; voice of Apostle Paul taken on in, 113

Methodism: of Apess, 147–48, 152, 161, 168, 170, 197n. 1, 199n. 16; Bailey and, 114; eighteenth-century, 39 (*see also* Marrant, John); Hastings and, 42, 172; Lee and, 119, 125, 136, 139. *See also* African Methodist Episcopal (AME) church
Methodist Episcopal Church (Philadelphia), 118
Methodist Error; or, Friendly Christian Advice to Those Methodists who indulge in extravagant emotions and bodily exercises (Watson), 125
metissage, notion of, 117–18
Michaelsen, Scott, 40, 146, 160, 198n. 9, 199n. 14, 199n. 15
Mielke, Laura, 199n. 13
minority perspectives, commonalities of voice and stance among diverse, 9–10
Miranda, José Porfirio, 18
missionaries, Christian, 21, 23, 30–31, 35–36, 146. *See also* Apess, William; Occom, Samson
Mohegans, Mason Controversy between colonists and, 23
Moraga, Cherrie, 39
Morse, Samuel, 127, 196n. 9
Moses story, Equiano's use of, 76–78
Mosquito and Ulua Indians, Equiano's interactions with, 80–81, 82

mujerista theologians, 17, 120
multicultural contact, 34, 36, 149, 191n. 6; Apess's description of conquest and exploitation of Native Americans, 156–58; borderlands and, 40; "contact zone," 9; Marrant's analysis shaped by, 47–49; multiple identities/subjectivities and, 39, 40, 44; spiritual receptivity and, 59; tradition of, 37
Murray, David, 188n. 1, 190n. 12, 199n. 16
mysticism, tradition of Christian, 97–98

Narrative of Lord's Wonderful Dealings with John Marrant, a Black, A (Marrant), 38–61: Aldridge's 1785 editor's preface to, 43, 44, 49–50; antislavery argument in, 58; biblical text invoked in, 42–43, 50–54; brutalization of slaves portrayed in, 55–58; complex rhetorical situation in, 42; concluding passage of, 59–60; encounter with Cherokees in, 41, 51–57; fluidity of identities of Marrant and his audience in, 43–44; on Indian violence/resistance, 47–49; interpretive framework of crucifixion of Jesus used in, 55–58; John Smith's captivity account compared to, 54–55; linguistic transformation imagined in, 60; popular appeal of, 38–39, 43–44; Potkay's and Burr's 1995 reissue, 44–46; reunion with his original family in, 44, 46–47, 55; scenes of violence shaping, 46–49, 53–59
Native Americans: African American missionary to: *see* Marrant, John; intellectual resistance, 197n. 1; literacy among, Protestant Christianity's emphasis on direct knowledge of Bible as primary motive for, 178; Mashpee Revolt, 148, 161–62, 198n. 4; Mason controversy, 23; self-determination among converts to Christianity, 34–35. *See also* Apess, William; Occom, Samson
Native American sovereignty, 150–51, 161–62, 170; Apess's substantiated assertion of, 150, 151; intellectual sovereignty, 34, 162

natural world, spiritual meaning inherent in, 27, 28
Nelson, Dana, 190n. 12
New England, interpretive presuppositions rooted in religious culture of colonial, 92
New England Christianity: Calvinism, 89; missionary enterprise with Native Americans, Occom's scathing indictment of, 25, 35–36; Puritanism, 7, 8, 37, 93, 195n. 10
"New Light" Christians, 89–90
Nielson, Donald, 198n. 4
Northampton revival, 4
novels, 15, 44, 126–27, 128, 140

Occom, Samson, 2, 6, 13, 19, 21–37, 89, 109, 138, 161, 163, 178, 180, 188n. 1, 188n. 8, 189n. 4, 189n. 6; Christianity as basis of ethnicity as Native American, 34–35; on conversion to Christianity, 29; Edwards compared with, 25–28; execution sermon for Moses Paul, 21, 188n. 1; fund-raising tour of England (1765-1768), 24; hardships and mistreatment by church and mission authorities, 23–24, 29–31, 35–36; hymnal of, 190n. 14; identification with white Christianity, 28–29; inadvertent role in founding of Dartmouth, 21, 23, 24; indictment of missionaries, 25, 35–36; lack of control and dependence on authorities of, 29–30, 35–36; Mason Controversy and, 23; as missionary, 21, 23; personal troubles, 24–25; racism experienced by, 22, 23, 28, 32, 33–34, 36; reasons for writing autobiography, 23–24; seeming self-hatred as chafing against powerlessness, 35–36; self-presentation, 27, 31, 36, 190n. 13; special concern for literacy, 23, 29, 189n. 7; unequal power dynamics recognized by, 115; Wheatley's correspondence with, 175–76. *See also* "Short Narrative of My Life, A" (Occom)
O'Connell, Barry, 146, 148, 153, 197n. 1, 198n. 5, 198n. 11
"Old Light" Christians, 89, 98

Olsen, Tillie, 117
"On Being Brought from Africa" (Wheatley), 175, 177
On Our Own Ground (O'Connell), 197n. 1, 198n. 5
Orban, Katalin, 66, 192n. 4
ordination, 41, 42, 46, 117, 143, 196n. 1, 197n. 12
outsider sensibility, 2, 3, 6, 8–9, 178; of Apess, 163; of Equiano, 66, 71, 73, 82, 83; of Lee, 123, 126, 145; of Marrant, 39, 47, 49, 50, 56, 59, 60
outsider-within stance, 181

Painter, Nell Irvin, 196n. 4, 197n. 11
Palmer, Phoebe, 197n. 12
passive voice, use of, 30
patriarchal nature of Christianity, 92–93: in Promise Keepers movement, 195n. 7
Paul, Apostle, 30; Baileys adoption of voice of, 113; Equiano's use of, 70; Lee's use of, 143; Occom's use of, 30-31
Paul, Moses, 21, 188n. 1
Payne, Rodger, 12, 14, 179–80
Pentecostal movement, 125
Pentecost story, 124
Pequot Indians, 148, 150, 156, 158, 198–99n. 12: Apess's reassertion of his Pequot identity, 162, 163–65, 170; women leaders, 198n. 3
personal authority by way of textual construction, sense of, 12
Personal Narrative (Edwards), 22, 27, 30, 109, 189n. 9
Peter and John, Equiano's identification with captive narrators, 71–72
Peyer, Bernd, 188n. 1, 189n. 5, 190n. 12
Philip, Wampanoag King, 154, 158
piety, Christian: appeal for early women and writers of color, 15–16; readerly response to, 14–15; twentieth-century critics of, 175; twin effects of pietism, 6–7
plantation violence portrayed by Marrant, 55–58: *See also* slavery
Pleck, Elizabeth, 194n. 2
Pocahontas, 54

Poems on Various Subjects, Religious and Moral (Wheatley), 173
political liberation, spiritual liberation and, 18
Potkay, Adam, 7, 38, 44, 45, 59, 63, 70, 77–78, 190n. 2, 192n. 4, 193n. 11
powerlessness: female, in popular novels of 1800s, 126–27; religious tradition disposing adherents to sense of, 106, 107, 108
Powers, Peter, 90
Pratt, Mary Louise, 9, 82
prayer, power of, 57
preaching/preachers, ministers/ministerial authority, 4, 23, 29, 41, 42, 43, 50, 71, 76, 87, 89, 95, 96, 98, 106, 108, 111, 130, 135–36, 180–81, 185; Allen, 118, 119, 120; Chauncey, 98; Edwards, 25, 137; Powers, 90; Wheelock, 21, 25; Whitefield, 5, 41, 70, 89; Williams, 132; women and: *see* Lee, Jarena
predestination, predestinarianism, 7, 82, 194n. 19
Promise Keepers movement, 195n. 7
Protestantism: dissent encouraged in, 7–8; early American, 7, 185–86; emphasis on language, 179; in evidence in autobiographical writings, 178
Protestant Reformation, 180
pulpit, significance of, 180
Puritanism, 7, 8; conversion narrative, 12; Puritan autobiographies, 195n. 10; representations of femininity and sexuality in, 93; zero-tolerance policy on dissent, 37. *See also* Occom, Samson

Quaker autobiography, 11, 12, 30, 33, 187n. 7

Raboteau, Albert, 58
race: Christianity experienced as outsider due to, 2, 3, 6; institutionalized Christian racial hierarchies, 118; Puritans' opposing views of, 7; skin color as physiognomic marker of, 160
race hatred framed as spiritual issue, 169
racial epithets, 167–68

racial identity framed as spiritual issue, 169
racial purity from exclusion of white blood, in Apess's narrative, 158
racial stereotypes, 152, 155, 189n. 4
racial violence, 64–65, 164–65: correction of readers' interpretive assumptions concerning, 183. *See also* slavery
racism: Apess's need to reassert Pequot identity due to, 163–65, 170; Equiano's confrontation of readers', 64; Occom's experience of, 22, 23, 28, 32, 33–34, 36; spiritual life-story genre converted into examination of causes and effects of Christian, 170
rape, 90; of female slaves, 75, 76; of Phebe Bailey by father, 90, 96–101
receptivity to Christianity, Marrant on Indians', 47, 48, 59
Reed, Ishmael, 193n. 15
Religion and Domestic Violence in Early New England (Bailey), 85
religiosity, readerly response to, 14–15
religious life-writing: as act of resistance, 13–14; context for traditions of American Protestant, 11–12; dominant mode of discourse in early American, 22–23; examination of causes and effects of racism through, 170; range of issues relevant to, 19
religious tradition: Lee's rejection of limits of, 144; opposition between scripture and, 140–41; other than Protestant Christianity in early America, presence of, 2–3; rethinking American religious history, 2–3, 42–43, 62–63, 66, 67–68, 92, 115, 179, 184. *See also* Catholicism
reluctant preacher, biblical tradition of, 139–40
Renza, Louis, 151
resistance: autobiography (life writing) as act of, 13–14; legitimation for, from biblical narratives enacting ideals, 15–16
resurrection accounts, women's ministerial roles in gospels', 144
retraditionalization, 161
retributive violence, Equiano's impulse for theology of, 77–78

reversals of Christian autobiography, 169–70
revivalist religion: autobiographical writing as extension of democratic theological inclinations in context of, 179; ecstatic experience and evangelical revivalism, 97–98; of Great Awakening, 3–5; inclusion of the marginalized in, sense of agency from, 182; loudness as characteristic of, 136; rhetorical enfranchisement within, 180–81; social order threatened by, 4–5
rhetorical enfranchisement, 180–81
Richards, Jeffrey, 187n. 2
Richardson, Leon, 24, 28
Ripley, Dorothy, 196n. 1
Robinson, Marius, 197n. 11
Rogal, Samuel, 199n. 2
Rowlandson, Mary, 86, 153, 190n. 1
Rowson, Susanna, 127
Ruether, Rosemary Radford, 143
Ruoff, LaVonne, 21, 149

Sabino, Robin, 191n. 1
Saénz, Richard, 39
Saffin, John, 7
Samuels, Wilfred, 191n. 1
Sayre, Gordon, 149, 161
Schueller, Malini Johar, 147, 187n. 6
scripture and tradition, opposition between, 140–41
Seasonable Thoughts (Chauncy), 195
seduction novels, 127
Segregated Sabbaths: Richard Allen and the Rise of Independent Black Churches, (1760–1840) (George), 196n. 1
Segundo, Juan Luis, 18
Sekora, John, 190n. 1
self: Apess's sense of, 151; Edwards's sense of religious, 27; Equiano's equivocal, 79; Marrant's multiple identities, 39, 40, 44; Occom's sense/presentation of, 27, 31, 36, 190n. 13; soul as spiritual or heavenly, 131; synecdochic, 36
self-loathing, female, 106, 107
Sewall, Samuel, 7, 8, 36
sexual violence: abuse/rape of Phebe Bailey by father, 90, 95, 96–101; incest, 98–99; inflicted on female

sexual violence (*continued*)
  slaves, 75, 76; in white conquest and exploitation of Native Americans, 158. *See also* Bailey, Abigail Abbot
Shea, Daniel B., 11–12, 23, 36, 87, 187n. 71
Shepard, Thomas, 85
"Short Narrative of My Life, A" (Occom), 22, 28–37: challenges to assumptions of superiority of Christian culture, 34; frequent use of passive voice in, 30; Poor Indian Boy story as template in, 32, 33–34; reasons for writing, 23–24; spiritual revelations as prefatory in, 28; ultimate revelation at end of, 31–33
"Sinners in the Hands of an Angry God" (Edwards), 137
slave narratives: earliest published, 190n. 1; function of portraits in, 192n. 8. *See also* Equiano, Olaudah
slavery, 42; baptism and, 7; Equiano's appreciation for Moses as liberator of slaves, 76–78; Equiano's position on, 63–64, 71–72, 79; Equiano's use of biblical literature of social justice in context of, 75–76; female slaves, sexual violence inflicted on, 75, 76; incompatibility of Christianity with, 83; opposition between slave masters and slaves regarding Christian teachings, 58; plantation violence portrayed by Marrant, 55–58; Puritans' opposing views of, 7; transition from widespread practices to race-based slave system, 191n. 3; Wheatley as, 172–74, 177; Woolman's Quaker social and political awareness of injustice of, 33
Slotkin, Richard, 191n. 8
Smith, Ethan, 85, 91–92, 106–8
Smith, John, 54
Smith, Sidonie, 13
Smith, Valerie, 191n. 1
Smith, Venture, 200n. 5
Smith-Rosenberg, Carroll, 196n. 8
social justice, Equiano's use of biblical literature of, 75–76
social order, revivalist Christianity as threatening to, 4–5

Sojourner Truth: a Life, a Symbol (Painter), 197n. 11
Song of Songs, 93
Son of the Forest, A (Apess), 148, 149, 153, 170; on abuse in childhood, 154–55, 156, 158–59, 163, 168; authenticity of Apess's spiritual identity in, 166–67; challenge to readers' unexamined presumptions about race/racial violence, 123, 183; concept of racial identity, pivotal moment in, 154–56; confused identity in, 159–60; conversion account in, 151–52; critical conversation about, 160–61, 162, 197n. 1; on effects of dispossession of Indians from their lands, history, and culture, 156–59; flight in forest, 155, 159–60, 162; frontispiece portrait and title page, 153; ideological journey required of readers in, 151–54; on mistreatment by whites due to Indian identity, 162–69; racial experiences presented in terms of skin color, 159–60; on reidentification with and reassertion of Pequot identity, 162, 163–65, 170; as scathing critique of mainstream Christianity, 170; sense of self and authority in, 151; voice of social protest developed in, 151
Southern Christian Leadership Conference, 8
Sovereign Selves (Carlson), 189n. 6
sovereignty: Apess's arguments for, 148, 149; Bailey's distinctions concerning, 101, 103; Calvinist preoccupation with, 36; distinctions concerning, 101, 103; hermeneutical, 34; intellectual, 34, 162; Native American, 150–51, 161–62, 170
spirit, language of, 7
spiritual autobiography, forms to be read as, 187n. 7
Spiritual Autobiography in Early America (Shea), 87
Spiritual Interrogations (Bassard), 188n. 8
spiritual liberation, political liberation and, 18
spiritual receptivity and cultural encounter, 59
stereotypes, racial, 152, 155, 189n. 4

Stevens, Scott Manning, 198n. 4, 198n. 7
Stowe, Harriet Beecher, 1–2, 3, 19, 180
submission, female, 88, 92–93, 95, 96, 103, 105
subversive religion, 185
suffering: despiritualization of Bailey's view of, 101; as God's vehicle for sanctification, 33, 94, 95; rejection of theology of divine authorship of, 33, 182–84. *See also* violence
"suffering servant" motif, 53, 191n. 7
synecdochic self, 36

Talking Book motif, 79, 193n. 15, 193n. 17; in Equiano's *Interesting Narrative*, 79–81
Taves, Ann, 85, 89–93, 98, 125, 136, 194n. 1, 194n. 5, 198n. 8
Tenney, Tabitha, 127
Teresa of Avila, 97, 137
Thomas, Helen, 17, 63
threat of cultural and linguistic erasure, identities articulated in context of, 40
Tiro, Karim, 198n. 2, 199n. 16
To Tell a Free Story (Andrews), 12–13
"To the University of Cambridge, in New England" (Wheatley), 177–78
tradition and scripture, opposition between, 140–41
transcendentalism, 27
transforming power of Christianity, material limits of, 83
Treatise Concerning Religious Affections, A (Edwards), 138, 190n. 10
Trevecca House, 42
Truth, Sojourner, 143, 196n. 4, 197n. 11
Turner, Victor, 190n. 13
typology, 49, 50, 87, 192n. 5, 196n. 7

Ulua Indians, 80–81, 82
Unchained Voices (Carretta), 191n. 5
universal priesthood, 181

VanDerBeets, Richard, 38
Van Lonkhuyzen, Harold W., 189n. 7
Velikova, Roumiana, 198n. 11
violence: Apess's childhood experiences of, 148; attempts to make spiritual sense of, 85–86; as both spiritual analogue and experiential reality, 182; Indian, in retaliation against white aggressions, 47–48, 156, 157–59; Marrant's religious concerns portrayed in context of, 46–49, 53–59; provocation of social critique by, 182, 183–84; racial, 64–65, 164–65, 183; retributive, Equiano's impulse for theology of, 77–78; sacralized in many Christian traditions, 99–100; sexual, inflicted on female slaves, 75, 76; as vehicle for religious meaning, 183–84; against women, patriarchal theology and, 92–93. *See also* domestic violence; slavery
Viswanathan, Gauri, 17
Vogel, Todd, 161, 200n. 6
voice; audibility, 136; divine, 135; gender and, 124

Walker, Alice, 175
Walpole, Horace, 42
Warrior, Robert Allen, 34, 150–51
Wars: American War for Independence, 6, 41; of 1812, 148; French and Indian War, 6
Watson, John Fanning, 125
Watts, Edward, 147, 187n. 6
Weaver, Jace, 34, 36, 162
Weinstein, Laurie, 189n. 7
Wesley, John, 7
Wheatley, John, 174
Wheatley, Phillis, 7, 19, 60, 122, 171–78, 180, 199n. 1, 199n. 3; authorial inquisition faced by, 172–74; correspondence with Samson Occom, 175–76; eighteenth-century responses to, 172–75; enslavement and purchase by Wheatleys, 172; expressions of piety grounded in experiences both of liberation and of racial exclusion and prohibition, 178–79; Jefferson's criticism of poetry of, 174–75; ministerial tones used by, 176–78; presumption of moral authority, 178; self-construction, 199n. 4; twentieth-century critics of piety of, 175; Whitefield poem, 172–74
Wheeler, Ephraim, 194n. 4
Wheelock, Eleazar, 21, 23, 24, 25, 30, 31, 34, 189n. 2; theories about properly Christianized Indian, 28–29

Whitefield, George, 3, 5, 6–7, 41, 42, 43, 70, 89, 172, 193n. 10; on race and slavery, 5; Wheatley's elegy for, 172–74
white supremacy movement, Christian, 8
Willard, Carla, 200n. 4
Willard, Frances, 197n. 12
Williams, Delores, 17–18, 99, 120
Williams, James, 195n. 9
Williams, John, 190n. 1
Williams, Richard, 132
Williams, Roger, 7, 8
Wollstonecraft, Mary, 6, 63, 175, 191n. 2
womanist theology, 17–18, 99, 120
woman suffrage, 6
women: of color, historical exclusion from traditional theology, 17–18; full ordination for, 197n. 12; itinerating preachers, 197; life-writing of, as enactments of resistance and self-definition, 13–14; in public ministry, Lee's argument for, 132, 140–44. *See also* Bailey, Abigail Abbot; Lee, Jarena; Wheatley, Phillis
Women and Redemption (Ruether), 143
women's rights. *See* Lee, Jarena
Wood, Forrest, 192n. 6
Wood, Mary, 148
Woolf, Virginia, 175
Woolman, John, 14–15, 33
Wretched of the Earth (Fanon), 9
Writing Indians (Wyss), 189n. 6
Wyss, Hilary, 17, 34, 189n. 6

Zacharias, 142–43
Zafar, Rafia, 39, 45, 59

EILEEN RAZZARI ELROD is an associate professor of English at Santa Clara University, where she teaches courses in American literature, women's studies, and writing. Her essays have appeared in *African American Review*, *Legacy: A Journal of American Women Writers*, *Prospects: An Annual of American Cultural Studies*, and other scholarly journals. She earned her PhD from the University of California at Davis. She lives with her husband and three children in San Jose, California.